Chelsea Child
Rose Gamble

Rose Gamble no longer lives in Chelsea but in an isolated Sussex cottage together with her husband and demanding Siamese cat. The war which 'swept away life as we had known it' brought all kinds of opportunities to families such as hers.

Rosie took a post-war teacher's training course, and taught art for some years before going with her husband, an engineer, to West Africa. There she worked as a buyer in a major bookselling organisation. Back home and unemployed, she broadcast some short pieces about her childhood in *Woman's Hour*. It was the great interest these five-minute broadcasts aroused which led to *Chelsea Child*.

D1339536

CHELSEA CHILD

ROSE GAMBLE

ARIEL BOOKS
BRITISH BROADCASTING CORPORATION

The BBC Woman's Hour serial based on this book
was abridged and produced by Pat McLoughlin

First published 1979
Reprinted in paperback 1982

Published by the British Broadcasting Corporation
35 Marylebone High Street London W1M 4AA

Typeset by Phoenix Photosetting, Chatham
Printed in England by Mackays of Chatham Ltd
Cover printed by Belmont, Northampton

This book is set in 10 on 11 point Ehrhardt Linotron

ISBN 0 563 20112 6

CONTENTS

ONE

Ethel's Ceiling

It was a narrow house, so squeezed between a row of little shops that it was almost overlooked. Its colour was the faded grey of a winter sky, and the scabs and cracks of old age showed through the flaked plaster and neglected paint. Here and there traces of decorative lettering clung to the wall, the sole reminder of the days when it had flourished as a Builders' Merchants and Plumbers. Its one patch of colour was the battered green front door which always stood open, and the darkness of the passage behind it suggested the entrance to an urban rabbit hole. In the early nineteen-twenties, the seven members of my family lived in the upstairs front room of this house. We were known as 'them Naylors', and the small room was to be our home for seven years.

Cracked brown oilcloth covered the narrow ground-floor passage but stopped short of the two flights of wooden stairs. At the top of the first flight was a dark square of landing, just wide enough for a door. Our room was at the top of the second flight, so every time we went in and out we had to pass that door on the landing, which was one of the terrors of my young life. It was never quite shut, so I'd belt up the stairs, put one foot on the landing and swing round to scoot up the second flight, holding my breath and blindly fighting the knob that opened our door. The relief I felt when I fell into our room was never understood.

'You're like a cartload of bloody 'orses, Rowie. Why can't you learn to come in properly?' was my usual welcome.

Mr Sackett lived in the room behind that door on the landing, and sometimes he stood silently there, just staring and breathing through the crack. He trundled around inside a droopy black overcoat that touched the floor, and indoors or out a dusty black bowler sat on the back of his head. At night times, when he crept out the back to the lav in the yard, he carried a tiny paraffin lamp in both hands on his chest. In the darkness this completely detached his head, so that his white moustache and white glassy eyes seemed to float in space. I never told anybody that I was afraid of Mr Sackett, and that I was certain that if I paused for a second by his door I'd be done for, but my brother Georgie knew how I felt, and he deliberately encouraged my fears.

'Old Sacky's dirty,' he whispered to me. 'He's so dirty he grows carrot tops on his chairs, an' his room is full of rags and bones.'

'How d'you know?'

'I seen inside.'

'You're a liar.'

'No I ain't. He's a rag an' bone man. I seen 'im with 'is barrer, an' he sleeps on the rags an' he eats the bones.'

Georgie was older than I was, so I believed almost everything he told me, and I could see Old Sacky squatting on rags among his carrots, scrunching bones. I got into such a state I wouldn't go down to the lav at night on my own, and I kicked up such a fuss one of my elder sisters had to take me.

One night I went down with Luli, clutching the back of her jersey while she carried the candle. We reached the scullery and trod on its soft beaten-earth floor and heard the tap dripping miserably into the yellow stone sink. In the corner stood the stone copper with a space underneath for burning firewood. There were always scuffling sounds under the copper where the rats dragged bits of charred paper. The lav was a shack in the corner of the yard, but first we had to pass the den of horrors. In daylight this was just an open shed covering a pile of assorted junk, but at night it was awesome to us, full of crouching shapes.

The lav door hung on one hinge so it had to be lifted as well as opened. Inside someone had covered the worst of the damp-blackened walls with two pictures. One, in a chipped gold plaster frame, showed a buxom lady, very thinly clad about the bosoms, placing a bleeding heart into a silver chalice. It was called 'Josephine'. We speculated on the bleeding heart. Georgie said it was what happened to you when they cut your tripes out, but Luli said that tripes were innards, and all your innards wouldn't go into such a daft little pot. Mum shut us all up by telling us that the lady was one of them nasty foreigners with dirty habits, and we wasn't to look. The other picture was like a framed set of sumptuous fag cards. It was bright with reds and blues, silver and gold, and showed rows and rows of brown-faced men with whiskers and beards, uniforms and turbans. It said 'The Ruling Princes of India' in green letters underneath, and although we had no idea where India was we each had our favourite prince, and their presence in the lav added a touch of glamour to an otherwise dismal occasion.

Just as Lu dragged open the lav door there was a terrible shriek. I screamed, Luli screamed, and we fought past each other, dropping the candle and running through the scullery to the stairs.

'What's up? What's all this noise?' Our Mum came running down to us.

'There's a ghost,' sobbed Luli, 'yellin' its 'ead off in the lav.' Grabbing hold of Mum, we all went back into the yard.

There was a fearful flapping and squawking noise. 'You daft 'aporths,' Mum said, laughing at us, 'it's just one of them ol' chickens got down the pan! Be quick, an' I'll wait for you.'

We didn't stop indoors much, not unless Mum was home. As the evenings grew dark, the first thing she did when she got in from work was to light the lamp and put it on the mantelpiece. Then we came in from whatever we were doing in the street, my two elder sisters Dodie and Luli, Georgie, myself, and later on, my young brother Joey. Mum cut a pile of bread on the clumsy little table that Dad had made which stood in front of the window. It was just big enough for Mum and Dad to sit at for their meals, but they had to sit sideways because it had a deep drawer underneath where we kept the knives and forks, the sewing things, the family papers in a tin box and a wodge of old newspapers. These were spread on the floor in front of the fireplace so that Mum could put down the sooty saucepans when she cooked our Sunday dinner. As we had no oven the dinner was always boiled. There was a big fender with a steel rim round the hearth and inside it stood the primus stove, the flat iron, the kettle and poker, the shovel and chopper. Everything had to be put in its proper place and facing the right way.

Dodie lit the primus stove, filling the room with the acrid smell of bubbling methylated spirit and then plunging us into the stink of paraffin vapour. She put the kettle on for cocoa while Luli spread the bread with marge. We had tinned milk in our tea, but cocoa was made with water and sugar. Joey and I had two rough little stools about six inches high that pulled out from under a plywood seated chair that was our table, and Georgie, Luli and Dodie always sat in a row on our one proper bed and ate off their laps. We had a good old jaw while we had our supper, Mum asking each of us what we'd been up to, and we telling her only the half of it.

Supper over, Dodie put the kettle on again for washing-up and for washing us. At the door end of the room Dad had made a long plywood shelf with a hole cut in the middle to fit the enamel bowl. A large china jug stood in the bowl and we took it in turns to keep it topped up from the scullery tap. Washing-up was a rotten job. We used carbolic soap, and all the ends were dropped into an empty cocoa tin with holes pierced in the bottom. You put the tin into the bowl and poured the boiling water into it, dunking it up and down to make the water soapy, then stood the wet tin on an old plate. The draining board was a tin tray. Everything soon got to taste of carbolic, but then it always did so you got used to it, and didn't complain, unless a thick bit of soap had been left on your cup and you hadn't done the wiping up.

Under the bowl stood the horrible galvanised iron slop bucket, hidden by a bit of curtain that Dodie had made. The slop bucket was a holy terror. We all hated lugging it down the stairs to the scullery and often as not wiping up the spills on the stairs, so it was nearly always brimming. Hidden behind the curtain it often got kicked, and would spill over and flood down the sloping floor towards the fireplace. The uncovered floor boards lapped up the flow and the scummy water disappeared between the cracks like rain on the desert. Everyone would shout 'Ethel's ceiling!' and grab anything to mop up. Ethel's ceiling, directly underneath us, was a map of stains from the contents of our slop bucket, and every time a new one appeared Mum would get invited into Ethel's room to have it pointed out. Ethel must have been a generous woman to live below us for so long with so little complaint.

Two narrow shelved cupboards were built in at each side of the flat, bedroom-type fireplace. One was stowed with Dad's tools, the bootmending gear, the paraffin can, firewood, the shoe-cleaning box, a bucket of coke and the few clothes Mum and Dad were not actually wearing. The other cupboard was for food, cooking pots and our cups and plates.

I don't know how the door of the room stayed on its hinges, peppered as it was with hooks. On these we each hung our coats, and on top of all swung a great cotton bag in which we kept the bread. Outside the window Mum had a little window box where she grew marigolds in the summer, and where she stuck Dad's fork in the dirt to get the smell of fish off it.

Nobody but Dad ever had fish, and we had what we called 'bread and smellit' whenever he had a herring for his tea on Saturday. It never occurred to us to expect to be included in his little luxuries, but Lu, who was the bravest and most outspoken, waited one Saturday until Dad had gone out, and then questioned Mum. As she wiped a piece of bread round his oily plate before washing it up she asked. "'Ere Mum, when are we gonner 'ave fish?'

'When you're grown up,' Mum answered. 'When you're all grown up and out to work, then we'll have a fine old time.'

'Pineapple chunks?' asked Lu.

'Every Sunday,' said Mum firmly.

I listened and watched, and decided that there were only two things I wanted to be, the first was grown up and the second was to be sure I grew up into a man, for I thought I could choose. It seemed to me that grown up men got the best of everything and could do just what they liked.

One Saturday Mum bought a couple of live eels for Dad, which at certain times of the year were even cheaper than herrings. She shook them out of the newspaper wrapping into our washing bowl, poured the jug of water over them and stood the bowl on the floor. The eels began to move and were soon swimming round and round the bowl, faster and faster until the water was a thrashing whirlpool. Suddenly they shot themselves clean over the rim of the bowl to squirm and wriggle on the floorboards. Lu and I shrieked with horror and leapt on the bed while Mum made a couple of furtive dashes at the eels, but she could not bring herself to pick them up.

'Gawd 'elp us,' she shouted at Lu, 'get orf there an' give me 'and! Get 'em back!' Lu and I were helpless with terror and disgust. 'Get Georgie, quick,' panted Mum, 'afore they goes down the floorboards.'

Lu flung herself across the room, leaving me screaming on the bed, and pelted downstairs shouting for Georgie. 'Stop screechin' for Chris'sake Rowie,' Mum yelled at me, poking at the eels with one foot to head them off from disappearing under the bed, for I was near hysteria.

The door burst open and of all people Ethel came into the room wrapped in a sacking apron and waving a huge pair of scissors. Lu stayed outside, snivelling on the landing, while Ethel dealt the death blow by calmly picking up each eel and cutting its head off. Lu and I ran down into the street and stayed there for hours until the eels were cooked, but Ethel had to go up to Mum again to see if there was enough salt in them, because Mum couldn't force herself to taste even the gravy. I made Lu promise me that I needn't have a wash that night because I didn't fancy having my face washed in the bowl that the eels had swum in.

The mantelpiece belonged to Dad and was out of bounds to us. The alarm clock that cost one and elevenpence stood in the middle, on its face otherwise it wouldn't go, and behind it was a packet of prickers for the primus and the hat pin Dad used for winkles. Joey and I used to take the heads from the winkles off Dad's plate and put them on our hands, frightening each other with scabby pox fingers. Once Joey put them on his bread, pretending they were currants, but they tasted awful. The winkle man came down our street on Sunday mornings with his pony and cart crying, 'Straight offa the boat!' in a hoarse, beery voice. He filled a cup with winkles right up to the top for a penny. Sometimes he cried, ''Apenny 'andful!' and for a halfpenny shoved a great fistful of rich green watercress into your arms.

The cut glass snuff box stood beside the clock and we stole pinches of snuff when Dad was out, smothering our noses in the brown powder to see which of us could do the most sneezes. Next to the snuff box Dad kept his penholder with a slender, silver-coloured nib and a threepenny bottle of ink, and beside that stood a white cardboard shoe box in which Mum carefully preserved his one stiff white collar and spotted bow tie.

He used the pen and ink when he earned a few shillings at home addressing envelopes in beautiful copperplate handwriting. He also wrote many letters applying for jobs, pressing a spare piece of paper between his hand and the writing so that no finger marks should spoil the finished letter. The envelope was every bit as important, the address exactly centred and the writing thick and thin with elegant capitals. The stamp had to be exactly straight, equidistant from the edges. When it was ready for posting he wrapped a piece of paper round it and sent one of us to the letter box, and his parting words were always the same: 'If you drop it – bring it back!' There were times though, when we hated his conceit about his writing. Practically every time there was a row he belittled Mum, repeating her faults over and over again, dragging up her ignorance and lack of schooling. 'Make your bloody mark,' he taunted, 'go on, learn to scratch your bloody name,' and he would take his pen from the mantelpiece and throw it down in front of her.

Mum kept the stiff collar rubbed up with bread so that it was clean when Dad went after a job. On the very end of the mantelpiece stood the candle for going out the back at night, and behind it was tucked a folded piece of emery paper for shining up the steel on the fender.

Dad had made shelves for each side of the window, and one was for our medicines. A tin of yellow basilicon ointment pulled the living daylights out of you if you had a fester, and syrup of figs sorted out your insides. Camphorated oil dealt with coughs, and permanganate of potash was used for sore throats and mouth ulcers. We pinched it for making invisible ink. Melrose was our misery. Our knees and hands were raw with chaps throughout most of the winter and the hard pink lump of Melrose was supposed to soothe and cure them. First it had to be warmed so that it became a soft paste, so Luli or Dodie held it in the candle flame until the edges became runny. Then they scrubbed it over our knees and hands. While it was soft and warm it went on smoothly, but as it cooled and dried it dragged over our cracked skin and we yelled. The candle flame left sooty streaks in the Melrose so our knees and the backs of our hands were pitted with grime for months.

Lu or Dodie washed Joey and me, sitting us up on the shelf beside the bowl, scrubbing at our sore knees with the bright red carbolic soap. We all used the same flannel and towel, except Dad.

The whole room was criss-crossed with the rough sisal string that came from the greengrocer's boxes and on this hung the airing. Hardly a day went by when bits of washing weren't over-head. This didn't worry us, but Dad used to lead off when he had to duck under the dampy clothes. Mum kept our hair clean and Dodie kept up our appearances. She patched and cut down and mended, and every night took our boots into the scullery to clean them, so they were ready for school in the morning. Dodie read a great deal, often dashing to the public library straight from school to read there until it was time to run home and get supper ready when Mum came in from work. When Dodie started work herself she got home too late to tell me stories in the evening, but as Joey became old enough I used to sit with him in the scullery while Dodie cleaned the boots early on Thursday evenings, which was her half-day, and on Sunday evenings too. While she rubbed and polished she told us stories, Joey and I sitting side by side on the cold scullery step while the candlelight flickered on the stone sink.

'Dodie,' Joey would say. 'Tell us something nice.'

'Don't know anything nice,' Dodie teased, every time.

'Yes, you do, course you do. Go on Dodie.' We rocked on the step hugging our knees until we all three shouted together, 'The Happy Traveller!'

Dodie knew it was our favourite and she never forgot a single detail in the retelling. It was about a sad orphan boy who ran away and was lost and starving, and was found in the nick of time by a handsome young man who was camping in the country with a tent and a fire and an open motor car. We knew the story backwards and waited for the moment when the boy, famished and exhausted to the point of death, opened his eyes as our hero spooned milk between his parched lips. It was sheer ecstasy and we lived every second. Sometimes we asked for something to make us frightened, and the shadows in the scullery crawled with figures from Grimms' Fairy Tales and there were goblins in the copper. Dodie told us about the books she was reading to herself. We heard about Sherlock Holmes, and about Little Nell, which I hated because nasty creepy Quilp was too much like Old Sacky, and he wasn't in a book, he was upstairs.

Dodie's own books were on the shelf by the medicine and she read them all to us. Most of them were her school prizes with labels inside saying, *Dora Naylor, for Progress and Conduct.* Lu told us that progress and conduct meant doing what you were told to without answering back, and that's why she hadn't got any prizes. After we had heard them for the first time, we thought Dodie's prizes were a bit soppy. One was called *Jessica's First Prayer,* and another was about *Tops, the Story of a Little Girl.*

As soon as it got near bedtime Mum would start to get fidgety if we dawdled about. She got anxious about getting the beds down and all of us tucked up out of the way before Dad came in from the pub. We knew this, and we all shared her worry of the mood he might be in when he came home. Putting the beds down was a rotten job, and we tried to put it off as long as we could, but once we started we were spurred on by the thought that he might come in and catch us still at it. Then there would be trouble and no mistake.

'Come on my ol' potherbs' – Mum often called us potherbs when she talked to us all at once – 'get the beds down.'

Taking up most of the wall oposite the window was an iron contraption of Edwardian vintage. It was a huge double bed that folded into three sections, secured at the top by an iron hook, and all our bedding was folded and stuffed inside it. Lu and Dodie got started.

Dodie said, 'Ready?' and we all shouted, 'Go!' While Lu thumped herself against the bed, Dodie arched her back and pushed her knee into it to relieve the pressure on the hook.

'Push harder, Lu,' gasped Dodie, 'I can't get it undone.'

'I am pushin'.'

'Give us a shove then, Mum,' cried Dodie. The three of them threw their weight at it, rocking it against the wall while Georgie,

Joey and I watched entranced because we never knew when it would suddenly gape open and shower everyone with the bed-clothes. Like Tower Bridge one end swung over Lu and Dodie and crashed down on to the floor with a terrible thud. Together we yelled: 'Ethel's ceiling!'

Once the big bed was undone, Lu and Dodie sorted out the pile of bedding, chucking pillows and bits of blanket at Georgie and me. We had to pile them up in the corner by the door and keep out of the way. To clear the centre of the room, Mum helped to swing the big bed round against the wall and the three of them heaved the huge dollop of shapeless flock mattress on to it. They worked on it like demons, diving and pecking with their hands until the lumps were shared out, more or less evenly. This was Mum and Dad's bed, and as soon as it was made Joey usually managed to leap on to it, dancing about and finishing with a huge jump, landing on his back flushed and laughing with his trousers round his ankles. Mum grabbed him and gave him a quick smack and flung him at Lu or Dodie, who always gave him a cuddle.

The next job was to get the bunks made for Georgie, Joey and me in what space was left in the middle of the room, and the odd bits of bedding left over on the floor in the corner were divided between us. Our two chairs were tied together for Joey, with the scrubbing board along one side to keep him from falling out. This contraption was pushed alongside Mum's bed. Joey had a pillow for his mattress and a little square cushion from the pram for his head. My bunk was Dad's armchair with the wooden back let down flat. As I didn't need a mattress, I got a pillow and a blanket and Mum's outdoor coat on top. Poor old Georgie had the saggy one, with knitted wire like chainmail looping its way over the folding iron frame. Its thin iron legs were like rapiers, and it was one of Georgie's jobs to remember to put the empty cocoa tin under the leg that stood on the soft bit of floorboard. He often dodged the bedmaking, messing about under the shed in the backyard with his scooter or counting his precious fag-cards, and so the placing of the tin was often forgotten. When this happened, and Georgie hopped into his bunk, there would be a horrible crunching sound as the iron spike shot through the rotten floor like butter, and then Mum really lost her temper. She pulled him out of his bed, worried sick that Ethel would complain once too often and chuck us out. 'Cripes! Now look what you've done, Georgie, another hole in Ethel's sodding ceiling! Where's the tin?'

Lu and Dodie had to move the bunk so that Mum could get to the cupboard, carefully lifting the leg back into our room, and then lowering it gently as Mum held the tin over the pitted wood. 'Now get into bed,' said Mum crossly, and we all joined in with her familiar words: 'and for Gawd's sake, lie still.'

Lu and Dodie had the proper bed, the single one in the corner with iron laths for the spring and a flock mattress – it must have been awful to sleep on because it got sat on so much during the evening. It was a bit much expecting Lu and Dodie to go to bed when we did because they were older than us, but with all the beds down there was nowhere to sit if they stayed up. To give them a little privacy they had a bit of curtain on a string in front of their bed.

Every other item we possessed was crammed under Lu and Dodie's bed. Pushed to the back were the various cardboard boxes belonging to Lu and Georgie, stuffed with precious rubbish. Lu folded and saved the clothes for our Guy Fawkes together with a halfpenny bright pink mask, cracked with rain. We made the guy in October and pushed it round the streets on our barrer, getting in a good two weeks' collecting before Guy Fawkes night. One night, we came home with our rattling cocoa tin to find Dad was waiting for us. He emptied it out on the table and counted seven pence in pennies and halfpennies. Furiously he backhanded Lu, who was standing nearest, catching her across the mouth. 'What else you got?' he said, in a terrible voice.

'That's all. Honest!' Lu held her face.

'You haven't been trying.'

'We did. We did try!' Lu's voice was thick with tears and temper. 'We bin out for ages an' there's 'undreds of other kids out with guys, an' no one ain't got no money to give us.' Dad swept the coppers up, put them in his pocket and stormed out. Sobbing, Lu ran down to the backyard and beat the living daylights out of our poor old guy.

Georgie's box was a rummage of withered conkers, beer bottle tops and bits of small bicycle parts that one day he intended to assemble. Dodie's straw pilgrim basket was filled with scraps of cloth, ends of wool, ribbon and rag, and cut-out pictures of ladies in posh clothes from the newspapers. Mum's long thin corset box held her treasures, a few brown photographs and some expired pawn tickets. Once she had a little twist of fur with two brown beady eyes, but she pawned it and we never saw it again. Right in front, ready to hand, was the rolled-up piece of singed blanket that Dodie spread on the table when she did the ironing, rubbing the soot from the fire off the iron on to a piece of rag and then sliding the iron over a bit of soap.

The mop lay just underneath the bed and stank of scummy floor water. Dad made us a new mop every so often. He cut a few rags into a square and nailed them in the middle to the end of a broom handle, protecting the end of the mop with a discarded round rubber heel. The floor was mopped over every day, but the floppy bunch of rags were too thick for us to wring out properly and there was never enough hot water to rinse it thoroughly. When it became too slippery and horrible, and the frayed rags disintegrated, Dad made a new one.

Every night Mum tucked us up, one at a time, and kissed the top of our heads. She shut the window, because Dad complained of the draught, then sat on the edge of her bed to wait for him to come home. The room grew quiet. I could hear Georgie's spring moving as he tried to get comfy and Joey was already asleep. Lu and Dodie were whispering behind their curtain. They had got hold of a little tin of face powder and had hidden it from Dad under the shed in the backyard, and were always talking about it. The thick and familiar smell settled over the room, the paraffin lamp, the coke fire, the carbolic soap and people, six of us and one to come. I pulled Mum's coat collar over my head to shut out the lamp-light, squeezed my eyes tight shut and tried to go to sleep before Dad came in. If there was a row, perhaps, with luck, I wouldn't wake up.

TWO
Our Street

Our street ran from the Kings Road down to the Embankment. At one end two buildings faced each other across the road, dedicated to the virtues of cleanliness and godliness, the public baths and the chapel, neither of which was sought with any regularity by us or the majority of our neighbours. The street was typical of Chelsea over the years, an abrupt assortment of graceful houses with cooks in the basements, pocked with corner shops and edged with slummy streets of artisans' dwellings. Poverty and elegance were separated by nothing more than a couple of kerbstones.

Next to the public baths, which we called 'the sheep dip', was a cul-de-sac, on one side the back of the Town Hall and on the other the Motor Works. We spent a lot of our spare time playing on the old cannons that defended the rear windows of local government and picking pink flowered weeds that grew there in the summer. Opposite the shops, where we lived, was a row of terraced cottages, and at the end of the shops a small terrace of workmen's dwellings ran into ours. All the houses were bugridden in summer, freezing in winter, for they had neither electricity nor gas, and rat-infested the whole year round.

A mysterious factory with a tall chimney which once had been an iron works stood on the corner, and then came another muddle of little shops, an upholsterer's, the greengrocer's and the fish and chip shop. On the next corner stood the dairy, and from then on a row of ladylike properties with fanlights swept down to the Embankment. Here there were trees and gardens and tall brick houses with white-framed windows and lovely ironwork facing the Thames.

Our house stood beside the sweet and paper shop, and the next best thing to having a ha'penny to spend was playing 'I-spy' through its tiny window. The floor of the window was layered with rows of grubby glass fluted dishes filled with tiger nuts that tasted like the insides of dusty cupboards, gritty spearmint toffee, aniseed balls, sherbet dabs and sun-faded jelly babies, all at a ha'penny an ounce. The quality stuff, the buttered brazils and satin cushions, was in tall glass jars up on the shelves, but we never paid any attention to them. At a penny an ounce it didn't occur to us to include them, not even when playing games through the window.

The butcher's jutted out on to the pavement past the sweet shop, but we never bought our meat there because Mum blamed all the rats in our scullery on the butcher. Across the road stood the boozer with fancy patterned frosty windows and liver-coloured walls, sickly with blotches where the paint and plaster had fallen away. The landlord owned a muscular bull terrier with a bald piggy face and uncertain temper, and a good deal of boasting went on in the pub about the prowess of this animal. Its reputation was tested on Sunday mornings when groups of men and boys assembled in the street, some of them with mongrel challengers growling and yelping at each other on bits of chain and rope. When the butcher crossed the road with live rats in a cage, there was pandemonium. The rats screamed as the eager bull terrier tried to attack the cage, the mongrels barking and straining upright on their leads. The men cursed, the boys climbed on to lamp posts and ledges, doors slammed and windows opened. We ran up our stairs and knelt on our table to lean out over the window box, shuddering with fearful excitement.

The first rat released would dart with a frantic bouncing run straight for the gutter to try to escape down the nearest drain. The bull terrier bolted after it and you could hear the thud as the dog's body bounced off the kerb. It tossed the rat high into the air and grabbed it as it fell stunned on to the road. A feather-tailed mongrel tried for the next rat, and lost it, pawing and yelping at the bars of the drain hole. Then two dogs were released and the fight over the rat and then with each other was vicious. The speed and ferocity of the dogs terrified me and I kept getting off the table, not wanting to look, and feeling sorry for the rotten old rats. We were all in Mum's way. She was trying to get the Sunday dinner ready, balancing the saucepans on two trivets over the fire, and when the riot in the street went on too long, she chucked us all out. I sat at the bottom of the stairs, but Lu and Georgie crept up the passage and went on watching round the front door.

The coffee stall had its pitch outside the public baths. Shining and trim by day, a little oasis of bright light at night, and all the time wafting out waves of spicy saveloy smells. The counter was strangely high, so the tall man who ran the stall stood remote from us surrounded by rows of white cups and piles of thick white plates. He wore a clean white coat that made his broad flat moustache look like a band of black paint across his face. Time after time we watched him lift half the hinged lid of a medical looking silver urn, plunge his hand into the steam and snap the lid down with a jerk to sever the brick red sausage from its mate. The rich smell of those saveloys that drifted from the silver urn started a tickle in one of my ears that ran down under my chin, and made my spit run.

We were sitting on the pavement one cold Saturday night, Georgie and I, with our backs pressed to the grating in the wall of the baths where the hot air was escaping from the boiler room, just feeling the warm and smelling the saveloys, when we saw Mr Dandy.

'You seen my Ginge?' he asked us.

'Nah!'

''Op down my place then, an' tell 'im to get a move on.'

We wasn't going to hop nowhere, so we went on pressing our backs into the grating and stared defiantly up at him.

'I 'aven't got nothing to give yer,' he said, knowing perfectly well that we'd do nothing for nothing. 'See my Ginge for me, and you can bring your barrer.'

'What for?'

'Juss you go an' fetch my Ginge an' you'll find out.' We ran down the street and banged on Ginger's door.

'What's up?'

'Your dad says you've gotta get a move on, an' he's waitin' for you up by the baths. 'Ere, Ginger, what we got to bring our barrer for?'

'Coke,' answered Ginger, wiping his nose upwards on the flat of his hand, 'my dad's got a job shovellin' coke for the boiler room.'

Georgie and I nipped home, and heaved our barrer from under the shed in the backyard. Everybody had to have a barrer and ours was a good one. It was made from a heavy box mounted on a plank. Two large ball bearings were fixed to the axle at the back of the box, and two on the extended plank in the front which swivelled, so the driver could sit on the edge of the box and steer with his feet. The wheels made a terrible noise clicking over the pavement cracks, so we usually chanced our luck and ran it along in the road.

'Shall we tell Mum?' I asked.

'Nah,' said Georgie, 'give 'er a surprise.'

We waited until Ginger came past our house pushing his mum's old pram. Together we ran to the cul-de-sac that went behind the baths and there, separated from the narrow pavement by iron railings, were three pointed mounds of undisturbed coke, just delivered. Mr Dandy, in shirtsleeves, waistcoat and stringed trousers, was leaning on a shovel, his bowler hat tipped backwards over his ears, his coat on the railings.

'Where the bloody 'ell you bin?' he started on Ginger.

'You never said what time to come,' Ginger grumbled.

'I'll clip your bloody ear, answerin' me back!' We didn't look at Ginger. It was not considered etiquette between us to listen to our mates getting told off by their mum or dad. 'Brought the sack?' demanded Mr Dandy.

'Yeah.'

'Well, chuck it over, and one of you nip and 'elp me.'

Ginger glared sulkily at his father, and we didn't want to be standing there all night, so Georgie shinned over the railings and held the sack open. Mr Dandy shovelled it half full and together they heaved the sack onto the railings and tipped it over, letting the coke fall straight into the pram. I wondered what Mrs Dandy would say! Ginger and I picked up the spillings while they filled the sack again, and when the pram was almost full, Mr Dandy dumped some into our barrer.

'Lovely stuff,' said Georgie to me, 'see how shiny it is?' I looked at it, coke to me was coke.

'Shove off,' said Mr Dandy, 'and Ginge, cover the pram with the sack and go straight home, and you two,' he glared at us, 'keep your bloody mouths shut.'

Back home we couldn't get the barrer down the step in the scullery when it was half filled with coke, so Georgie got a sack and the shovel and I fetched the bucket from the fender. When we had finished we were dirtier than usual, and Dodie told me off.

'Georgie,' said Mum, 'where did you get this coke? Did you nick it?'

'Course not!'

'Where did it come from then?'

'We done someone a favour, an' he give it to us.'

Between us, and in our various ways we all made small contributions to the family's needs, and on the whole Mum couldn't afford to question our methods too closely, but she had a knack of knowing when something was a bit fishy.

'Be careful, Georgie. I don't want to have you in trouble.'

It was just our luck wasn't it, that Mum should run into Mrs Dandy in the street a couple of days later.

'Hubby still out?' Mum asked.

'Don't talk to me about my old man,' said Mrs Dandy, bitterly. ''E's bin out, in and out again, all in one week. 'E's back 'ome now, readin' the paper like 'e's on 'is 'olidays.'

'I'm that sorry,' murmured our Mum, 'I didn't know he'd had a start.'

'Start an' finish,' Mrs Dandy complained. 'He got a job up the baths, stoker in the boiler room. Couldn't keep it five minutes though, could 'e? 'Ad to start knockin' off the coke, didn't 'e? 'Arf the bloody street gets the coke, an' my ole man gets the push.' Mum's eyes narrowed as she suddenly remembered the bucket of coke in our fender. She straightened her face and pressed Mrs Dandy's hand.

'Never mind love. You still cleanin'?'

'Yeh, I'm just off to do a bit now. Got a lovely lady up Redcliffe Square.'

'Things will have to start getting better soon,' said Mum.

'I know one thing for sure,' answered Mrs Dandy as they parted, 'the can't get no worse.'

When Mum came in from work that night she looked very solemn at Georgie and me. 'I got something to say to you two,' she said, 'I met Mrs Dandy today.'

'Yes Mum?' said Georgie, wondering.

'And I found out where that coke came from. Do you know that Mr Dandy has lost his job?'

'Yes Mum,' we said together, and Georgie added, 'Ginger told us.'

'And did he tell you why?'

'Yes Mum,' said Georgie, 'but we didn't ask him to give us the coke, honest. Rowie and me was up the baths smellin' the coffee stall, an' Mr Dandy told us to go an' fetch 'is Ginger, an' then 'e gave us the coke.'

'All right,' Mum sat down. 'Now listen to me, the pair of you. You will never get something for nothing in this life. Just you remember that. One way or the other, you always have to pay. Do you understand?'

'Yes Mum,' we said. She fished in her purse and found three ha'pennies.

'There you are,' she smiled at us, 'get yourselves a saveloy between you, and we'll say no more about it. And don't bring it back here,' she called after us as we sped down our stairs, 'eat it in the street. Your father can't stand the smell of them in the house.'

We sat by the warm grating, peeling the thick skin from the hot peppery saveloy, putting off the moment of the first bite.

'Georgie,' I said, 'what did Mum give us the three'apence for?'

'You ain't arf a pudden'ead. She just told us you don't get somethin' for nothin'. Well, she got the coke didn't she, so it's cost her a saveloy.'

All the terraced houses round us were the same, having two rooms up, two down and a narrow room over the scullery, and most of them housed two or more families. Front doorsteps were hearthstoned white, wooden kitchen chairs were propped outside for gossip in the summer and all the kids got together for huge communal games in the road, for motor traffic was scarce. Many people kept caged birds, linnets and canaries, and in the summer hung their cages on the brick walls outside the front room windows. It was lovely, in the hot evenings, playing hop-scotch and listening to the birds.

The street had its watchers too, the consumptives sitting up all day beside open windows having the fresh air treatment, too near to death to take up space in hospital. One by one they disappeared and the curtains would be drawn for a few days. A strange quiet hung over the street on the day of a funeral. Everyone turned out, women stood in groups with their heads together, hands pressed against their mouths, and the kids dared each other to touch the hearse. Black-plumed horses stamped on the wood block road and the mourners came out of the house stiff and vacant, staring right through the familiar faces of their neighbours. It was terribly important for the bereaved family to appear head to toe in black, and they would pawn and go into debt for months to keep up the expected appearances.

Old Skewer's bottle and jar shop stood next to the butcher's. He accepted clean empties from the public, paying a farthing for a pound jam jar, a ha'penny on a two-pound jar and a ha'penny on most bottles, which he stored in crates in his backyard for collection once a week by the manufacturer's agent. One day, a boy climbed over the backyard walls and got among the crates, pinched a couple of bottles and stuffed them down his shirt. He walked casually into the shop and collected a penny for his daring. Word flew round, and in no time kids of all ages were scrambling over the walls and dodging across the yards all hell bent for the back of the bottle shop. It was a complete give-away when half a dozen of them charged into the shop all at the same time, out of breath, covered in brick dust and pulling bottles out of their coats.

Old Skewer suddenly saw the fraud and lashed out in all directions like a windmill. He chased round the counter losing his bowler hat, bashing at anyone he could reach. In the panic some kids got wedged in the doorway and Old Skewer barged into them, sending them flying all over the road. He chased them, hopping with fury and bellowing threats as they tore down the street chucking his bowler hat to each other. Things went a bit quiet after that, nobody had the cheek to take anything in to him, not even a legitimate jam jar.

Our favourite shop joined on to Old Skewer's, it was Antonio's the hokey-pokey shop. For a ha'penny he dropped a soft dollop of ice cream into a thick oval shaped glass on a classy stem, and when you sucked it out of the glass it was just like licking from an eye bath. The glasses were chipped, and the ice cream should have killed us for it was made on the premises, but it was custardy and sweet and we craved for it. Antonio had a gigantic waxed moustache and an enormous belly that burst through his shirt buttons, and a dirty tea towel was stuffed through his braces. He watched us lick the glass clean, often two or three of us sharing one glass, then he dunked it into a chipped enamel bowl of cold water standing handy on the counter, whisked the towel from his braces and polished it with a flourish, holding it up to the light like a maître d'hôtel scrutinising crystal.

Antonio also had a sarsaparilla machine, like an inverted gold-fish bowl with a cranky handle that pumped gas into the water. It made a spectacular sound, a riotous gurgling of breaking bubbles that sent us off into fits of dirty giggles. We were helpless with tears of laughter when Ginger said that Antonio 'was letting Charlie out of prison'. The drinks were a lurid pink and green and sent burps down your nose and bit your tongue. Sometimes trays of thick bread pudding stood on the counter for a penny a lump. It was grey and soggy, heavy on spice and mean on sultanas.

The dairy marked the boundary between us and the nobs, and we hardly ever had reason to go there. It was clean and fresh with a sharp black and white diamond floor and in the window stood a painted china stork with china frogs at its feet. The dairy employed a nippy little man in polished black leggings who pushed a cart round the street and sold milk from a churn with a yellow brass lid. People took their jugs out to him and he dipped a measure into the churn on a long milky handle. If he liked you he'd give you a little drop extra. 'The poor sods he don't,' said Georgie, 'gets a drop less.' We rarely bought fresh milk, it went off too quickly.

Another regular street trader was a raw-faced bony man, bent under a yoke from which hung two great drums. 'Cer-har-bolic! You wannit!' he shouted, and he did a roaring trade, though Mum thought lysol did the job better than carbolic. There was no humbug between us, women and kids queued up with empty bottles showing each other their bites.

'Beat the bugs,' shouted old Carbolic, as he filled a bottle for twopence, 'and bugger the fleas! Thank you lady.' We had a good go at the bugs once a week, though in the summer we had to pounce nearly every day. On Sunday mornings, as soon as we got up, Mum stripped the bunks and beds one at a time and Lu or Dodie dripped the lysol along the laths. Mum had a lighted candle in one hand and a hammer in the other. As the bugs emerged she shrivelled them in the candle flame and if one fell to the floor she dotted it one with the hammer. We all joined in, Joey on his knees by Mum, sharp-eyed and excited, while Georgie and I had to shake the bedding. We had no hopes of getting rid of them permanently, but we kept up quite an interesting battle. Bugs lurked and multiplied between the layers of historic wallpaper and migrated with deadly regularity between rooms and properties, and nothing would shift them until eventually the whole block was bulldozed to the ground.

The street had its memories and reminders of the Great War. One of the regular traders lifted his barrow with a rope round his neck attached to the shafts and served with one hand, an empty sleeve pinned across his chest; another man walked slowly, breathing with his mouth open, and we were shy of him because it was whispered that he had been gassed. We really didn't know what this meant, but Georgie had a picture from a magazine of weary-looking soldiers with their heads bent, holding on to each other's shoulders and looking lost. The war seemed like a great shadow that the grown-ups wouldn't talk about. Wooden boards were nailed up on some of the corner houses with names painted on them in memory of the men from the local streets who had died in the war.

We were looking at one of the boards one day, just reading the names, when an old boy walking with a stick stopped behind us.

'They made their rendezvous with death,' he said, pointing at the board with his stick, 'at some disputed barricade.' We stared at him, he looked at us, shaking his head, and then he went on his way.

'What's up with 'im?'

''E's barmy!'

'No 'e ain't,' said Ginger, ''e's on about all them blokes what got killed in the war.'

'Why don't 'e say so then, daft old sod?'

'Rotten though, innit?' said Ginger.

'What is?'

''Avin' their names up where they lived, like 'avin' ghosts 'angin' around. I bet they clank up the road in the night, draggin' their kit bags.'

'Shut up Ginger! You'll give Lil the creeps, she don't like the dark.' Ginger covered his head with his arms as Lil bashed at him and we ran off, soon forgetting the soldiers and the boards.

Unemployed ex-servicemen often stood outside the pub playing mouthorgans and banjos, but there was one special lot known as the Sallies that had worked up an act, and their visits were a rare treat. They came with a barrel organ, half a dozen emaciated men in shabby overcoats and old macs, and they stood quietly talking and smoking fag ends, letting the crowd gather round them. Abruptly, as the tumbling shrill music began, they swept us roughly out of the road, and each selected their own place. With slow, deliberate artistry they took off their coats, dropping them at their feet, and stood quite still, slowly raising their arms to the music and turning their heads sharply over one shoulder.

The crowd gasped! It didn't matter how many times we had seen it, we were always shocked. Every man was dressed like a woman! Faces were painted with powder and rouge, ear-rings and beads trembled, bare arms hung with bangles. Their necklines were low, bodices tight and flat, short skirts flared, and their thin, high-muscled legs tiptoed in slender shoes with high heels. As the tune changed to 'Valencia' they flung themselves into the dance, circling and stamping, fingers clicking and backs arching, a whirl of reds and greens, purples and pink, the silk fringes on their frocks whipping to and fro.

'Christ! 'E's got 'is leg right up past 'is ear'ole.'

High kicks were held as they circled on one foot, and leaping into the air they landed with the splits. Sometimes they sang snatches of the tune in high voices, falling back to let one of them dance a solo, then joining in again when they felt like it. We watched every move, dumb at their skill, intoxicated by the excitement of it all, and knowing somehow that it was a bit wicked.

When any old busker came down the street with a barrel organ we joined in, jigging about and singing the songs, but not with the Sallies. They wouldn't stand for any mucking about with their act, not from anyone. When a few pennies jingled down from one of the windows, it was usual for one of the nearest kids to run and pick them up and hand them to the busker, but if you attempted to do this for the Sallies, a muscular arm slung you into the gutter, and the pennies disappeared in a flash down his bodice. They had no time for kids or niceties, and were out strictly for cash.

When they had gone, once more a straggling group of ordinary men, the street seemed quiet and grey for a moment, then all the kids came alive and jumped into the road, hopping about holding one foot in both hands and barging into each other, singing and shouting and collapsing with laughter.

Sometimes the fancy would take us to try and see Lady Chantry. It was a sort of challenge, a dare to step into the other world. She lived in the big house right at the bottom of our street, the front of it facing the river. The side of her house and garden that edged our street had a beautiful iron gate in the tall brick wall, and we stood outside it, a grubby handful of curious young females.

'Yoo, hoo! Lady Chantry!' sang Luli, in a high childish voice. We waited. 'Yooo, hooo! Ladeee Chantreee!' she repeated, while the rest of us held our breath, ready to run.

'It's all right,' said Lu, 'she don't mind. 'Ang on.' We stared through the black pattern of leaves and birds on the gate, and fingered the gold-painted knob by the keyhole. Inside we could see a small patch of grass spotted with daisies surrounded by a stone path. Directly opposite the gate was a brick archway.

'She ain't comin',' said Nellie.

'She prob'ly ain't in.'

'I'm goin' 'ome.' Reen was fed up already. 'I don't wanna see 'er anyway, posh ole cat!'

''Old on!' commanded Lu, 'there y'are, I told yer!' A very cross woman in a huge white pinny came stamping towards us round the path and unlocked the gate. For a moment she glared at us, then jerked her head and we shuffled inside as she banged the gate behind us, leaving us standing on the grass in an untidy huddle.

Bright eyed, Lu turned to look at the arch and we all did the same, and after a long time, just like turning the page of a book, she was suddenly there. Luli bobbed a curtsey, it seemed proper, and Reen giggled. Lady Chantry glided towards us and moved her hand for us to be seated. We dropped on to the grass and the maid brought a fragile white chair for the lady. I was so nervous I began to dig out a daisy with my fingers and I tried to hide it up my sleeve. I ducked behind Lu's shoulder and looked at Lady Chantry to see if she had noticed. She was old, older than my mum, and ever so thin, but pretty and clean and like a china ornament. Her frock was black, but a lot of white lace went up all round her neck to her piled-up white hair, and a bunch of silvery things hung on a black ribbon from her waist. I couldn't see her shoes because her frock touched the ground.

'I hope you're all right,' said Lu politely.

'You're not supposed to say nothink till you're spoke to,' hissed Nellie.

'Thank you,' said Lady Chantry, 'I am quite well.'

'You don't mind us comin'?'

'I am pleased to see you, and your friends.'

'There you are!' Lu turned round to us. 'I told you she don't mind.'

'What we come 'ere for then?' asked Flo.

''Cause we're payin' a call, ain't we,' answered Lu, getting cross. No one was being much help with the conversation. She had got us in, and now the problem was how to get out.

'I must now say good afternoon to you,' said Lady Chantry, rising slowly to her feet, and as she went through the arch she turned and smiled faintly at us, and was gone. In a moment the maid had bundled us out of the gate, and we exploded into shouts, ran and jumped, pushing each other into the gutter. Luli was bursting with pride.

'See, you lot!' she yelled, and tucking her skirt into her bloomer legs she went up the wall, standing on her hands, banging her boots on the brickwork. 'I know a real posh lady I do,' her voice sounding funny, upside-down, 'and I ain't frightened to talk to 'er, neiver!'

'You're a rotten show off,' screamed Nellie back at her, and ran off home by herself, before Lu could bash her. I took the daisy home and gave it to my Mum.

Ivy Potter lived in the end house of the terrace opposite us. She left her front door open most of the time, and her back door was often open too, so you could look right through. Joey and I liked staring through Ivy's house because out the back there was always sunshine, and it shone on grass and plants, and Joey was convinced that it was the way into the country. We never did get into Ivy's country, but I often had to go into her front room.

I had caught measles and Mum said I should have been kept in the dark. But as we all lived in one room she had nowhere to put me, and a measle spot developed in the middle of my left eye. From then on for several years I had weak runny eyes, and went to school holding a bit of towel over them to keep the light out. When they were worse than usual I had to stop home, and Ivy offered to look after me.

She drew the curtains in her front room and made me lie down on the sofa, every morning and every afternoon. The sofa, with one sloping end, was stuffed with horsehair and covered in black slippery stuff, and no matter how I braced myself I always slid down and finished up lying flat with my eyes just a few inches above the floor. Every time Ivy came in to look at me, I pretended to be asleep and closed my eyes, but it was no good, at the last minute I always looked. The horror of Ivy's clapper just had to be looked at. The hems of her pinafore and skirt and petticoats were directly on my eye level as I lay on that detested sofa, and I could see her one proper foot in its cloth boot and the other foot dangling short, wrapped in an old black sock, swinging to and fro like a silent tongue in the bell of her skirts.

Ivy was quiet and dark, just like her front room. Years of leaning on her crutch had made her thin body twist sideways. She was a good woman, kind to me, and the sole support and comforter of her old parents. Every Sunday she made her slow way up to the Methodist Chapel, and she always invited us to their magic lantern evenings.

The chapel was the centre of adventure and culture. It was dominated by a true Christian Soldier of a parson known to everyone as the Old Warrior because he was never seen without his war medals right across his chest. He could let fly, and often did, clouting at random at the chaos of kids fighting to get into the busted charabanc on one of his brave outings to Wimbledon Common; then he would close his eyes and loudly beg God's forgiveness for his words and deeds, in front of everyone. Sometimes he would stop short and add 'and thoughts, O Lord,' then belt a boy behind the ear. The Band of Hope, the Sunday school and the scouts all operated from the chapel, and church parade was strict and smart. The drums and bugle band played, colours flew, and even if the uniforms were patchy, the parade round the streets went in fine style, with dogs and kids running behind and people watching from windows.

The real benefactress of the street was Mrs Daniels, and we and many other families would have foundered without her. Some of us got parish relief from time to time, most of our fathers were unemployed and nobody owned anything that would pawn for more than a few shillings. The only place where we could get something to tide us over was Mrs Daniel's shop, which gave sparing but life-saving credit.

The front room of her house was crammed with groceries, and she obliged as no other shop would by selling minute quantities. By Wednesday or Thursday, we were sent running to her for a penn'orth of tea or sugar. She would put a dollop of tinned milk or pickles in a cup for a penny, while rice and split peas were done up in newspaper screws of two and four ounces. She didn't mind being knocked up late at night for a baby's dummy, hastily torn off a display board hanging from the ceiling. She was a lovely understanding woman, and knew the ins and outs of everyone's troubles. She could calculate to a penny how much tick she could allow each family, and what their prospects were for settling up.

Off the street ran a pretty little grove of really old dilapidated cottages, picturesque in summer with nasturtiums and coloured creepers, freezing and damp in the winter. The front gardens had wooden fences and gates that stood straight on to the dirt and stones of the road. We often played down there, making mud pies, and Lu sometimes helped Mrs Bellows, who earned a living for her family as a washerwoman. All the rooms in Mrs Bellows' house were strung with washing lines, and a massive old mangle took up half the scullery. Many a night in the winter her kids went to bed with wet washing hung above them, and Elsie, the eldest, who was in Lu's class at school, got the rheumatics.

'I dunno wot I done to deserve this,' said Ma Bellows to our Lu one day, who was helping with the mangling.

'Deserve what?' asked Lu.

'That posh woman, comin' 'ere to complain about my Elsie. Bloody cheek!'

'What posh woman?'

'All dolled up she was. Come from the Town 'All I think.'

'What she on about?'

'Sez I've got ter stop 'angin' the washin' in the kids' bedroom. Ain't it marvellous! 'Ow am I goin' ter get it dry, I asks 'er. It's our livin', I sez.'

'Them posh women. Nosey bloody parkers,' answered Lu, entering into the spirit of the conversation, and knowing that Mum couldn't hear her. 'What she say then?'

'She said it's my fault my Elsie's ill.' Mrs Bellows pushed back her hair and looked helplessly at Lu. 'I'll tell you one thing my girl, and you can mark my words. It's not the idle rich that worries me, it's the bleedin' busy ones you gotta watch!'

THREE

On the Parish

We were newcomers to the street. Some of our neighbours had lived in the area for generations, their small dwellings surviving the great clearance that took place just before the 1914 War, when Chelsea was improved. We arrived in Chelsea in 1919 via Limehouse and Richmond, and settled into two shabby rooms in a small street just north of the Kings Road.

Mum was having a particularly rough time just then. Her married life had been a series of downward steps, and whenever she reached a new crisis, she always managed to combine it with being pregnant. Because her diet consisted largely of bread, tea and potatoes, she was a plump little woman, with bright round eyes and long brown hair, which she wore in plaits twisted over her head in two circles. She was like a street sparrow, foraging to feed and protect us with neither thought nor energy for anything else. She sang her funny old songs to us and laughed with us after her day's work as a cleaner was done. She entered into conspiracies with us to conceal our misdeeds and mistakes from Dad, often getting a swipe across the face from him for her pains when he found us out. She loved us and provided for us, she schemed and struggled to keep us together. Our devotion to her created an indestructible family unity.

Her own childhood had taught her a thing or two about survival, for her father died when she was a baby and her mother had to go back into service as a cook. The solution in the 1880s for any woman in such circumstances was to farm her baby out with a family sufficiently hard up to accept another child for a few shillings a week. Unfortunately, the family that accepted our Mum was worse than most. By the time she was nine years old she was a household drudge who had hardly ever been sent to school, and at thirteen she went into service as a kitchenmaid, her total possessions being a clean change of underclothes in a basket and a straw bonnet in a paper bag. She married my father when she was eighteen and her firstborn son died. She went on to have fourteen pregnancies, all the while coping with erratic flights from rooms to rooms that resulted from Dad's unemployment, losing her furniture and possessions on the way. In spite of dangerous stillbirths attended by local amateur midwives and numerous miscarriages, five of her children grew up. She had no vanities, but now and again a pretty pattern would catch her eye, perhaps on a scrap of cloth in Dodie's basket or on a roll of lino standing outside the ironmonger's 'I'd like a frock of that,' she would say, showing just for a moment that she still had an occasional thought for herself.

Dad was a thin, wiry man, with a heavily-lined strong face. We knew nothing at all about his family or where he came from, and we never asked. In fact, we never spoke to him spontaneously about anything, and because we were all afraid of him, kept out of his way as much as we could. He brought us up by the force of his authority and he completely dominated Mum by his overbearing personality and physical strength. He had no friends that we knew of, and apart from an abrupt and decidedly upper-class politeness to neighbours, which he used to keep them at their distance, he was never familiar with anyone in the street. There was a distinct air of superiority about him, in spite of his shabby appearance.

When he met Mum he was a seaman in sail, and this influenced the way we lived. Our room had to be kept ship-shape and everything put in its appointed place. Our worn washing line ran through a block and the ends were spliced. The mop, broom, poker, and chopper all sported Turk's heads and dad made the sennit mat in front of the hearth from rope ends. Cupboards were lockers, beds were bunks, and if we messed up a job we made 'heavy weather' of it, and if the sugar pot or the coke bucket or any other container was empty, we said 'there's a southerly wind in the bread barge'. We jumped to it at his command and a strict routine for living was laid down. He called us 'guttersnipes' and allowed none of the free and easy ways of the streets. Slang was forbidden, and we were made to repeat 'I beg your pardon' instead of a casual 'sorry'. We did not bang the door nor speak during mealtimes, sketchy though they were. Chores were done over again until they were done thoroughly, and we all learned the meaning of punctuality.

His attitude to the new freedoms of life in the nineteen-twenties was utterly Victorian, and he disapproved of women with short hair, short skirts and make-up. The growing popularity of the picture shows was, as far as he was concerned, another sign of decadence. 'Thank God,' he used to say, 'that I am old-fashioned.' There were rare occasions, perhaps after dinner on Sunday, when he would suddenly sing a music hall song, knowing all the words and the tune, winking his eyes and working his elbows to the rhythm. We were too shy of this embarrassing spectacle to join in, but we learned all his songs and the antics that went with them. As soon as we were on our own we copied him, slapping our feet and jerking our bums like Little Titch, and swaggering like Vesta Tilley.

He spent a lot of his days 'up the City', and we were thankful that he went to the pub every evening, Mum often ill affording a shilling to make sure he went out. The worst rows happened at night, after he came in. Sometimes a trivial incident that had happened during the day would be brought up until it grew all out of proportion, and we were kept awake while he nagged and bullied. When something had gone wrong outside, we always knew, for he came home with an air of suppressed fury about him. His face was white and he muttered to himself. For a short time there would be a sickening silence, and we kept still in our bunks hoping he would put the lamp out and go to bed. The signal was a crash as he slammed his fist on the table, chucking his supper off the plate, and we were off. It did not matter what subject he chose, he had brought his anger home and we were ready made to take it. Lu and Dodie and sometimes even Georgie got out of bed to protect Mum, things got smashed, there was a terrible noise and everyone was crying. Funnily enough, we nearly always had a drop of tea during a really bad row. During one of the lulls in the activity, Lu or Dodie managed to get the kettle on, and I knelt up in my bunk tasting my tears in the comforting hot tea.

In the morning we awoke to the alarm and the sound of Dad pumping the primus, as he squatted in the hearth in long wrinkled underpants. After a row the atmosphere was tense and worse than usually quiet, so we made up the beds and got out of the house as quickly as we could, puffy-eyed and sleepy. We never knew whether or not Dad would be there when we came home from school at dinner time. Sometimes he was, sullenly mending the broken bits of furniture, but now and again he packed his tools and cleared off for a few days, only to reappear without a word. Family fights were not at all uncommon and ours were no worse than average, so the neighbours neither interfered nor commented. Most were probably the result of long unemployment, lack of privacy and booze.

Dad hung about on the fringe of the wharfing and shipping world, but the times were depressed and openings scarce. He had neither the appearance nor the contacts to get the kind of job he wanted. For reasons better known to himself, he did not own an insurance card, so there was no threat of a menial job from the Labour Exchange, and no dole either. He used his wits, sometimes picking up a few shillings, but he made promises he could not keep and tried to sell things he did not own. We were trained to say that he was out when anyone came asking for him, and one persistent man referred to him as a 'bloody pirate'. Sometimes he had to clear out altogether for a few days, then Lu or Dodie were sent grumbling to meet him outside a church near Victoria with a sixpence from Mum wrapped in a bit of paper. Dad hated poverty and despised everything about the way we lived, but he was hopelessly enmeshed in both and it made him angry, all the time. Mum simply saw to it that we lived from day to day.

We grew up leading a double life, one with Dad and the other without him. We could switch from wary obedience to boisterous cheerfulness at the banging of a door. Our real freedom was the street, where we were daring and adventurous, inventive and noisy. We were part of the intricate life outside, curious about everything and nosey about everyone. We played all the seasonal games, naturally using the local slang and speech, and we were quick to find the means of earning or saving a penny.

Just three weeks before I was born, Dad had gone to Southend to try and get a job with the men who owned the sailing boats. They were large open boats, about thirty to forty feet long with a gaff mainsail and foresail. In the season they took trippers off the beach for a sail to the end of the pier and back. The owners usually took on a nautical-looking front man, to tout for customers and inspire briny confidence, a part tailor-made for Dad. Mum had a job washing up in a café and was seriously behind with the rent for the two rooms. One blustery morning she got home to find that her landlady, Mrs Butler, had put a padlock on her door, and she realised that she had come to the end of yet another of her lodgings. When something like this happened that was too big for her to tackle, Mum didn't make a fuss, but just sat down to find a way round it with a calm and resigned simplicity born of long practice. Her first thoughts were for her 'ol' potherbs'.

Dodie was away from home having the scarlet fever in the Seagrave hospital, so she was all right for the present. No need to worry about her. Luli and Georgie had gone to school and would be home any minute for their dinner, and there it was, a basin of pea soup, locked up inside the room. She waited outside the house for them, and took Georgie to the café where she worked and asked if they would take care of him, just for the afternoon. Mum needed a quiet place to sit down and have a think what to do, so she took Luli to the churchyard at St Lukes and found an empty bench. The chilly wind fluttered the bits of litter wedged between the starved privet bushes as Mum sat there, rubbing her thumb to and fro along the broken flap of her empty purse, the only outward sign that she was worried. Lu's voice came thinly from among the gravestones where she played a solitary game.

'Right then Lu,' called Mum, 'come on, we've a lot to do.' She got awkwardly to her feet, and tucking Lu's cold hand under her arm crossed the Kings Road to the street that led down to the Embankment, knowing that there were several clusters of little houses around there that might have a spare room. Half-way down the street she saw just what she was looking for, a postcard propped between the lace curtains of a small front-room window. She lifted the knocker on the green front door and for the first time clapped eyes on Ethel.

'Yes love?' Ethel stood in the narrow passage, sleeves rolled up, an apron round her thin body. She took in Mum's condition at a glance.

'You got a card in the window. Is the room still to let?'

'Yes love, six bob a week, share lav. Couple of beds up there but not much else.'

'Could we move in today?'

'No reason why not,' said Ethel kindly, 'six bob and it's yours. Have you got any more kids?'

'My boy, Georgie.' Mum thought it better not to mention Dodie just then, time to worry about that later on. 'Keep the room for me, would you please? I'll be back with the money after tea. Mrs Naylor's the name, my husband's away just for the present.'

'After tea then,' said Ethel. Mum breathed a thankful sigh and set about finding the six bob.

'Mum, I n'arf hungry,' whined Luli.

'You'll have to wait a bit,' said Mum, 'be a good girl and don't worry me.' Together they went back to the street where they had lived to see Mrs Carter, the moneylender. She sat at her open window and transacted business straight into the street.

'I need to borrow a shilling, please Mrs Carter,' said Mum.

'Penny a day interest Mrs Naylor.'

'I know,' answered Mum, 'I'll let you have it back tonight.'

'Righto then dearie, a shillin' it is.' Mum put the coin carefully into her purse and she and Lu walked down to the Embankment, over Battersea Bridge to The Latchmere then on to an old-established drapers' shop, where goods were sold on instalment. Luli breathed in the posh smell of new cardboard boxes and watched the metal balls whizzing across the shop on wires, operated so casually by wavy-haired ladies in black dresses. Mum went through a door leading into the back of the shop and signed for a pair of sheets at fifteen shillings for the pair, promising to pay a shilling a week and giving the new room as her address. The down payment was made with Mrs Carter's loan.

With the sheets under her arm, Mum and Lu returned to Chelsea and went straight to the pawn shop. There were several to choose from. One specialised in jewellery and bric-à-brac and others took more lowly items. Mum went to the smallest, run by a withered little man who already possessed a few of her things, the pledges long since expired. The shop was hung about outside with lumpy suits of clothes swinging sadly in the wind, boots tied in fruity bunches decorated the door, and on the pavement stood a rusty mangle, a wooden cased gramophone with a dark green horn, trestle tables of books and boxes of assorted tools. They slipped into one of the brown varnished booths, Lu heaving herself up to rest her chin on the high counter to look at the shelves of clocks.

'Get down Lu,' whispered Mum crossly, 'you'll scratch the paint.'

'I can't see!'

'There's nothing to see. Now hold your noise,' but Lu could just see the dome of uncle's little bald head as he presented himself. He wasn't much taller than Mum, and their eyes met over the polished surface when she placed the sheets on the counter.

'Ahhh, sheets!' sighed uncle. 'Sorry Missis, can't do much for you with sheets, not much in my line.' Mum knew this was the build-up for a poor price, and was prepared to argue.

'Brand new,' she said, 'still got the ribbon on.'

'Shockin' poor quality though,' he replied, reaching up to finger the miserly hem. (Course they are, said Mum to herself, they're not worth it at half the price. One wash and they'll look like bandage.)

'Last for years,' Mum said aloud.

'Not worth more than a dollar to me, Missis.'

'Can't you make it ten bob?' Uncle drew in his breath with a loud hissing sound.

'No. Tell you what, seven and six, final. Not a ha'penny more.' Mum tried to keep the relief out of her face as she accepted the money and the ticket, and went straight to Ethel's house.

'I've brought the rent,' said Mum, as Ethel opened the door, 'six bob's right isn't it? Could we have a look at the room now?'

'Upstairs front,' said Ethel, walking up the passage, 'you can use the copper in the scullery, lav's out the back. I'll see if I can find you a key, but we hardly never lock the door.' Mum and Lu went up the wooden stairs and stood in the room that was to be our home for the next seven years.

'What's that?' asked Lu. 'What's it for?'

'Heavens, I haven't seen one of those for twenty years,' said Mum, 'not since I shared in service. It's a bed, you daft 'aporth. It's a big double bed that folds up out of the way. My word, it won't half come in handy! We are in luck, Lu, I never expected beds.'

'This one's all lumps,' said Lu, sitting on the single bed in the corner.

'You've seen a flock mattress before! It only wants a good thump and a shake out. Lu, I never thought I'd be this pleased,' said Mum cheerfully. 'Now you stop here and have a sit down while I go and fetch Georgie.'

Lu stared hatefully between the cage-like bars of the horrid double bed then backed away and poked her tongue out at it. She had taken an instant dislike to it, and her struggles with it over the years to come were to confirm her first impression. She stood by the window, looking curiously at the new street, watching the daylight beginning to fade and felt her tummy rumbling.

Mum moved as quickly as she could back to her old street, collected Georgie from the café and stopped by Mrs Carter's window. She repaid the shilling and the penny interest and still had five pence left.

'I've had to move,' she informed Mrs Carter.

'Yers dear, I had heard.'

'I expect Mr Naylor to be home in a day or two. You might let him know that we're in Manor Street now, next to the sweet-shop.'

'Righto dear. You goin' to manage all right?'

'I should think so,' answered Mum wearily, 'we usually do. Thanks for your help Mrs Carter.'

'Tata dear, all the best.'

Taking Georgie by the hand, they crossed the road and knocked on their old front door. Mrs Butler stood across the threshold. She had some compassion for Mum, and was a kindly woman, but rent was rent, and she hand no intention of letting the Naylor family back into the house. Mum explained about the basin of soup.

'Wait a minute,' she said and went upstairs. Mum and Georgie stood on the doorstep until Mrs Butler returned carrying the basin and one of our blankets. 'There you are Mrs Naylor. Have you got anywhere to go?' Mum nodded. 'Come round in the morning then,' she said, 'and collect your things.'

Georgie was too full of café tea to want any more food, so Luli and Mum shared the thick pea soup, sucking dollops of it from their fingers, then Mum cuddled them up under the blanket on the little bed and Georgie went to sleep, while Lu and Mum talked.

''Ere, Mum,' said Lu, 'why didn't you borrow all the six bob from Mrs Carter, instead of us hafting to go all the way to Battersea for them sheets?'

'Good girl Lu. Now just you hark to me and I'll learn you something. A shilling a day borrowed at a penny a day interest for one week is seven pence, right?'

'Right Mum.'

'Six shillings borrowed for a week makes the interest come to three and sixpence, doesn't it?'

'Yes Mum.'

'Now, how much each week do we have to pay for the sheets?'

'A shillin' a week.'

'Well then, it's not how much money we owe, but how much we have to find each week to pay back that matters. I could never find three and six a week to pay just for interest, not on top of everything else, and still have the six bob to find. But we can easily find a shilling, see?'

'Yes, I see now. I could probably earn nearly a shillin' easy, runnin' errands.'

'Another thing,' said Mum, 'we might have to miss out now an' then, and I don't suppose they'll send a man all the way over here, not juss for a shillin'.'

'P'raps not. Does that mean we got to go to Battersea every week?'

'It would stop the man coming here.'

'Good,' said Lu, 'I like muckin' about on the bridge, an' I want to see them ladies whizzing the money across the shop.'

Mum tucked the blanket round George and leaned back against

the wall. 'Lie down now love, I'm tired, an' you must be. Your father will probably come up with something, he knows I'm due soon and he'll be home presently. We'll get some of our things tomorrow.'

So we became established, and a month later I was brought home from St Luke's hospital to add another demanding presence to the already overburdened room.

When I was getting on to be three years old, Mum went into St George's hospital to have Joey, so Lu and Dodie contrived to get some things ready for the new baby. Dodie made a long flannel gown at school and her teacher let her bring it home without paying for the material, and they unravelled a green jersey and made a shawl. Between them they knitted a bonnet and boots and made a flannel binder with blanket-stitched edging. Everything was carefully folded into a paper bag ready to be taken to Mum, but a few days before she was to come home, Dad had a visitor. He was a persistent man, tougher than most, for he disbelieved that Dad was out, pushed his way up the stairs and confronted him in our room. There was a terrible scene, so Dodie bundled us all down into the yard to wait until the man went away. Instead, after a long time, Dad himself came down carrying the paper bag, and he told Dodie to take it to uncle's

'I can't. I'm not old enough,' cried Dodie.

'Do as you're bloody well told,' he shouted, 'and bring the money straight upstairs.' Dodie went, and soon came back into the yard with the bag of baby clothes.

'I told you,' she said, frightened, 'uncle won't take 'em off me.'

'Good!' Lu was crying with temper and disappointment.

'I'll have to go up and tell him.' Miserably, Dodie went upstairs and tapped on our door. Dad flung it open and saw from her face that there was no money. He wrote a note on a piece of paper and signed it, which Dodie immediately read. It said, 'Please do the best you can.' She returned to the pawn shop but uncle still refused and Dodie came home again, in a worse state than before.

'I daren't go upstairs again Lu.'

'I'll go,' said Lu. 'I'm glad he can't pawn 'em. He ain't got no right to.' Dad was furious. He snatched the bag from Lu and slammed out of the house, leaving the strange man alone in our room. I don't know how much uncle paid for the pathetic little bundle but it must have been enough, because soon after Dad returned, the man left. We stayed out in the yard for a long time, Dodie quiet and miserable, and Lu furiously angry.

'Poor little bugger,' she said. 'He ain't a week old yet an' 'e's had all his clothes nicked.'

I didn't know who the little bugger was and I didn't understand what was going on. I only knew that Mum had gone away and I looked for her all the time. Lu and Dodie took care of me as they always did. In the mornings they left me with Ivy Potter and collected me at dinner time on their way home from school. Each time we went into our room I was all ready to see Mum there. In the afternoon I stayed at home with Dad. He used to crush up a lump of salt into a saucepan lid and give me dozen split peas and I played at making patterns. Sometimes he went out and would not let me stay indoors by myself, so I played outside in the street until Lu or Dodie came home. I spent most of the time squatting under Ethel's window, looking up the street, waiting for Mum.

Dad cooked our dinner. Every day he boiled a suet duff in a cloth and whacked great steaming dollops on our tin plates. The colour was dishcloth and the outside wet and slimy. The inside texture collapsed into dense layers until it congealed into a solid middle. Sometimes we got a spoonful of black treacle on it and sometimes a dip into the sugar jar. On Saturday he made dandy funk, a reminder of his sea-going days, pounding a couple of penny arrowroot biscuits and mixing the crumbs with mashed potato, dotted with fatty scraps of boiled salt beef. When Mum was home, we smothered dandy funk with a twopenny ha'penny bottle of 'Daddies' Favourite' sauce, with Georgie glorifying the occasion by reading aloud the exotic ingredients printed on the label. Dad wouldn't let us put salt or even pepper on it. He said such a thing was an insult to the cook! His masterpiece on Sunday was sausage stew. The joy of finding a piece of sausage among the drenched potherbs had to be savoured and we left these tasty bits until last, and ate them with our eyes shut.

At tea time we just had a cup of tea, but if Dad was out Lu quickly cut a couple of slices of bread and spread them with condensed milk, which we shared in the street. Once she made us toast by pressing the bread to the asbestos mat over the primus stove, and we squabbled over the burnt bits, because she said it tasted like liquorice, but it didn't. We usually had our proper tea when Mum came in from work, bread and marge with sometimes jam and occasionally fish paste. We took a saucer to Mrs Daniels and she scooped two penn'orth of it out of an enamel pie dish. It was rich and strongly flavoured and the top was covered with flat discs of yellow fat. Dad gave us fried bread and cocoa, and instead of letting us muck about after tea he made us get the beds down straight away and by seven o'clock we were washed and in bed. He went out as usual, and we sat up listening to other kids still out playing in the street. Dodie read to us, and as it got dark she knelt on the end of her bed with her book on the table propped up by the candle. Every night Georgie asked Luli when Mum was coming home, and at last she said, 'Tomorrow'.

'Good,' said Georgie.

'An' we're goin' to have a surprise.'

'I know.'

'No you don't.'

'Yes I do,' Georgie argued, 'we're goin' to have another baby.'

'Ow, not that, we're goin' to 'ave pancakes.'

'Who sez?'

'Me an' Dodie. We're goin' to make pancakes for a treat for Mum comin' home.'

I waited and waited all the next day, and she didn't come. When Lu and Dodie came home from school I was a heap of misery.

'It's all right, love,' Dodie cuddled me. 'She's coming soon. Come on upstairs and help us get ready.' They tipped some of the water out of our big jug that stood in the washing bowl and Lu poured flour out of a paper bag. Dodie began to stir, pressing the spoon against the insides of the jug to see that there were no lumps.

'That's not pancakes,' Georgie looked disappointed. 'That's for makin' paperchains.'

'Shut up!' said Lu. Dodie went on stirring and peering into the jug.

'I think you're supposed to have an egg,' she said.

'What for?'

'To make it bubbly.'

'We ain't got no eggs,' said Lu, 'stir it faster.' Dodie beat hard with the spoon and lifted it out to drip back into the jug. It looked exactly like paste. Georgie put his finger in and licked.

'It don't taste like nothing,' he said.

'Then it must taste like something,' Dodie shouted at him.

'No it don't,' grumbled Georgie. 'It don't taste like nothing.'

'Now,' said Lu, 'we got to hurry up. Dodie, you light the fire. Georgie and Rowie, wipe your faces over, clear everything up, put our plates in the fender to get warm and get out the frying pan.'

'What you goin' to do then?' asked Georgie.

'I'm goin' out for some sherbet.'

'What for?' asked Dodie.

'To make the pancakes bubbly. How much money we got?' Mum had left a shilling with Dodie in case anything cropped up, and Dodie had kept it hidden in her work basket under the bed. She dragged the basket out, unwrapped a grubby piece of paper and counted.

'A tanner, three pennies and two ha'pennies.'

'Give us 'a'pn'y.' Lu bounced down our stairs and Dodie took the stub of pencil from the rim of the candlestick, crossed out tenpence on the bit of paper and wrote ninepence halfpenny, and put it back. She gave me the damp face flannel to wipe my face and hands, lit the fire and began to clean up the mess on the table. Georgie put the plates in the fender as Luli came bursting into the room with a cone of newspaper twisted at the bottom. 'You can all have one dab,' she said. We each licked one of our thumbs and took turns to press it into the fine white powder, rolling it round to gather as much as we could on to the wet bits, then sucked slowly.

'I love sherbet,' Georgie said, 'specially when it makes burps come down my nose.' Lu tipped the remainder into the jug and we all watched to see what would happen.

'Give it a stir Dodie,' said Lu. Dodie gently poked the insides of the jug and there was a convulsive heave, then a white volcano erupted over the top. We shrieked, and ran our fingers up the outsides, pushing the thick rivers back over the rim.

'That'll do lovely,' said Dodie. 'What we got to fry them in?'

'Marge,' Lu answered.

We were ready, kettle on the fire, waiting for Mum. We were cheerful, excited and fluent again, the barren days of living with Dad had simply melted away. Dodie put her tammy on and took Georgie with her to the bus stop and I stayed indoors to wait with Luli.

'Where's Dad?' I asked her.

'Gone to fetch Mum home.'

'Will he come in? Will we have pancakes if he comes in?'

'A course not! We'll have to wait till he goes up the pub,' said Lu. 'I'd better put the frying pan away, just in case,' and she also stood the jug of pancake mixture back in the washing bowl.

We heard them tramping up the stairs. Lu opened the door. Mum came in first and I stared at her. For just a second she looked different, and then, all of a sudden she was just the same, wearing her shiny sideways hat the colour of an old penny. She carried a bundle against her chest, and was smiling at us.

'All right then love?' she said to Lu.

'Yes Mum,' Lu answered. 'Let me have him.' Mum handed the bundle over to Lu and bent down to me.

'Been a good girl then?'

'Yes Mum.' She put her arms round me and kissed the top of my head.

'Now then Dodie, what about a cup?' Dodie lit the primus and put the already warm kettle to boil.

'He's lovely, Mum,' said Lu. 'Fair inne? Still goin' to call him Joey?'

'That's what your father wants.'

'Is Dad comin' in yet?'

'No,' said Mum, 'I don't think so. He left me at the bus stop when he saw Dodie. He's had enough of you lot, and told me to get Joey settled down. He won't be in till bedtime.'

'Good,' said Luli. 'Dodie, out the frying pan. We got a surprise for you, Mum.' The pancakes were a surprise for everyone. We sprinkled them with sugar and tried to roll them up, but they were stiff as board and cracked and broke into bits. Some were thick and some were thin, and they were dry as wadding and about the same colour. We didn't care, but ate the lot with greasy fingers, all talking at once, telling Mum everything, while our new baby learned to sleep through the noise.

By the time tea was over everything felt just like it always had done, so I went down into the street by myself to chalk on the pavement. The paving stones outside our house were real stone of slightly different colours made up in odd squares and rectangles and just right for pictures. We used lumps of plaster for drawing which Lu and Georgie found among the rubble in the ruins in Flood Street. I chose a space and sat down to draw, utterly content. I always drew the same picture, a house with windows and a door and a chimney with smoke. I put a circle up in one corner with spokes all round it to show the sunshine, and two toffee apple trees, one on each side. Sometimes I drew what I thought was a bird on top of a tree and sometimes an unrecognisable cat by the door. By the time Lu stuck her head out of the window and shouted to me to come and wash for bed, I had smothered the pavement with scribble and forgotten that Mum had ever been away.

Joey slipped into the family routine without any trouble, except at night when he cried. This made Dad angry and he shouted at Mum, so Luli had to get dressed and take Joey out into the street and walk about with him until he dropped off, sometimes ever so late. In the end Mum had to get him a dummy which she pinned on his clothes and whenever he started to yell, one of us shoved it into his mouth. If he spat it out we dipped it into the sugar or the condensed milk. That made him shut up.

We could not get used to Mum being home all day, and Lu and Dodie soon realised how worried she was. Dad went out, and hung about on the pier, sometimes earning a few shillings by sculling an owner out to the private boats which were moored just below Albert Bridge. Luli ran errands and hearthstoned doorsteps for twopence a time, but without Mum bringing in regular wages, we were desperately short of money. Our mid-day meal was reduced to a plate of boiled oatmeal with a sprinkle of sugar and our meal at night was the usual bread and marge, but with no extras. Mum still managed to feed Joey herself. While she had been in hospital her cleaning jobs had been snapped up and there was no hope of getting her foot back in those doors, for competition among charwomen at sixpence an hour was fierce. Her one real anxiety was that we should fall behind with the rent again.

'We got to raise the wind, somehow,' she said to Lu.

'Ain't there anything left for uncle's?'

'No. Honestly Lu, we've nothing fit to take.'

'We're on the floor, ain't we, Mum.'

'Just about, love.'

'Can't we work the sheet lark again?'

'I've thought of that. We already owe Mrs Daniels, an' I don't want any more debts if I can help it.' Lu watched Mum's fingers pleating and unpleating her skirt over her knees.

'What we goin' to do then?'

'There's nothing else for it,' Mum said, 'I shall have to try to get on the Guardians until I can get a start.'

'Oh Mum, we've never bin on the Guardians!'

'I don't suppose they'll have us. Your father hasn't got an unemployment card. They always ask if you have a card, it's the only way you can prove you're out of work.'

'Then he ought to go to the Guardians, not you Mum.'

'Use your loaf, Lu! You know what he thinks about the Guardians, he'll have a row with them and get chucked out. Then where shall we be?' We had all heard Dad going off about the Guardians. 'What the hell are they for?' he'd shout, banging on the table. 'To guard the poor from starvation or guard the worthy taxpayer from the predatory poor?'

Without saying a word to Dad, Mum and Georgie nipped up

to Arthur Street next morning where the Board of Guardians sat in judgment. The Board was made up of gentlefolk of the parish who had to try and decide if the appeals for relief were genuine. Some Boards, notably the one in Poplar, gave limited financial assistance, but in Chelsea parish relief consisted of a box of basic groceries and tickets for milk and fuel.

Mum's hopes dropped when she saw the crowd of men and women, some carrying children, queueing outside. Slowly they inched forward until at last she took Georgie's hand as they passed through the main door and entered a room lined with wooden benches and chairs. They took their places on one of the benches and leaned back against the brown painted wall. People sat quietly, and Mum could hear the questions put to the couple standing before the long wooden table, and the murmur of their mumbled replies. The interviews were brief and Mum kept moving up as newcomers arrived. Georgie wanted to go to the lav, but Mum shook her head, determined not to miss her place. An elderly lady with a nice face asked Mum's name and address and told her to be ready, and her name was called.

Mum faced the Board, looking only at the silver-haired gentleman across the centre of the table. The first questions were simple enough. No, she'd never applied to the Board of Guardians before, no, not in any other parish. She told them how much rent she paid for our room and the names and ages of all the family, and why, because of the recent arrival of Joey, she was out of work, just for the time being. Then, as she expected, came the tricky ones.

'Mrs Naylor, is your husband registered as unemployed?'

'What was his trade, or profession?'

'Where, and when, did he last seek employment?'

'What proof have you of this?'

How could Mum put into a few words the complex pattern of Dad's character, and in front of strangers? Dad and his affairs did not fit into the ideas held by the Board of the typical working man. There was nothing typical about Dad. 'Mr Naylor,' she said earnestly, 'was in the shipping line of things, and while he's looking for a position, he picks up what work he can, but things are very quiet just now. He sort of employs himself like.'

'When did your husband last have regular employment?' asked one of the ladies behind the table.

'Not since the war, m'm. But I can get work, and I shall get fixed up,' she assured them, 'within a few days. My eldest girl leaves school this Christmas, so we shan't come here regular. I just need a bit to tide us over.'

The Guardians came up trumps. Mum and Georgie came home with a stout cardboard box containing tea, sugar, flour, oatmeal and treacle, and relief tickets for marge and bread. The marge ticket had to be taken to a special shop which had a printed notice on the wall saying, 'Relief Tickets Taken Here', but they made you wait at the back of the shop until they had served all the cash customers first. We collected the bread from the workhouse where it was baked by the inmates. Colossal loaves they were, double length tins, and wrapped in a give-away yellow paper, so everyone knew you were on the Guardian's bread. Workhouse men were easily recognisable by their thick grey suits and stiff unshiny hobnailed boots, but not the women. I never knowingly saw a workhouse woman, but we heard the bell tolled every night at six o'clock. 'That's a reminder,' Dad said to us, 'to mind out you keep this side of the bloody gates.'

We were on the Guardians for about three weeks. The second week Mum got a ticket for coal to the value of three and sixpence-One or two greengrocers around us sold small bags of coal, so Mum managed to swap it for vegetables. She also got a ticket for a pint of fresh milk a day, which we fetched in turns in a jug from the diary on Chelsea Common.

Then our luck turned. Mum got a job at twenty-five shillings a week, and we were solvent.

FOUR

God Bless the Prince of Wales

Towards the top of our street stood a red brick house with pointed gables and long windows edged with a pattern of stone slabs. A flight of grey stone steps led up to the front door and a row of black iron railings guarded the drop to the area in front of the gloomy basement window. This house was taken over by a group of volunteers and opened as a baby clinic and mothercraft centre. It was here that Mum got her job. The volunteers were real ladies who talked in clear cultured voices and knew exactly what they were going to say before they said it. Not that they were bossy or condescending, they simply had a distinct air of assurance about them that distinguished them from the dozens of ill-nourished and shabby women who flocked to the clinic with their young children.

The ladies wore flowered overalls that buttoned down the front like coats instead of the cross-over pinnies that we were used to, and they kept their hats on even though they were indoors all day. Their shoes were different too, narrow, firm, and there were no gaps between where their shoes finished and their stockings started. Small children see a lot of feet. Most of the women down our street wore shoes that were squashed out side-ways, collapsed around the misshapen feet inside, and with heels so worn that they trod on the sides. No one bought shoes out of boxes, for we never looked beyond the bunches that were strung up in pairs outside the door of the shoe shop, and priced from two shillings and elevenpence. Some families belonged to a weekly boot club, but the proceeds were invariably spent on the men and children.

The ladies at the clinic were kind but businesslike, and typical of the long tradition of upper-class British women who became aware of social needs and cared sufficiently to do something practical to help. It was no trifling part-time charity job for them. They worked hard, and some of them were there for years and years.

Mum's job was to keep the whole place clean, wash the medicine bottles, make tea for the doctor and staff and help hump the prams up the front door steps. She started at eight in the morning and worked until six in the evening, with an hour off for dinner, so she could nip home and save us from Dad's duff. She had Saturday afternoon off from one o'clock and all day Sunday, although she could earn a bit extra if she did the clinic washing over the weekend. She usually did this on Sunday evening, but sometimes Luli went instead to give her a break. Georgie used to take me to stare through the railings to watch Lu scrubbing at the towels and nappies in the big sink in front of the basement window, waiting to see how long it would take her to look up and see us and give us a soapy wave.

The ladies brought cast-off baby clothes to the clinic which they gave away. They were obviously from their posh friends because the buttonholes were silk stitched and there were often three buttons close together where one would have done. Undernourishment was one of the most common problems, so the clinic supplied cheap or even free packets of dried milk powder, tins of cod liver oil and malt, and bottles of Parrish's food, a bright pink iron tonic. Joey did well out of all this bounty and I was just small enough to squeeze into a couple of delicate little dresses. I insisted on wearing these in the winter over my jersey and thick drawers, and Lu said I looked like a tea cosy. Mum brought home a curious garment for me to wear underneath which she said was called a liberty bodice. I think it was supposed to join up with something else lower down because there were buttons round the bottom edge, but I never found out what they were for.

With the arrival of Joey, things began to happen to our family. First Mum had got this marvellously secure and regular job, and then Dodie left school and with a great stroke of luck found a job straight away. My turn came next, and I started in the bottom class of the infant school. The child population in our part of London had fallen at the beginning of the 1920s and the schools were able to take pupils from the age of three.

Luli was in the big girls' department at the same school and so I set out with her on a freezing cold spring morning. With one hand I clutched the elbow of her sleeve and in the other I held a brown paper bag with my name written on it. Inside was a thick slice of bread and marge that Dad had cut into four pieces and pressed together, marge sides inwards, for my lunch at playtime in lieu of breakfast. It was fine trotting behind Lu, listening to her talking to her friends and shouting to them across the street, being wrapped up and going somewhere, instead of holding up my feet at home while Dad mopped the dusty floorboards. The school had two stone entrance gates close together, one marked *Boys* and the other *Girls and Infants,* and as we came up to them I stopped dead. Lu tugged me forward but I put my chin down and held back. Around the gates, running in and out were dozens of huge, brawling, noisy kids, shoving and shouting, chasing and barging, enormous boys with great red knees and stringy-haired girls with gaping stockings and loud voices. I didn't know any of them and I could not pass between them. 'Oh, come on Rowie,' Lu dragged my hand, 'you said you wanted to come to school.'

'I don't like it.'

''Ere, Reen,' called Lu to one of her friends, 'take 'er other 'and.' Squashed between Lu and Reen I drew my whole self inwards as we pushed our way through the *Girls and Infants* and into the grey asphalt playground. It was a small inadequate space, but to me it was a vast battlefield alive with chains of big girls with linked hands who chased, cornered and captured their victims, their mouths opened by an endless excited scream. I clung to Lu and slunk behind her.

'Come on, love,' she said to me. 'I'll show you the lavs.' In the grey brick wall that divided our playground from the big boys over seven years old, were two narrow openings, one each for boys and girls. 'This one's ourn,' said Lu, 'the one nearest the gate an' don't you forget, 'cos it's wicked to go into the boys' lav.' A lot of girls were standing around the entrance and Lu fiercely pushed a way through for us into the narrow gangway, open to the sky. On one side was the brick wall and on the other stood six shabby green painted doors that left a gap eighteen inches or so from the floor and three feet from the half-roof. The doors banged as girls flitted in and out and at the end of the gangway we stared into an empty lav. Ginger shiny bricks separated it from the one next door and a piece of frayed cord had been tied to the chain so that small children could reach. 'If anyone looks under the door at you,' said Lu, 'shout at 'em.'

'It's all dirty, Lu,' I said, 'innit.'

'A 'course it is,' Lu answered cheerfully. 'It's 'cos it's froze. They all gets froze when it's cold an' the chains don't pull. You'd better go now.'

'I don't want to.'

'Now look 'ere Rowie. You can't just run in an' out whenever you want to. It's not like 'ome, you 'ave to put your 'and up an' ask.'

'I know,' I said. 'Dodie's already told me.'

'And mind you put your scarf over your 'ead if it's rainin'.'

We dodged across the playground where a small semicircular stone sink was fixed to the wall with a button built into the brickwork. 'You push this 'ere,' said Lu, pressing the button, 'an' if you're lucky water comes outa' that spout. Drink under the spout an' don't use the cup.' There was an iron staple in the wall holding a galvanised chain and on the end swung the metal beaker, that showed its history by a myriad of dents and scratches. 'You never know,' said Lu darkly, ''oo's drunk outa' that!'

'I can't reach the spout,' I said.

'Put your 'ands under, daft,' said Lu, 'an' drink out of them.'

''Oo pushes the button then?' I asked.

'Don't be bloody awkward, Rowie. You gotta tongue in your 'ead, ask someone! Now then, I'll show you the shed.' This was the only other feature of the playground that I had not seen, but before we got there a bell rang, long and loud. It was a quarter to nine. 'Stand still,' whispered Lu. Everyone stopped like statues in mid-hop and mid-shriek and there was an uncanny grey silence. A lady teacher stamped her feet in the cold wind, her bright brown coat and shining brass bell the only colours in the drab scene. She glared round the playground to see if she could catch anyone wobbling, then with a swing of her arm, rang the bell again. Out of the muddle, long lines took shape. Lu bundled me into a queue by the wall, muttered, 'don't talk, and follow them. See you dinner time.' and left me. When the bell rang for the third time, my line toddled off first and I noticed that they put one finger across their lips, so I did the same, and we kept on doing it until we stopped in a long green tiled corridor. Our teacher was waiting for us and the first words I heard her say were, 'hands down.'

Her voice was soft but it carried a commanding edge, and she made the word 'down' have two syllables. She was very tall, angular and flat chested. She had a pale sandy face, pale brown eyes, and hair the colour of weak tea pulled back into a scrap of a bun on her thin neck. She wore a straight green overall with brown lisle stockings and long thin brown shoes with a strap over the instep. Her name was Miss Bland and I watched every move she made, followed each word she spoke, so I could repeat every detail when I got home. She was the first posh person I had ever been closely associated with, and I was fuddled with awe, stupid with embarrassment and terrified that she would actually speak to me. This gulf between us and our teachers continued throughout my schooldays, for we could never accept that they were real people. They knew everything, had complete authority over us and at all costs were to be kept in total ignorance of our private lives outside school.

Because we were so small we had a low wooden peg stand outside our classroom, but all the other classes used the proper cloakrooms, with glass panes above the green tiles and three chipped glazed sinks. Under Miss Bland's unfussed eye, we struggled with our motley collection of wrappings, and at last I was to see the vast, cold, cream and brown-coloured classroom with gigantic slabs of windows taller than our house. My first feeling was one of utter despair because there were no desks, but then I was seated at a small flat table with another new girl called Vera in a tiny chair with a curved back. I liked the chair so much it made up for the disappointment. We had to put our lunch bags on the table in front of us and sit up with both our hands on the table, fingers locked to stop the fidgets, while Miss Bland went through the solemn ritual of calling the register. This ceremony was observed throughout the school with hushed formality, the teachers concentrating on keeping the brown paper-covered documents immaculate. They blotted, and changed pens with long thin nibs, angling the red 'present' marks and then blue ones for latecomers. The red ink in the white china inkwell let into the corner of Miss Bland's table took on a supreme significance and was used for no other purpose. Absentees received a carefully penned and elongated blue nought.

We lined up to place our paper bags into a cane wastepaper basket, Miss Bland checking that our names were clearly written. When it came to my greasy little bag she said, 'What excellent writing,' and I had a little spurt of pride in my Dad, which came as something of a surprise.

The infant school was for ages three to seven and consisted of only four classes of around forty children in each. We were allocated the whole of the ground floor of the school and when we were all assembled in the hall, it was barely half full. Our headmistress might have been made of parchment. She had a yellow powdered face and flat paper-sculptured hair. She wore beige, and walked stiff-necked and stiff-kneed with her feet pointing sideways in toffee-coloured shiny shoes. The kids call her Old Ma Pegtop. Sometimes she smiled at a pretty or nicely-dressed little girl, but her obsession was with royalty. Her desk was in the corner of the hall and was partially screened from the draughty doors by four hinged pieces of polished wood. This was plastered with newspaper cuttings and photographs of King George, Queen Mary and Old Pegtop's favourite, the Prince of Wales. We marched into the hall for prayers to the thump of the piano and stood for the whole time. We whined through the hymn, picking up the words and tunes of *All Things Bright and Beautiful* and *Fight the Good Fight* on alternate days, and then gasped through The Lord's Prayer with hands together and eyes closed. A resounding smack punctuated the prayer every so often as a teacher crept along the lines and slapped the back of a boy's head who was caught peeping through his fingers.

After prayers we had a bulletin on the health and activities of the Royal Family and then we had to show our handkerchiefs. A few hands went up waving proper ones with hemmed edges. 'Now, rag!' Up went a few more displaying crumpled bits of cloth. 'It will not do,' boomed Old Pegtop. 'I insist that your mothers can find a piece of good clean rag.' Then she got on to her camphor campaign. 'Each of you,' she said, 'can find the means to buy a piece of camphor,' and she held up a little piece about half an inch cube. 'Tie it into the corner of your handkerchief, and then we shall all smell delightful and keep free from the tishoos. March, out!' I took this instruction as a royal command and made Lu and Dodie's life a misery until I had a piece of camphor, which cost a penny at the chemist's, tied into the corner of my rag, which was pinned to the front of my jersey. All was well until it went into the copper with the washing.

For the first few mornings on our way back to the classroom Miss Bland kept us in the corridor at the coat pegs, learning to put on our coats and shoes. 'We are not babies any more,' she said. We struggled with torn sleeve linings, big jackets with sleeves rolled back that served as overcoats, laces and wrong feet. Several children had no socks and many more had newspaper stuffed inside the soles of their shoes. Once in the classroom, we started with counting. The monitor gave out flat tin boxes, so worn and used that the paint had faded and the metal was shiny. They rattled, and inside were ten thin sticks of wood about three inches long and an eighth of an inch square. They were coloured red and blue and green and yellow, and I loved them. I sorted out my colours and made patterns and piled them up. Together with Miss Bland we held up one, then two, and learned to count. We held up two and two and counted to four and took one away and counted three. We had millboards, supposedly black, but grey and greasy with age. We slowly copied figures from one to ten with slaty chalk, spitting on the shiny boards to make the chalk stick. Around the walls Miss Bland hung home-made posters. The first one was a picture of a big green apple with the capital and small letter 'a', and so on through books, cats and dogs to zebras. After counting we made 'a' and 'b' sounds, and got to work on the phonetic alphabet. On the other side of our millboards the chalk whizzed across the surface as we learned to make our letters. The three 'r's were to be the solid foundation of our lessons throughout the infants.

At playtime I was given my paper bag and ventured alone into the playground. After the orderly classrooms, the playground was bedlam. I watched what the other kids were doing. Most of them played chasing, pushing each other clean off their feet. Others jumped up and down with a continuous shout into each other's faces. Long strings of small boys chunted behind each other, playing trains, winding their way through the crowds. Some just squatted down against the walls, their faces pinched, their hands drawn up into their sleeves. I wandered over to the shed, which was for shelter, for we were sent out to play whatever the weather. It was simply a roof built over a corner where two of the playground walls joined, with the open side supported by brick columns. One of the walls had been painted with dark green paint, and along the bottom ran a wooden bench about eighteen inches high. The bench was the scene of the simplest and most excitingly savage game I had ever seen. A boy, or a girl, leapt on the bench, and leaned hard against the wall with braced legs. It was the object of one or a group of several other kids to nudge, push, shove or pull him off, and for the quickest to hop up and take his place. Four or five of these games were going on at the same time all along the bench. Kids shot up and disappeared like skittles. They landed on the bench skilfully shoving a knee behind the defender in one movement and levered him off, giving him a wild push to send him on his way sprawling on the asphalt. Some were bodily yanked by the arms and twisted to the ground with jersey sleeves stretching a foot over their hands. One lot all fell down as two girls came hurtling together off the bench on top of them, screeching with grazed knees and bashed fingers. Noses ran, boots, socks and trousers were scuffed with grey dust, bloomer legs trailed over knees and the noise reached fever pitch as the games got faster and faster. The bell rang, and just as in the morning everyone stood still as stone, panting and grinning, red-faced and filthy. The din of children's voices echoed for a moment round the shed and then in the stillness there was the faint clap of a pigeon's wing. At the second bell I stole into my line still carrying my unopened paper bag. I hadn't remembered to go to the lav either.

After playtime we began to learn to tell the time with a big cardboard clock face, and then to memorise short poems, repeating each line after Miss Bland as she walked among us, nodding her head in time with the halting words. Sometimes she read us stories, some by Beatrix Potter and one about two posh kids who lived in a house with a garden and a cook and a nurse and a cat called Tabitha. She asked questions about the stories, drawing the words out of us, and when we had fashioned the answer between us, we all had to say it together. Every morning she played the piano and sang to us in a thin wobbly voice. Her favourite was about a foxglove.

'Foxglove, foxglove, what do you see?
The cool green wood and the bumble bee.'

Foxgloves and bees and cool green woods were way outside anything I could visualise, and the more she sang it the more I wanted to know what it was all about. I said 'foxglove' and 'bumble' all the way home, 'bumble', 'bumble', 'bumble', and I asked Mum what they were.

'Well love,' she said, 'in the country there are all trees an' that, and underneath the trees these foxglove flowers are growing. They're ever so mauve. Now then, buzzin' all over the place there are these big brown an' yeller flies, but they look like velvet, an' they go in the flowers to eat their dinner.'

'Mum,' I said, 'where is the country?'

'On a train,' she said. 'A long way.'

'Can we go?'

'Course we can love, one of these fine days.' I knew what that meant already. It meant it's something nice to talk about.

Bit by bit, from songs and poems, stories and pictures in books, I began to build up a feeling about the country, but I couldn't find out where it was. Some things I did know. It would have red toadstools with white spots and sitting up rabbits, and everyone walked about with a cow on a piece of string.

At twelve o'clock the bell monitor swung the brass bell outside our door, and half in my coat I ran to the playground and there was Lu. I felt I hadn't seen her for days and clung to her hand all the way home. We were back again by twenty to two, and after the register Miss Bland opened the long cupboard and gave each of us a thin rolled-up straw mat. We spread them on the floor in neat rows and then sat on our own mat until we were tidily arranged. Then Miss Bland said, 'Lie do-own,' and flat on our backs we went to sleep or doze or fidget until playtime. This was terrible, worse than Ivy's sofa. I stared into Vera's face staring into mine. It was cold and draughty, and I put my hands under my arms. The door opened, someone had come into the classroom. I couldn't see, so I sat up to look. Suddenly the room was filled with the sound of my name. 'Rose, Rose Naylor, what do you think you are doing?' I crashed back on my mat with such force that I banged my head and saw Vera catch her bottom lip in her teeth. Now I wouldn't go to sleep, never. My name had been said in front of everyone, and I squirmed with shame.

After playtime we had a circular game, either Lucy Locket or Farmer's in the Dell or Ring o'Roses, and then back to words, words words. We recited what we had learned that day, Mary, Mary, or Simple Simon. We remembered the alphabet and counted to ten. Slowly the things we were taught became locked inside us and we never forgot them. I was taken at four o'clock to wait on a little bench until half-past, when the big school came out. A couple of other kids sat with me, and Miss Bland told us not to move, so we didn't.

Friday was the day I counted to and waited for. All day I behaved impeccably, hoping to catch Miss Bland's eye by doing everything especially well. At half-past three on Friday afternoon we had two special treats, on alternate weeks. The first was the rocking horse and the other was the percussion band. The horse was a huge dappled grey with red nostrils and a coarse flowing mane and tail. At each end of the horse were round cane baskets. As the horse swung to and fro the baskets moved gently up and down. We sat on the floor round the horse and Miss Bland chose one boy to sit on the saddle and a girl to sit in each basket. I sat up tall, but the first week I wasn't chosen, although there was time for about four rides each fortnight. The following Friday we sat on the floor, this time round the piano. Miss Bland distributed three drums, three tambourines and three triangles. The boys got the drums, three girls were given the tambourines and the triangles were shared, girls held the triangles and three boys were given the strikers. I held a triangle and my partner with the striker was a daft kid called Eric. Miss Bland played a tune, emphasising the rhythm, and we clashed and banged out of time. Eric had no idea, so I started hitting my triangle against the little metal bar that dangled from his fingers. He began to hit me, so I pushed him but Miss Bland still played and the other kids banged the drums. Every night in my bunk I used to shut my eyes and pretend I was in the rocking horse basket bashing a tambourine. I never did get a tambourine, but I had lots of rides in the basket and I didn't think much of it.

The pulse of the school was the sing-song tempo of learning by heart. Tables – pounds, shillings and pence, weights and measures, inches, feet and yards – flowed from every door and window. Poems and spellings were chanted over and over from the blackboard, every breath taken at precisely the same moment, every eye on the red and white cardboard pointer that tapped its way from word to word. By the time I was six I was in the top class of the infants, where we knew up to our six times table, wrote in printed letters, did mental arithmetic and dictation and could read sufficiently well to 'go up' into the big school. We could add, subtract, multiply and divide in two figures. I was also carting Joey to school, and tucking his dummy up his jersey to help him through his afternoon sleep in the babies' class.

We were completely unaware of the state of affairs in the London County Council, of the chronic shortage of money, and accepted the strict training in the care of school equipment as a matter of course. We had no exercise books and received half a sheet of paper from the monitor for dictation. This was collected at the end of the lesson and redistributed the next day for use on the other side. For arithmetic the sheets were cut lengthways, and we worked our sums down the narrow strip of paper. If we wanted a second piece we had to hold up our paper to show it had been properly used on both sides. All through the infants school we worked in pencil, and these were counted as they were collected and locked in the cupboard. We had very few books, and those we did have were limp bound for economy. They were distributed, collected, counted and locked away after each lesson. We used Fundamental Arithmetic, Fundamental English and a series of readers. The reading books had a few pictures, but the only colour was yellow. Discipline was an inherited atmosphere. Our elderly teachers needed little more than their firm voices and experienced eye to maintain the formal routine. Every moment of time in the classrooms was filled with work. There were no discussions, no pots of paint and there was no acting. We rarely left our seats, except for one half hour a week when the girls did country dancing and the boys had team games in the playground.

Once we left the babies' class we had real desks, massively made on a solid iron frame with a sloping top and fixed bench that was designed for two children to sit side by side. The class-rooms were stepped so that each row of children could be clearly seen above each other. Our normal sitting position was up straight with arms crossed behind our backs, but when our teacher wanted five minutes to herself the order was 'heads down'. We folded our arms on the desk top and lay our heads sideways on our wrists, breathing the dirt-grained smell of the wood.

Old Pegtop really let herself go on Empire day. Many girls wore a bow of red or blue ribbon on their hair. At home we threaded cotton through any bits of red, white or blue paper we could find and pulled them into rosettes, which, on this day of days, we were allowed to wear on our frocks. We had ordinary lessons until playtime, then the infants assembled in the hall where we sang the National Anthem. Four chosen girls from the top class wore additions over their clothes suggesting national costumes. The Scottish girl had a piece of tartan cloth pinned to one shoulder, the Welsh girl wore a white pinny and a black cardboard stove hat, the Irish girl was enveloped in a green cotton shawl and the English girl was given a sailor collar and carried a cardboard trident. They each sang a verse and a chorus from *Ye banks and braes, Land of my fathers, By Killarney's Lakes and Fells* and *D'ye ken John Peel,* in thin, nasal voices. The Union Jack sagged between sepia photographs of King George V and Queen Mary, and arranged on the floor beneath the portraits were the three aspidistras that usually stood on the hall window sills, their leaves freshly washed for the occasion. In single file the entire infant school bobbed round the hall to the tune of 'Land of Hope and Glory,' thumped repeatedly by Miss Bland on the upright piano. As we reached the flag we were supposed to salute smartly, but it was too much for some of the little kids when the moment arrived. Several used both hands, some waved 'bye, bye', while Old Pegtop nodded and smiled. The ceremony ended with the singing of *God Bless the Prince of Wales,* and then we had a half holiday. We sauntered home in the sunshine that always blessed Empire Day, with no understanding of anything we had done, but aware that we were exceptional because we were English.

May day was even better. After playtime in the morning, we assembled in the hall and sat on the floor to watch the top-class girls hopping around in plimsolls or socks with spuds in the heels, 'Gathering Peascods' or 'Sellinger's Rounding'. Then came the great moment when they bolted the maypole into the brass plates in the middle of the hall floor and the red, blue, white and yellow ribbons were shaken out. Selected boys and girls tripped to the piano, the girls wearing white frocks and peering through nodding bunches of artificial posies fixed insecurely to their hair. What an incredible ritual it was! Under the benign eye of the London County Council, five ageing spinsters and a hundred or so crummy kids watched their chosen young men and maidens prance around the symbol of fertility.

When I was old enough to leave the infant school, I was thrilled at the idea of being a junior. I couldn't wait to have an inkwell in my desk and do joined-up writing with a pen. There were alarming stories, though, about the men teachers in the junior school, especially the headmaster, Old Crawley Lordy. They said he crept about the corridors with a cane hidden up his sleeve. I changed my role from a cocky know-all top-class infant to the bottom of the unknown juniors, a lesson in life no one can learn too soon.

Dodie had learned the lesson, in fact she had crammed plenty of bitter ones into her short life. When she was thirteen she left school to look for work, because Mum could wait no longer for the bit of money she would earn. It was lucky that Dodie's birthday fell during the holidays, and as she was held in such high regard by the headmistress, she was allowed to leave at the end of the Christmas term.

Because she was the eldest Dodie had always been very close to Mum, being with her through all the downward moves and evictions from the two respectable rooms in Limehouse where Mum had started her married life. Dodie always had the newest baby to look after, and understood from an early age when Mum was worried, in debt or pregnant. She sensed Dad's moods better than any of us, and she knew about death too. When Dodie was nine years old, Lu was seven and Georgie three, they were living in the two rooms just north of the Kings Road. Mum was due to have another baby and she sent Dodie hurrying to fetch a neighbour. That night the baby was born dead while the three children listened in the next room. The woman who had come to help wrapped the dead infant in a cloth and left. Dodie took care of Mum as best she could, and put Georgie and Lu to bed on the kitchen table, where they normally slept. A man from the undertaker's came the next day and Dodie handed him the little bundle and half a crown. 'Tell your mother,' the man said, 'that I'll pop him in with someone else.' It took Dodie a long time to accept the idea of her little brother being buried with a stranger, but she never said anything about it to Mum, or Lu. When I was born two years later I had both Dodie and Lu to care for me and I could have wished for nobody better.

School for Dodie and Lu was a chronicle of absenteeism resulting in dreaded visits from the 'school gawd man'. His correct title was that of 'School Board Man', but he was raised to the diety of 'gawd' by the wrath with which he descended when he found an absentee running errands in the streets or, as in our case, pushing a pram. Dodie was bright and industrious, always top of her class, and was held up as an example to Lu who trundled along a couple of classes behind. Both girls had a reputation for singing and were in the choir, joyfully sending *Nymphs and Shepherds* rolling over the rooftops. Because they were so small they were put into the front row of the choir, standing erect with the little fingers of each hand linked in front of them, their eyes riveted on their teacher-conductor. When they were left out of the London School Choirs festival at the Albert Hall because neither of them had a white frock, Dodie was sickly quiet and Lu rampaging with temper. In our house, misery and disappointment was inexpressible.

Their clothes were no worse than those worn by many of the other girls, but that made it no less a problem. Shoes were the biggest worry, because there was no way to make a cast-off pair fit. There was one time when Lu had to slop to school in a pair that she had fished out of Ethel's dustbin. When she came home that day she made us laugh, prancing about in her stockinged feet. 'We 'ave to march into prayers,' she said, slipping her feet into the awful old shoes, 'like this,' and she lifted each foot up leaving the shoes behind. 'An' ol' Miss Bish sends me back for muckin' about. Looked over 'er ol' glassis at me she did. "Head up, Louise," she said. "Swing your arms, Louise." So I did, an' I marched clean outa me shoes. She bent down then an' looked right through 'er glassis proper, an' there was Ethel's ol' shoes starin' back at 'er.'

'What she say?' asked Georgie, giggling.

'She told me to pick 'em up an' walk into prayers quietly. Fat lot a' chance she'd got. All the others 'ad gone in by this time see, an' I wasn't goin' into the hall with them all watchin' me, 'specially carryin' me shoes, not for ol' Miss Bish nor no one.'

'Go on then,' said Georgie. 'What didjer do?'

'I picked 'em up,' said Lu, laughing, 'an' I run, straight back into me classroom an' I stayed there on me own all through prayers. An' when ol' Miss Bish come back, she never said nothing.'

'You n'alf got a nerve,' Georgie gazed at Lu with pride. It was a rare thing to defy a teacher.

When Mum was charring, before she got the job at the clinic, she often brought home odds and ends given her by her employers. Dodie took charge of them, sorting out which could be made use of and which were worth trying to pawn or sell. Lu fell in love with a disastrous black and yellow dance dress, the skirt heavily encrusted with jet beads. On Lu, the knee-length dress sagged towards the floor, and when she walked the beads whacked her calves. She wore it to school over a green jersey, and when she sat down at her desk in class the weight of the skirt fell between her knees and hit the floor with a resounding thud, to the delight of the girls around her. The dream of Lu's collection was her coat, a chic affair in tweed, originally designed to wrap round and fasten low on the hip with one gigantic button. After Dodie's alterations it hung sadly on Lu, and the button walloped between her knees like a cannon ball.

Dodie's plunge from the top of her class to the bottom of starting work happened when she saw a postcard in the window of a tobacconist's shop in the Kings Road. 'Cashier wanted', it said, and gave the name of a nearby greengrocer. She made up her mind on the spot and went straight to the shop, which was near Sloane Square. For a moment she looked at the pyramids of polished fruit and washed veg, punctuated by bunches of grapes and hands of bananas and the unexpected row of pineapples hanging from hooks. She also noticed that the shop had an opening into the florist's next door, which not only had dark green pots of flowers, but also great cascades of flowering branches and made-up displays of flowers in baskets, the likes of which she'd never seen. She ran her eye over the prices and realised that the shop was pretty classy. Taking a breath, Dodie plunged in.

'Yes missie?' A man in a brown overall bent down to her.

'I want to see the gov'ner,' said Dodie, 'please.'

'Who?'

'The man in charge. I've come about the job.'

'You've what? Oh, hang on a minute,' he said as he went out to the back of the shop. Dodie stared into a pile of tomatoes, pretending to be a customer, and had an overwhelming urge to rush out into the road, but before she could escape the assistant beckoned to her.

Mr Chisholm, the owner of the shop, could hardly believe his eyes. A child stood before him who couldn't be more than twelve. Long wavy hair fell over her shoulders from beneath a blue knitted tammy. Some old girl's cut-down coat broadened her shoulders and stopped short above a brown cotton skirt that just showed her knees in black woollen stockings, before they disappeared into clumpy boots. 'What's your name?' he asked.

'Dora Naylor.'

'And how old are you Dora Naylor?'

'Fourteen on Tuesday.'

'Left school?'

'Yes.' Dodie's blue eyes stared fiercely up at the man, who was quietly amused at this determined little figure.

'Do you think you can be a cashier?' he asked.

'Of course I can.'

'And what makes you think so?'

'Because I'm good at sums.'

'Do you know anything about keeping books?'

'No. No sir,' said Dodie, desperately remembering her manners.

'We'll have a look at your writing. Put down the name and address of your school and where you live,' Mr Chisholm said, 'and we'll see.'

Dodie waited every day for the postman. After a week a note was dropped in the passage one evening by one of the shop assistants on his way home to Battersea. Ethel found it and called up the stairs while we were making the beds. Dodie flew down and raced back, and suddenly afraid of the contents, gave the envelope to Mum. 'Open it Dodie, it's your letter,' said Mum. We watched her read it to herself and then she smiled.

'He says yes! Oh Mum, I've got the job! Look everyone, read it. I've got a job.' Dodie hugged Mum, and Mum kissed Joey. Lu picked me up and whirled me round and Georgie jumped up and down shouting, 'Dodie's got a start. Dodie's got a job,' and Ethel banged on her ceiling. Dodie plaited her hair and Mum showed her how to pin it up as she started off for work the following Monday. Her hours were from eight in the morning until seven at night with an hour off for lunch. She had a half-day on Thursday and worked until eight o'clock on Saturday night. Her wages were to be ten shillings for a fifty-six-hour week.

'It's no good,' said Mr Chisholm, 'she can't be seen.' Dodie was sitting on the high stool in the cash booth, stretching her back and lifting her chin, trying to see over the top of the till.

'S'all right sir, I can manage.' Dodie was desperate to please.

'I'll fetch something to bunk me up a bit, an' I'll move the stool an' sit sideways.' As with everything else she did, Dodie flung herself heart and soul into her job. She was quick and obliging, polite and smiling with both the customers and staff. It wasn't enough to sit behind the cash register. She mastered the books, learned to serve and began to do small jobs in the florist's department. This she enjoyed above everything and they discovered that she had a talent for making wreaths and bouquets. Mr Chisholm owned several properties in the area and he trusted Dodie to collect the rents, making entries in the books in her neat precise hand. She ran all the way home at lunch time, ate her dinner in twenty minutes and ran all the way back to the shop. She proudly gave every penny of her wages to Mum, but what with all the dashing about at dinner time and walking to collect the rents she came to a decision. 'What I need,' she said to herself, 'is a bike.' She certainly did, but she was going to have to wait for it.

Soon after Dodie started work, something almost happened to Joey. With everyone at work or at school, and no one knowing where Dad would be, the care of Joey was a real problem. It was solved by one of the ladies at the clinic giving Mum a huge and very beautiful old-fashioned pram, with enormous wheels and handlebars. It was far too big to push through our narrow passage to the backyard, so it had to stay outside on the pavement, and Dad anchored it to the bars that guarded Ethel's front-room window with a nifty piece of splicing. Every morning, after having his bottle, Joey was put into the pram with a home-made harness to prevent him from falling out, and there he stayed until dinner time when he was fed and changed and put back for the afternoon until Lu came home from school.

A lot of people passing regularly up and down our street got to know Joey and many of them stopped to talk to him, including two very posh ladies. One evening, Ethel called up the stairs to Mum to say that someone was at the door for her. Mum went down and was taken aback at the sight of two beautifully-dressed women. They were hesitant and smiling and began to say how much they admired the little boy whom they had got to know, and what was his name, and could they come indoors and talk about him. Mum couldn't allow this, because we were in the middle of putting the beds down and anyway we never had visitors, not even people we knew. Couldn't they talk outside, Mum asked, but they said no, for what they had to say was rather important. The gave Mum their card and Mum reluctantly agreed, to get rid of them, that she would call on them.

Lu, Dodie and Mum talked about the ladies. 'They're posh all right,' Mum said, 'but they talk different. I wonder what they're up to?' Lu, ever hopeful and stuffed with romantic ideas, thought they might be Dad's unknown relations, and that they'd found us and we were all going to be rich like them. Georgie told Lu she was barmy. Dodie wondered if they wanted to be Joey's godmothers. None of us had a godmother and we felt we'd lost out on the chance of a bit of magic, and there was a surge of optimism at Dodie's idea. One thing was certain, the ladies had to be kept a secret from Dad. There was no knowing what he'd get up to if there was a chance of making a few bob out of them. In the end, Mum decided that she and Dodie would find out what it was all about the following Thursday afternoon, on Dodie's half-day off from work. Dodie hung about outside the clinic until Mum could slip out, and by four o'clock they were outside a big house in Onslow Gardens, where the door was opened by a uniformed maid. They were shown into a drawing-room where they refused tea, as neither of them felt able to deal with anything other than the unaccustomed surroundings. Sitting on the edge of a brocade chair and clutching her purse, Mum paid attention.

'Mrs Naylor, we are only visiting in England, our home is in Canada.'

'Yes 'm,' said Mum automatically.

'This is my sister Miss Everly, and I am Mrs Childers.'

'Mrs Childers,' Mum repeated the name, nodding.

'We have become very fond of your little boy, Joey. Now please tell us, why is he left alone outside your house so much?'

'Well 'm,' Mum was a bit affronted, 'it's because there's no one at home all the time, that's why.' She looked to Dodie for help.

'Mum goes to work you see,' explained Dodie quietly and clearly, 'and I have just started in a shop, and my sister Luli is still at school.'

'What about your husband, Mrs Naylor?' smiled Miss Everly.

'He's at home sometimes an' he looks to Joey, an' if the weather is bad our neighbour takes him in. I'm sure Joey is quite well, 'm.'

'But he doesn't appear to have anything to play with, no one to talk to him,' said Mrs Childers.

'Oh, Joey's happy enough 'm. The girls play with him the minute they're home, an' everyone knows him.'

'Mrs Naylor, would you consider Joey's future? You have other children, and I know things are not easy. We should be happy, so very happy if you would let us take care of Joey.'

'You mean take him to Canada?'

'Of course. He would have a wonderful home there.'

'For good?'

'We often come to England. We could try it for a while, and see how Joey settles down.'

Mum let out a deep breath and looked down at her hands. She was completely out of her depth, surprised and shocked, and had no idea what to say next. Dodie wanted to go, she just wanted to get Mum and herself out of the place and safely home, so she stood up, too upset to look at anyone but Mum and heard herself saying, 'Thank you very much, but we must be getting back.'

Mrs Childers took them to the door. 'Thank you both for coming. I do want you to think about what we have said. It is for Joey's good.'

Mum walked quickly with Dodie hopping every so often to keep up. They were nearly home before Mum said, 'Dodie, how far is Canada?' Dodie remembered the sticky varnished map, coloured pink and blue hanging on a pole over the blackboard.

'It's miles and miles Mum, over the Atlantic Ocean, on top of America.'

Lu rushed me home from school that day, she was half daft with excitement and impatience. I stopped in the street to play with Joey while Lu went indoors to make his bottle. When she heard Mum and Dodie coming up the stairs she flung the door open. 'Tell us,' she cried, 'What did they say, what did they want?' Her bright face became puzzled when there were no answering smiles and she watched Dodie slump on to the edge of the bed.

'They want Joey,' said Dodie quietly.

'What jer mean?' Lu was startled. 'What jer mean, they want Joey?'

'They want to take him,' Dodie stared at Lu, 'to Canada.'

'What for?' Lu rounded on them. 'They can't! They bloody well can't, can they Mum?'

'Course not. Course they can't,' said Dodie, and at last she began to cry, 'can they Mum?'

'No,' Mum said, 'not if we don't want them to.'

'We don't, do we Mum! Not for a million thousand rotten pounds,' yelled Lu. 'Who do they think they are?' She was angry and frightened and rushed down the stairs, unstrapped the astonished Joey and hugged the breath out of him. She stumbled with him up to our room and thrust him at Mum. 'There,' she cried, tears running down her face, 'don't you dare say they can have him!' Mum put Joey over her shoulder and patted his lumpy wet nappy.

'Sh! It's all right love, sh! It's all right,' she murmured to him as he began to yell. 'Now stop making all this fuss the two of you.' Her voice was strained, it always went like that when she was upset. 'Lu, go out and find Rowie and Georgie, an' Dodie get the kettle on, just look at the time! I don't know what you've been thinking of Lu, you should have brought Joey up long before now, he's all wet.'

The ladies must have stopped by Joey several times after that because we found a white woolly rabbit with pink eyes in his pram, and then he had a yellow mug and saucer with black hens painted on them. Mum never went back to the house in Onslow Gardens, and the ladies never called on us again.

FIVE

A Penn'orth of Potherbs

The jumble sales held at Mum's clinic were a blessing to everyone because the stuff was good and the prices low. Soon after she started working there, Mum became an expert at hovering in the background when loads of jumble were delivered and sorted, so she could get a preview of the clothes she needed for us. One particular Saturday morning, when Joey was only a few months old, Mum saw a bath standing among the cardboard boxes. It was an elegant little brown and cream hip bath, the sort of bath that stood in front of the fire in a lady's bedroom. Mum wanted it so badly. The thought that someone else might grab it on the day of the sale was unbearable, so she knocked it off. She stuffed her duster into her overall pocket, picked the bath up and marched it straight out of the door, down the street, up our stairs, and plonked it in the middle of our room. In a sudden panic she rushed back to the clinic.

It was understandable. The nearest thing we had to a bath was half a barrel which was kept in the scullery. It was a heavy, splintery lump of permanently sodden wood with the bung stuffed up. It was as much as Mum could do to lift it empty, so it had to be filled and baled out with a saucepan. We bathed in it in the summer, but in the winter the scullery was freezing.

Dodie was indoors minding Joey when Mum appeared with the bath and sat astonished as Mum left without saying a word. The first I knew about it was Dodie's head sticking out of the window, shouting at me to come in quick. I called Georgie and we raced upstairs just as Lu arrived humping a bag of shopping. We all stood and stared at the bath, touching it. With a delighted smile, Dodie gently put Joey into it. I got in too, and then we all took it in turns, Lu making us take our boots off. We sang and laughed, getting in and out, and created such a din that we didn't hear Dad come in. He shouted, and at once we got up and stood still.

'Where did this come from?' he asked.

'Mum just brought it home,' whispered Dodie. I knew what he was going to do, we all did, and I hoped and wished that Mum would come home and stop him, but she didn't.

'Right then Luli,' said Dad sharply, 'it should be worth a few bob,' and he sent her out there and then to sell it, and told her not to come back without five shillings. For a moment nobody moved. 'Come on,' Dad was angry, 'let's get going!' Somehow we manhandled it down the stairs, turned it over and raised it up as high as we could so that Lu could duck under. She spread out her arms as we lowered it on to her head, and we watched her skinny legs stagger as the great brown shape lurched between the wall and the kerb.

She dawdled outside the pawn shop where uncle displayed his more popular goods on trestle tables underneath streaky green blinds.

'Uncle!' she called. 'Uncle, d'you wanna buy a barf?' The shrewd little pawnbroker appeared in his doorway, so Lu piped up again, 'How much?'

'What for?'

'Me barf.'

'Don't want it.'

'Go on,' wheedled Luli, 'it's posh. Never bin used.'

'Half a crown.'

'That all?'

'Half a crown.'

'Mingy ole nit,' yelled Lu, as she shuffled away towards Arthur Street where there were a couple of cheap junk shops and a yard where the rag and bone men off loaded their barrows. There were usually a few hangers-on loitering around the yard, their carts in the kerb, picking up a bob or two out of a bit of totting and dealing. Luli hung about outside the first shop until she saw a man moving about inside.

'Wanna barf?' she called.

''Ad one.'

'Jer wanna buy one?' she bawled.

'No.' The shop next door was shut. Lu peered through the dirty, crammed window from under the bath, but there was not a sign of life. One of the men in the yard ambled across the cobbles and leaned against the wall, a flat, stained fag-end stuck to his lip.

'Ole Lumber might buy it,' he said.

'Where is 'e?' asked Lu hopefully.

'Out. Took the 'orse this mornin'. Back ternight.'

'That's no good. I can't 'ang about all day, me Dad's waitin'.'

'I might 'ave it.'

'How much?'

'Give yer three an' a tanner.'

'My Dad sez it's worth five bob.'

'Not to me it ain't.'

'Go on,' said Lu, 'give us a dollar.'

'Knocked it off?' he asked with a smirk, and strolled back into the yard leaving Lu staring miserably after him.

'Bloody cheek,' she said to herself, 'well, that's it then. Last hope, the cats' meat shop.' This was down the passage near the World's End, a gloomy little den where an elderly woman sold lumps of offal for cat and dog food. Horrible purple and yellow innards dangled on hooks round the wall. She also bought rags, weighing them on an ancient flat machine, and sometimes empty bottles and odds and ends. Lu stood by the scabby door, just ajar, where a single step led down into the room.

''Ere, missis, do you wanna buy a barf?' The old girl blinked through the door.

'What do you think I want with a bath?'

'I wanna sell it.'

'Not to me you don't. No good to me. No call for a bath.'

Lu was tired, fed up, and wondering what to do next.

Georgie and I stayed out in the street after Lu had gone. We were mending the axle in his ball bearing scooter with a stick of firewood when we saw a grown-up woman running towards us. It was Mum, still in her clinic overall.

'Quick,' she said to us, 'help me get the bath back. They've missed it.'

'We can't! Lu's got it. Dad's sent her out to sell it.'

'Stop her. Go on, both of you, find her and fetch it back, an' hurry up. Go on, Georgie, run!'

I chased after Georgie, first to uncle's and then to the junk shops. She wasn't there. We were out of breath and still running past St Luke's churchyard when Georgie shouted, 'Look, there's Lu.' She was flopped on the end of one of the benches, and the bath, with a terrible big scratch on it, was lopsided on someone's grave.

'Quick Lu,' panted Georgie, 'we gotta get it back.'

'Where to? What's up?' Lu shot to her feet.

'Mum's bin home,' said Georgie, dragging the bath off the flat tombstone, 'they've missed it up the clinic an' we've got to get it back.' Together we carried it over the road and past the Town

Hall and hesitated as we saw Mum standing on the clinic steps. She jerked her head at us and in a panic we bumped it up and through the door.

'Scarper,' she whispered, and we fled home.

They made me go upstairs by myself to see if Dad was still in. I raced past rotten Old Sacky's door and found Dodie with Joey, so I climbed on our table and bawled out of the window, 'It's all right, he's out!'

Luli and Georgie came upstairs and Luli flopped on the bed to tell Dodie what had happened.

'Dad won't half go off,' said Dodie.

'Bugger him!' said Lu. 'What happens if Mum gets the sack?'

'Lu, you shouldn't swear.'

'Well, so would you if you'd had to cart that rotten bath about all the morning.'

Dodie peeled the spuds and soon after one o'clock Mum came home, and bustled about getting the dinner. We waited for her to say something.

'Mum,' said Georgie, 'did you get the sack?'

'No, love.'

'What am I goin' to tell Dad then, about the five bob?' asked Lu.

'Nothing. Leave it to me, and I don't want to hear another word about that bath,' said Mum firmly, 'not from any of you.'

The great achievement for any family down our street was to have regular wages. Odd jobs were about, but the way to keep on your feet was to know what was coming in. After putting by money for the rent, coke, paraffin and meth, we had about six-teen shillings to see us through, so very little was spent on any-thing but food. Going on a bus was a rare treat, and everything else we wanted had to be made out of what we could scrounge or what 'floated against the tide'. This was one of Dad's expressions which we were quick to adopt.

As there was little or no refrigeration in any of the shops, a lot of food was sold cheaply just before it went 'off', and Luli was the expert in the family at knowing just where and when to take advantage of this. She kept her eye on the bacon slicer in the posh grocers, where the first slice off the rusty brown sides of bacon was discarded for the discerning customer, and which piled up round the machine with odd scraps of fat. As soon as Lu reckoned it was worth the price, she whizzed in with twopence and a tin plate, and often got the lot, sometimes with a knuckle-bone on top for her cheek. She never missed a quick look into the glass tops of the biscuit boxes on display in front of the counter, judging to the moment when the grocer would put out a fresh box, and buying up the broken bits in the old one. She got a basin of cracked eggs, demanding no runny ones and no ducks', and in the middle of the week looked around for a twopenny cod's head, pretending for pride's sake that it was for our non-existent cat, and Mum would boil it and turn it into fishcakes. We had to be careful though, as our food cupboard was next to the fire and had no ventilation, so we had to buy nearly every day, and cheap meat was wiped with a vinegar cloth and cooked straight away to save its life.

Potatoes cost sixpence for seven pounds, balls of flour they were called, and Lu wouldn't take little ones. She hung around the greengrocer until her mate was free to serve her. He was a shrunken little man with baggy red eyes and a wet moustache, and his trousers drooped forwards on dismal braces and hung in folds over his curiously misshapen boots, in which he lifted up each foot as though it was the last thing he'd ever do. Lu called him Hoppy.

'Any specs 'Op?' asked Lu cheerfully.

''Ang on cocky bird, an' I'll 'ave a butchers.' Hoppy trod warily to the back of the open shop, a thing he wouldn't do for every-one, and returned presently with an apple box. They peered into it and then at each other, Lu trying to hide her delight at the pile of over-ripe tomatoes, brown bananas, bruised cooking apples and soft dented oranges. 'Awright?' Hoppy pushed his bowler back on his head.

'Yeh,' said Lu, ''ow much?'

''Ow about fourpence?' suggested Hoppy.

'Come off it 'Op.' Lu gave him a beaming smile. 'Threepence, box an' all.'

Hoppy showed his gums in a sweet grin and rolled his eyes upwards at Lu's cheek. 'Throopence! You'll 'ave me the sack one o' these days,' he said.

'They won't never sack you 'Oppy,' sauced Lu as she handed over three pennies. 'Make a fortune for 'em you do, the prices you charge.'

'Yeh!' shouted Hoppy after her. 'Rollin' in it we are. I'll wear me top 'at termorrer. Tata!'

We ate a lot of bread, and a fresh loaf from the baker cost fourpence halfpenny, so a couple of times a week we had to go to a shop in the Fulham Road where they sold off stale bread very early in the morning. The job was passed down the family and when Georgie started collecting newspapers for the shop next door, it came to me. Stale bread cut into slices more economically than new bread, and absorbed less marge, and for sixpence you got at least three large loaves and with a bit of luck a couple of rubbery rolls as well, so many families around us went regularly up to Snelling's. Just before six o'clock, a droopy bunch of kids dawdled along in twos and threes, cold and sleepy, carrying sacks and bags and money wrapped up in bits of paper. There was a depressing hunchiness about the queue that stretched out beyond the shuttered shops. People waited anxiously, counting the heads in front of them, hoping they would be served before the stale bread ran out.

In the winter, puddles of gaslight fell across the road and outlined those in the front of the queue as Ma Snelling thumped down the shutters and opened the door, letting the customers in a few at a time. The baker stood with his fingers spread on the unpolished counter, an open cash drawer beside him, its two circular wooden scoops inside worn to a dull shine, pennies in one and silver in the other. Behind him, stacked on shelves, the stale bread. The system was brisk and simple. He swept each sixpence into the open drawer, turned and collected up an armful of bread and dumped it on the counter. With his other hand he shoved it along to the end, and you were served, no choosing, no wrapping, no conversation. You trundled along to your pile and scooped it into your bag as the person behind you got the same rapid treatment.

We waited for each other outside the shop, feeling in the bags to see who had the most bread, and breaking off knobbly bits to eat on the way home as we dragged and bumped the bags along the streets.

We didn't have to get up so early to go to the butcher's, Bartletts, because they started serving at half-past seven, which meant it was sometimes a scramble to get to school on time. One butcher near us sold off meat that would not keep through the weekend by holding auction sales on Saturday night, where you could pick up a ripe leg of mutton for less than a couple of bob, but Bartletts got rid of theirs by making up sixpenny parcels. They tidied up joints for one more day in the window and the trimmings went into a parcel. Sometimes they wrapped up a lump of purply dark brisket, or thin salt belly, limp as tripe and peppered with sawdust. Now and again you might get a couple of coarse breasts of mutton a yard long, with luck unchopped so they could be boned and rolled, or a hunk of flank.

One Friday I put down my sixpence and the butcher whacked an extra large parcel in front of me. As I struggled to shove it into my bag the newspaper uncurled, and I caught a glimpse of whiskery hair. I looked up at the man behind the counter but he wasn't looking at me. I was finished with, I had been served. It wasn't right and I wanted to say something but the queue was pushing forward and I was in the way. I humped the bag outside, still looking back at the butcher, hoping he might say something, and waited for my friend Winnie.

'What you got, Win?' I asked.

''Ang on, let's have a look.' She put her bag on the pavement and squatted down to fish among the newspaper. 'Looks like scrag,' she said, 'yeh, couple of necks a' mutton. Another bloody stew! What you got?'

'I dunno. It's got 'air.'

''Air? You prob'ly got rabbits.'

'No, I ain't Win. I know it ain't rabbits!'

'Well for gawd's sake 'ave a look.' Slowly I parted the paper and stared into a wide open eye.

'It's an 'ead!' I cried. 'Win, I've got an 'ead!'

'Never!'

'I 'ave.'

'What sort?'

'Pig's. It's got eyes, an' teeth, an' ear'oles. Everything. What am I goin' to do?'

'Take it back. Go on, tell 'im that 'eads ain't proper meat.'

'My Dad won't half go on.'

'Take it back.'

'You take it, Win.'

'No fear, it's your 'ead. 'Ere, show us.' Together we looked at the half-smiling grimace on the face of the pig, and then through the window at the busy butcher. Customers were still shuffling through the door.

'I can't,' I said. 'We're not proper customers are we? You can't choose your meat, can you, when you have a tanner parcel?'

'Well 'urry up,' said Winnie, 'or I'm goin'. We'll n'arf be late.' I took one last desperate look through the window and then ran. I ran all the way home, up our stairs, dumped the bag on the table and fled to school.

I was blank with worry all the morning. I had *wasted* a tanner. I had spent a tanner and not got any proper meat. There was bound to be a row and it would be my fault. Why didn't I take it back? Because I was windy, windy of telling the butcher I didn't want it. Then I remembered I hadn't brought Joey to school but at playtime I was relieved to find him sitting by himself on the bench under the shed eating his bread.

'Where you bin?' he asked me.

'Who brought you to school?'

'Lu. Where you bin?'

'Did Dad say anything about the meat?'

'I dunno. Haven't you got your bread?'

'No.'

Joey broke his bit and gave half to me. 'Rowie, where you bin?'

'I bin to Bartlett's,' I said, 'an' I got home late.' The bell rang, and we got into our lines.

By dinner time I had made up my mind to run away. I'd take Joey home first and then run away, and I'd be lost and ill and starving in a shop doorway, and they'd be so pleased to find me that everything would be all right. I left Joey on the pavement by our front door and watched him go upstairs, then I crossed the road and sat on Ivy Potter's front wall and stared up at our window. I wanted to go in. I wanted my dinner, but I couldn't go indoors, so I stayed there. Our window opened and Mum looked out over the window box.

'Rowie!' she called. I didn't answer, I couldn't, and started crying.

'Rowie, what's up?'

I slid down on to the pavement, helpless. The next minute Mum was stooping over me, wearing her clinic overall. 'Come on now love, tell me what's the matter.'

'It's the 'ead,' I sobbed. 'I got a pig's 'ead, and I should've took it back.'

'You daft 'aporth!' Mum was smiling, and wiped my face on the skirt of her overall. 'Come on now, come in and have your dinner. You'll make me late back for work.'

'What about the 'ead then?'

'You had a proper bit of luck,' said Mum. 'Enough on that head for two dinners.'

'I ain't goin' to 'ave any!' I cried. 'I seen its face!'

'You won't recognise it now,' Mum laughed down at me. 'Dad's cooked it.' She took my hand and led me, hiccuping with sobs, up to our room. I sat down on my stool opposite Joey. Luli and Georgie were sitting on the bed side by side, busily eating from plates balanced on their laps.

'What we got?' I whispered to Joey.

'Meat, gravy an' taters.'

'I don't want no meat Mum,' I said, 'nor gravy neither.'

'You'll eat what you're given, and eat it properly,' Dad said sharply. Our big saucepan stood inside the fender, close to the fire to keep its contents warm. Mum bent down to spoon some gravy over the spuds on my plate, but she didn't give me any meat.

Our fireplace was narrow and small, and only suitable for what it was originally designed for, to put a flicker of warmth into the little room. Dad had fixed two trivets to the top bar so that we could balance half a kettle and the edge of a saucepan over the fire. When we had to, we burned coke, but we eked this out with driftwood from the Thames and stolen road blocks. The acquisition of the road blocks, or tar blocks as we called them, was the sole responsibility of the kids, no adults ever got involved.

The roads around us were built with solid wood blocks, perfectly fitted and coated with tar and rolled with stone chippings. At the first sign of a road gang in the neighbourhood the word went round, and spies sauntered on street corners to estimate the size of the job. If a tarpaulin hut was put up it meant that a lot of men would be employed and there would be a good chance for a tar block raid. We watched the navvies spike the surface of the road with a heavy iron bar which was pointed or chiselled at one end and flattened at the other. Five or six men stripped to their shirt sleeves, with string tied under the knees of their trousers, surrounded the spike, and each one held a long-handled fourteen-pound hammer. The first man swung his hammer in a circle behind him, whirling it over his shoulder, and brought it down smack on the head of the spike. As he pulled his hammer away at the end of the strike the next man hit the spike, and so on round the team. As soon as the first man's hammer was above his head again it was his turn to smash it down. The spike drove into the road under a constant series of rhythmic blows with no more than a second between them. I loved watching the navvies. Their movements were accurate and powerful and their hammers made a pattern as they kept perfect time circling and striking. The sound of the hammers was like a peal of bells that didn't ring.

When the spike was several inches into the road, one of the men knocked it with a sideways blow and the road was broken ready for the pickaxes. As they cleared the top surface the old broken road blocks were piled into an untidy heap. The site was steadily growing. The mountain of blue-grey stone chippings slid from the back of a chunky, ochre-coloured open cart, drawn by a massive black horse. Heavy poles were lowered on to three-legged crutches to mark out the road works and divert the traffic. The positioning of the nightwatchman's hut was of great importance to us, and we noticed how far it was from the nearest street corner and which way the entrance faced. The watchman's brazier was delivered with a generous pile of coke, and his night-lamps with a drum of paraffin. At last the bounty arrived, a huge load of sweet-smelling wood blocks, stained with something that smelt of Stockholm tar. They were about nine inches long by three inches square and were stacked into a neat wooden wall under the innocently watchful eyes of half a dozen kids.

There was a good deal of rivalry between the local kids, depending on which road was being repaired, and we had to guard against poaching on our territory. We couldn't pinch road blocks in the summertime, we needed to be hidden in darkness, but when the conditions were right we rarely missed an opportunity. To be successful, a raid had to be planned by a group, there was little chance of nicking a load on your own. I didn't go on a raid until I was six, and then I was only used as one of the decoys.

My first raid was on a February evening, and over a dozen of us met down Manor Gardens with a muster of two prams and five barrers. The biggest boy and the most experienced was Wally, and he took charge. He looked over the transport critically and said that one of the prams was no good because the wheels were buckled and it would slow us down. 'Take it over there,' he said. It was Ginger's pram and he began to argue. 'Shut up Ginge,' demanded Wally. 'You can nark up the watchman, an' you'll get your share.' With this, Ginger had to be content. 'Now, you four little kids,' said Wally, which included me, 'get over there with the pram.' Ginger wasn't having this.

'I ain't 'avin' that lot wi' me,' he complained. 'I ain't a bleedin' nursemaid. I can do it on me own.'

'They gotta learn, ain't they?' shouted Wally, as we looked from one to the other. 'You can do as what I tells yer Ginge, or you can push off, please yourself.' Ginger kicked his pram wheels and sulked against the wall.

Lu and Georgie had brought our barrer and it looked the best of the bunch. Wally said there must be two kids to each barrer as loading would have to be quick and the run down the road afterwards had to be fast. 'If you're on your own you'll hold us up,' he said, 'so get yerself a mate.' He came over to Ginger and the four of us who were to be with him. 'You lot,' he said patiently, 'start muckin' about down the street till you get to the watchman. Give 'im a bit of lip. Run the ol' pram up an' try an' nick a bit of 'is coke, 'e'll think that's what you're after. Get 'im ratty, an' once 'e's out of 'is 'ut get 'im to chase yer an' keep 'im goin'. Then the barrers'll nip round the corner, pile up an' scarper. Orright?'

'Yeh,' we said.

Lu came over to me. 'Don't you forget, Rowie,' she said. 'As soon as that nightwatchman leaves his hut, you're to run straight 'ome, an' don't you forget. I don't want you gettin' caught or lost, an' 'avin' to come an' look for you.' I was too excited to listen. It was pitch dark as Ginger led us down the street and we mucked about round a lamp post for a minute before wandering noisily down to the faint red lamps lining the road works. I could smell the throaty tang of the coke fire and just make out the watchman sitting in his hut with something over his knees. Alfie chucked his ball so that it bounced just outside the hut, and as he ran to get it he kicked the pile of coke.

'Sod off!' shouted the watchman.

'Keep yer 'air on,' bawled Ginger.

''Ere, mister. Giss a drop a' tea,' called Vi, who was holding my hand tightly.

'Yeh,' jeered Ginger. 'Giss a drop a' tea, mister.' The watchman stood up, dropping his knee covering on to the floor. He was an old man and not very lively on his feet.

'Clear orf the lot of yer,' he shouted, 'or I'll be after yer!'

Alfie made a dirty noise and Ginger cried: 'Come on, nick 'is coke. I got the pram!' The watchman made a threatening growl and took a couple of doddery steps towards us. We retreated, jeering and laughing. He came hopping after us, waving his stick, and we jumped about in front of him. 'Go on Vi,' Ginger was yelling, 'get some of 'is coke.'

Round the corner burst the armada of barrows, Lu and Georgie in the lead. They pelted to the wall of new blocks and frantically grabbed armfuls. The old nightwatchman turned and hobbled towards them, roaring threats to protect the Council's property. The pram and one of the barrows fled back round the corner, but our barrow and Wally's were still loading. I stood rooted, waiting for them to be caught. At the last minute Georgie pulled the rope in front of our barrow and ran straight at the watchman. He tottered back out of the way and went on to try to catch Wally. As Lu and Georgie came up to me, they stopped and finished loading our barrow with the old and damaged blocks. Lu caught my arm as I stood stupidly watching, and together we ran, pushing our barrow back to Manor Gardens. Everyone turned up, Wally, all the transport and the decoys.

'Who got windy?' demanded Wally.

'Well,' said Charlie, 'he was comin' straight for us.'

'Charlie should've done what we done,' said Lu. 'We filled up with old blocks.'

'You done well, Ginge,' Wally grinned at him.

'Yeh,' said Ginger, 'Alfie an' Vi was all right an' all.'

'Wot about the share out,' asked Reen, ''cos I gotta go 'ome in a minute,'

'So've we,' said Lu. All the blocks were tipped into the road and sorted. Wally allocated our shares and we ran all the way home, late, with half a barrow load of mixed blocks, some new and some old.

The next day Mum put a couple of blocks on our fire and they sent a solid column of yellow smoke up the chimney that you could cut with a knife. Little flames began to lick round them and suddenly there was a loud bang! They were old blocks, and the bits of stone embedded in them had exploded and shot out in fragments all over the room. Dad leapt out of his chair and caught Lu a heavy clout round the ear. 'How many times have I told you,' he shouted, 'not to bring home old blocks! Look at the bloody mess they make!' Lu glared at Georgie, Georgie looked at me and I looked at Lu and we all looked at Mum. She frowned at us and faintly shook her head, so we didn't answer him back.

Lu earned a sixpence here and threepence there doing simple charring jobs. She was quick and efficient and started on door-steps, but was soon doing stairs and landings and cleaning brass. When she was thirteen she picked up a regular job on Saturday afternoons. She tidied up the living quarters behind an un-successful little toy shop owned by Mr and Mrs Morrison. They were a stooped and elderly couple, and Mrs Morrison, thin and faded, spent more and more of her life in a rickety wheel chair.

Lu scrubbed their kitchen floor, swept and dusted the living-room that opened straight into the shop, washed up and ran errands. Week by week they introduced extra duties, and Lu found herself 'just popping a wet cloth over the outsides of the windows' and 'just pushing Mrs Morrison out in her wheelchair for a bit of air.' Always obliging, and hopeful of one day getting an increase in her wages, Lu struggled with both the old chair and Mrs Morrison's strange fancies. One foggy Saturday after-noon she wrapped the old lady up and manoeuvred the chair out into the street. 'Where to Mrs M?' she asked. 'Down the embankment, 'ave a look at the ducks?'

'No, no dear.' Lu's face fell as Mrs Morrison answered, as she always did. 'Take me round the cemetery.'

'Wot about the shops Mrs M? Cheer you up a bit, like,' suggested Lu, but it was always the same. Old Mrs Morrison insisted on the cemetery.

'Rotten miserable 'ole,' thought Lu. 'Gives me the proper willies goin' up there.' Obediently, Lu wrestled with the old chair, shaking the life out of Mrs Morrison as she bumped her up and down the kerbstones, until they reached the grey stone entrance to the grey stone cemetery. On the way Lu chattered and sang a bit, trying to put a spark of life into the old lady, but as soon as they were on the smooth path among the quiet, still gravestones, Lu trod carefully and talked in whispers. 'If she wants to stop,' said Lu to herself, 'I ain't goin' to. I ain't goin' to watch another funeral.' Quickening her pace, Lu decided that she had had enough, 'Come on Mrs M,' she said, 'time for tea. 'Ow about a nice bit a' jam on toast?'

She made Mrs Morrison's tea, and just as she was leaving to come home she stopped to watch Mr Morrison arranging a kite in the centre of the shop window. It was shaped like a bird, a great yellow and black bird with the head of an eagle. She was full of it when she came home, talked about nothing else.

''Ow much is it Lu?' asked Georgie.

'I dunno,' Lu answered. 'Pounds and pounds I should reckon.'

'Couldn't you make one, Georgie?' I asked.

'Easy!' said Georgie. 'Let's go an' 'ave a look at it.' The next morning being Sunday, we all stared into Mr Morrison's window. ''At's just about the biggest kite I ever seen,' said Georgie. 'It's bigger'n Joey.' We went on looking at it and we all knew that nothing we made would be any good unless it looked just like that great fierce bird. 'Come on,' said Georgie. 'Let's start now,' and we chased him home. Luli didn't come with us, she stayed behind staring into the window.

'S'posin',' she thought, 'just supposin' I don't 'ave any wages, an' I push Mrs Morrison up the cemetery every day for nothin', 'ow long would it take me to earn the kite? Bloody years! I don't even know 'ow much it is. Old Morrison wouldn't 'ave that. I wonder if I could pinch it? No, t'aint worth it. I know, I'll borrer it, that's what I'll do, I'll just borrer it for one Sunday.'

We went kite mad. The pavement outside our house was

smothered in bits of newspaper and whittled down wood. We belted up and down the road with knotted bits of string dragging and bumping a tattered collection of hopeless experiments.

Two weeks went by and the kite had disappeared, gone. A fairy bicycle stood in the window and we didn't give it a second glance. Lu was frantic, where was it? Could someone have bought it? On Saturday she rushed early to the Morrisons. "Allo Mrs M,' she said, 'I'll 'urry up with the housework, then where shall we go? Up the cemetery? 'Ow's Mr Morrison, all right?' Bustling and desperately chatty, Lu could wait no longer. 'I see the kite's gone, 'ave you sold it then?'

'No dear,' replied Mrs Morrison. 'It's back on the shelf, far too expensive for people round here. It was silly of Arthur to buy it.' Lu shut her eyes with relief, and set to busily to get through the afternoon, wondering how she was going to get her hands on the kite. Her opportunity came when Mr Morrison left the shop empty to spend a few minutes in the living-room having a cup of tea with his wife.

'How about me dustin' round the shop a bit?' suggested Lu. 'I'll be ever so careful.'

'It can do with it,' answered Mr Morrison. 'Pop in there now Luli, while I have my tea, and if a customer comes in, call me.' Lu waved her bit of dusting rag vaguely at the dingy shelves while she searched for the kite, and started with a tiny gasp as she found the box on a shelf near the floor. She raised the lid and saw the yellow and black folds. Instinctively she pushed the box to the end of the shelf near the living-room door as Mr Morrison returned to the shop. 'Nearly closing time, Luli,' he said. 'Here's your sixpence. Off home with you.' Lu hesitated. Mrs Morrison's back was briefly turned and Mrs Morrison was nodding in her chair. She grabbed the box and ran. It was done.

She hid the kite under the shed in the backyard, and on Sunday after dinner we all went up Battersea Park, Lu pushing Joey's pram with a long shape on top, wrapped in a piece of blanket. We opened the box in the middle of a wide grassy space and quarrelled and argued over the struts and strings. We couldn't put it together. Several big boys and men joined in, and people with dogs stopped to watch, and soon there was quite a crowd. At last, we all stood back. A strange man was holding our kite and another man had taken the string. The first man ran until he was a long way off, and the second man shouted 'Let go!' He ran, jerking the string, and the kite moved slowly and uncertainly just above the ground, lifted a little and hovered, then it suddenly rose up and up, soaring like a thunderbird. I held my breath and my heart rose with the kite and I found myself jumping up and down. I looked at Joey. He hadn't moved, he was standing absolutely still with his head back watching the kite, his hands clasped on his chest.

The man handed the string to Lu. It jerked her hands above her head and she screamed, 'I can't hold it! It don't half pull!' She let Georgie try, and he braced himself against the power of the kite.

'It's marvellous!' he shouted. 'It's alive, it's just like it's alive!' I put my hand on the string and gave it a pull while Georgie held it, and the yellow-black bird soared above my head. Joey squatted on the grass and watched. Sometimes the kite began to fall.

'Wind in,' shouted the onlookers, 'go on son, wind in fast, keep it up!'

Lu screamed, 'Don't let it come down Georgie,' and Georgie struggled to pull in and wind, and it soared again, high and remote.

More people came to watch and Joey and I shouted at them, 'It's ours! It's our kite!' For the moment, we really believed it was.

Suddenly it got late, and we were all on our own. Lu and Georgie had run about a lot, and we seemed to be too near the trees. The string touched a high branch and the kite fell to earth quickly, so quickly that Georgie couldn't wind in fast enough, and we all tried to pull the string. We trampled on it in our anxiety to help, and around us was a great heap of muddled tangle. We tried to sort it out and to smooth the kite back into its folds, but the whole thing had grown too big for its box. 'Let's go 'ome,' said Georgie. 'We can pack it up proper at 'ome. It was good, wasn't it, Lu!'

The kite looked even bigger in the backyard, and the string remained hopelessly knotted. Lu began to realise what lay ahead.

'Georgie,' she said, 'I gotta get it back.'

'You can't. Not till you go there next Saturday.'

'I never thought about gettin' it back.'

'Wot you goin' to do?'

'I dunno. S'posin' old Morrison misses it, an' comes round here askin'.'

'If Dad finds out he'll murder yer.'

'Yeh.'

'Tell yer what,' said Georgie, 'take it back tomorrer. Take it back an' tell 'im what you done. That you just borrered it.'

'Will you come with us?'

'Course! Nip 'ome sharpish from school an' then we'll be back again before Mum comes in.'

After school on Monday, Lu and Georgie knocked on the side door of Mr Morrison's shop. Mr Morrison took the battered, bulging box from them and listened to what Lu had to say.

'I am ashamed of you Luli,' he said. 'And so will Mrs Morrison be ashamed of you.' There was nothing more Lu could say, so she lowered her eyes from Mr Morrison's face. 'Of course,' he went on, 'we can't have you back now. It wouldn't be the same.'

'Yes Mr Morrison,' whispered Lu. 'Thank you Mr Morrison.' Lu was still standing on the doorstep when the door was closed in her face, and Georgie touched her arm and turned her towards home. She was white and frightened at what she had done, and at losing her job.

'That kite,' Georgie said cheerfully. 'It didn't 'arf pull. Worth it, wasn't it Lu?'

'Yeh,' Lu smiled, and then brightened up. She began to run and as she ran she jumped. 'Tell yer something Georgie,' she shouted back at him.

'What?' Georgie chased after her and caught her up.

'I won't never 'ave to go up that rotten cemetery again.' She put her arm round Georgie's shoulders. 'I won't go up that cemetery any more, not as long as I live.' Suddenly realising what she had said she laughed and pushed Georgie clean off the pavement. 'Did you 'ear what I said Georgie? Not as long as I live! I just made a joke!' They ran home, shouting.

Dad took little or no notice of Georgie, and Joey was seven years his junior, so he was swamped at home by Mum and his three sisters. He turned to the streets for male company and I envied him his incredible freedom. No one asked him where he was going or where he had been, and I soon realised that this was yet another advantage of being a boy. Sometimes he came home with a grazed face or soaking wet hair, and I knew what he'd been up to. The big boys swam in the Thames from the steps by Battersea Bridge and they dared the younger ones to dive into the oily brown water. I had seen them crouching naked on the inch of trellised ironwork that projected beyond the banister chains, egged on by jeers and threats. Georgie was small and slight and hovered, barely accepted, on the fringe of the gang, but he was quite fearless and would do anything to prove his courage. He pinched rides by hanging under the coal carts and heaved himself into the back of horse-drawn vans by grabbing the rope that dangled above the tailboard.

When the ice cart rumbled into the street it attracted a pack of determined kids like a magnet. The driver pulled the horses up right outside the pub and opposite the butcher's. He knew we were there to steal bits of ice and he always made a couple of threatening runs at us so that we scattered and edged forward again like the tide the moment his back was turned. Swearing and cussing at us, he dragged a great block of ice, wrapped in sacking, to the tail of the cart with a ferocious-looking pointed ice pick. Then he edged the block on to his shoulder, which was protected by a piece of dark stained leather. With his head forced over almost at right angles, he loped with a swingy shuffle into the pub. The moment he disappeared inside, Georgie was the first and often the only boy to climb up into the cart. He darted among the blocks, feeling for slivers of ice on the muddy sawdust floor, and handed dripping pieces down to us. Now and again he saved a small dissolving piece for me and I put it all in my mouth at once and crunched it up. It tasted like sack smell.

Georgie tried so hard to grow. At night he took off his shirt and washed in a bucket of cold water in the backyard. He had a loose page of print torn from an old copy of the *Boy's Own Paper*, which showed an expressionless gentleman with a pointed waxed moustache illustrating boxing stances. Georgie propped it up on the scullery window sill and circled round the yard, pumping his skinny white arms and snorting fiercely down his nose. Whenever he let me, I hung about in the yard to watch this ritual. He also had a zed-shaped piece of metal that he squeezed twenty times in each hand. One night, I was sitting on the scullery step, watching him, and he said, 'How many can you count up to?'

''Undreds,' I answered.

'Right then.' Georgie took up the piece of metal. 'Watch my muscle, this one up 'ere in my arm, an' count 'ow many times it moves.'

'What for?'

'It makes yer strong. I'm in trainin','

'Go on then,' I said. 'Show us.' Georgie squeezed the metal. It closed a fraction, his arm stiffened and a tiny bulge appeared. 'One!' I shouted. Georgie did it again. His face was strained and his arm trembled by the time I got to seven, and he staggered forward, panting. 'Seven. Tha's all.'

'You missed some out.'

'No I never! What you in trainin' for?'

'Everythin',' said Georgie, casually.

'Can I do it?' I wanted to do everything that Georgie did.

'No. You're a girl, ain'tcher.'

'I can fight Eric Stringer,' I boasted.

'Everyone can fight 'im.'

To reward me for my devoted admiration, Georgie occasionally let me climb on the roof of our shed with him to gloat secretly at his hoard of special things. These were wrapped in bits of rag, and hidden between the roof planks and the sheets of corrugated iron. His most treasured possession was a tin bicycle lamp with a wick and paraffin. We lit it one night and held it to warm our hands, and the smell of the cheap black paint on the hot metal made me sick, all down Georgie.

He had a protective and deep affection for Mum, and did his bit to help her make ends meet. As soon as he was old enough he started earning regular money and gave her all his wages. He was nearly ten when he got into the newspaper business. The sweet shop next door to us sold the popular morning papers, and it was Georgie's job to get up early, scoot to Sloane Square and collect them ready for sale by seven o'clock. His regular timekeeping, speed, and enthusiasm was noticed by the distributor, and he offered Georgie a job on the evening papers, delivering parcels to several local shops.

On a dusky evening, Sloane Square was a fine sight. It towered darkly above the even chain of street lamps, and brighter spots of light from the shops fell upon the homegoing crowds. Buses honked their short staccato horns as the Chocolate Expresses raced the red Generals for scrambling passengers. Vans hooted, taxis tooted, cyclists thumbed their tinny bells, and underneath was the steady rhythm of the clopping of running carthorses. The steps of the Royal Court Theatre was the distribution spot for the evening papers. They were alive with chattering, scrapping delivery boys and feeble-minded old men, who hung about in the hope of earning a few pennies by being the first to spot the delivery vans. Tension built up and competition was fierce between the lookouts as the cry went up 'Newses are up!'

'Here comes the News. Evenin' News is first!' The News van rattled into the square, the doors were jerked open before it had stopped and the bundles flung at the feet of the pouncing boys. Knives whipped through the coarse string and the boys fought to be the first away to deliver to the shops. In the heat of the bustle another cry rang out. 'Star's up! Look alive. Here comes the Star!'

The Star bundles, with a parcel of placards, thudded on the pavement, and as the van raced away the boys frantically counted and sorted. A small boy ran through the traffic that circled the graceful square crying: 'Here she comes! Standard's up! I seen the Standard!'

Georgie had fifteen shops on his round and it took him an hour from the arrival of the first van to the final delivery of all three papers. He swerved through the crowds on his ball bearing scooter, his crowning moment when he placed a placard inside the wire frame outside a paper shop. He was paid one and six-pence a week, 'in coin Ma,' as he used to say as he handed it over on Saturday night.

In the summer he joined one of his mates and pushed Antonio's ice cream cart round the streets on Saturdays and Sundays. The cart looked like a fair ground exhibit with twirled shafts and candy twist canopy supports painted in red, gold and green. Georgie and Bert shouted "Okey Pokey, penny a lump! The more you eats, the more you jump!' as they trudged along the streets shoving the heavy cart, searching for customers.

'What we wants,' said Bert, 'is a bloody good street accident.'

In the winter, Georgie and Bert worked for an enterprising woman who lived in Shawfield Street. She cooked a pile of sausages and a mountain of mash and packed the lot into a couple of hay boxes on a converted coster barrow. Bert pushed and Georgie shouted: 'Banger'n masho! All 'ot an' lovely!' They stuck to the better parts of Chelsea, and occasionally sold a dollop of spud with a couple of sausages stuck artistically into the mound to women and kids who came running with dinner plates. Somehow the idea didn't catch on. Georgie wore over-long short trousers and a darned jersey, and Bert was unsavoury in a khaki boiler suit.

'What we wants,' said Georgie as they gloomily pushed the barrow round Poulton Square, 'is chef's 'ats.'

Jobs were passed on between the boys as the older ones started work or found one that was better paid. In this way, Georgie fell into a good one when the sausage and mash business went bankrupt. A gentleman in Upper Cheyne Row, feeling the pinch no doubt, sacked his handyman, and hopefully employed Georgie to do the job on a fraction of the pay. His hours were from seven to eight in the morning and from five to seven o'clock in the evening. He was paid five shillings a week, and for this kind of money, Georgie cheerfully handed on his paper jobs.

His morning duties included stoking the boiler and dumping the ashes, emptying the household rubbish into the bins and rubbing up the front door. In the evening the yard had to be swept, all the boots and shoes cleaned, and the steel knives put through the cleaner and grinder. Georgie was happy, the gentleman satisfied and the five shillings welcomed every week at home until the day came when it was decided to maintain the archaic water softener. The gentleman elected to do it himself, with Georgie's help. It was attached to an outside wall, and they shovelled in the salt and spun the numerous cocks, working contentedly together, each relying on the other's approval of their hopeful guesswork. They created utter chaos. Water, that might have come direct from the Red Sea, seeped and flowed from every part of the house. A distraught and quivering lady pointed into the direction in which Georgie was commanded to go, and never return. The unfortunate gentleman had no such luck.

While we all lived in our one room, I was too young to have a job, but I was well practised in scrounging. One evening, early in March, Lu was giving my face a quick lick over with the damp flannel and I told her Ginger was waiting downstairs for me.

'Mind you're back before it gets dark,' said Lu. I escaped cheerfully down the stairs and there was Ginger sitting on the lino in our passage, leaning against the open front door.

'What we gonna do, Ginge?' I asked.

'Let's try up the copin'. See if we can get a chip.' As Ginger got to his feet he hitched his baggy knee-length trousers under his armpits and heaved down his shrunk jersey to keep them in place. His shaved head was almost bald, except for the tuft above his forehead. We called this popular hairstyle a 'Fourpenny 'eaven', because the price was fourpence at the barber's, and God was supposed to yank the boy up to heaven by the solitary tuft of hair, in His own good time.

Half-way down our street was a derelict patch of land with hardly a trace of the old cottages that once stood there. One thing remained, a chunk of thick brick wall about three feet high, right on the edge of the rough ground near the pavement. This we called 'the coping', and it was our meeting place.

Directly opposite stood the shabby little fish and chip shop, to us a paradise of rich, steamy smells. We climbed on the coping, dangling our boots over the edge, and concentrated like a pair of predatory sparrows on the open shop door.

''Ere comes ol' Sherbet,' I whispered to Ginger.

''E ain't no good,' Ginger muttered without turning his head. The proprietor of our sweet shop entered the fish shop, received a whopping great parcel over the high counter, and went treading neatly down the street without a glance at us. A chilly wind blew, and we pulled our hands up into our sleeves and banged our heels. We waited and watched until two kids appeared, a whiny girl and her little sister. They entered the fish shop and we watched every movement they made through the cloudy window, until they reappeared carrying a newspaper bundle, already staining with grease and vinegar. Ginger went into action. 'Giss a chip, Dolly,' he shouted.

'Can't. They're my Mum's.'

'Go on Doll,' wheedled Ginger. 'Giss one.'

'No!'

'Mingy.'

'Get yer own chips.' Superior with possession they flounced to the corner, and Dolly poked her fingers through the paper and flourished a chip at us before she and her sister fled.

'Moo,' said Ginger. 'I bet they wasn't 'er Mum's.'

Two of our mates arrived, hands in pockets, kicking the kerb.

''Ad a chip yet?' asked Alfie.

'Nah,' Ginger answered. 'There ain't bin 'ardly no customers. Got any money?'

'Some 'opes,' said Alfie, 'shove up.' Reluctantly we made room for them beside us, and then there were four of us staring at the shop. Our chances were slim now, no one could be expected to hand out *four* chips.

''Ow about askin' for some cracklin'?' suggested Alfie.

'Too early,' Ginger was gloomy. 'They ain't bin open long.'

'You're windy!'

'No I ain't. I asked 'er lars week, an' I got some.'

'Go on then, ask 'er now.'

'You ask 'er.'

'I'll ask,' I said, 'but it's for me an' Ginger. We got 'ere first.' I put my head round the fish shop door, breathing the exquisite pungent warmth. As the lumps of fish bubbled in the deep fat, bits of batter broke off and were fried into crispy bits of brittle crunch that we called 'cracklin'. Sometimes Mrs Lea sieved some out for us with her long scoop and wrapped it up in a bit of newspaper, and we had the cheek to put her free salt and vinegar on it.

'Got any cracklin' please,' I asked, not very loudly. Mrs Lea's back was towards me and I half hoped she hadn't heard, but the odours were too much for me and I got braver.

'Mrs Lea, any cracklin' goin' yet?'

'Sorry duck,' Mrs Lea turned round to me. 'It's too early, we've only just put the first lot in. Come back later an' I'll find you a bit.'

'I can't stop out any later.'

'Sorry then love.' I went back to the coping.

'None yet,' I said, 'it's too early.'

'Then we'll 'ang on,' decided Alfie.

An old man on a bicycle came slowly towards us. He had one hand on the handlebars while the other supported a long pole on his shoulder. At the top of the pole was a tiny spark and a hook. He got off his bike awkwardly, propped it against the lamp post and we watched him grope about with the pole, trying to catch the gas lever. With a faint pop, a soft yellow glow shone down on us from the lamp, making the street suddenly darker.

'I got to go home,' I said, remembering Lu. Nobody took any notice, so I slipped off the coping and ran past the shops, now shuttered with peeling wooden boards. As usual, I shut my eyes and pelted past Old Sacky's door and fell into our room, warm with people and the roaring primus stove. Dodie was washing Joey and they talked and laughed secretly together. Georgie was concentrated over a line of cups, stirring cocoa and sugar into each one. Mum smiled at me from the clumsy little table where she was cutting bread and marge.

'I told you not to stop out late,' Lu started on me. 'I bet you bin cadgin' chips again, 'aven't you?' They all paused to look at me.

'I like chips,' I started to whine, 'an' we never 'ave any. I tried to get some cracklin' to put vinegar on, an' Mrs Lea said it was too early, an' Ginger is still there an' I bet he'll get some.'

'You know what Dad will say if he catches you at it, don't you?' Lu was still cross.

'That's enough Lu,' said Mum. 'I'll tell you what. We'll have two penn'orth of fish paste on Saturday, an' Rowie can go and get it. Nice strong taste, fish paste.'

SIX

Touch Collar, Never Swaller

We were intensely superstitious, and it is hardly surprising that much of the nonsense in which we unquestioningly believed was concerned with sickness, dying, death, misfortune and downright disaster.

It was not a rare occurrence, particularly near the stall at the top of our street or in the Fulham market, to see a cut flower lying on the ground, and if one of the younger children went to touch it, the rest of us dragged him back gasping 'pick up a flower, pick up a fever!' On the other hand, if something edible was similarly abandoned and you had the good fortune to pounce on it before anyone else, you could justifiably eat it as long as you first said the protective words, 'waste not, want not, pick it up and eat it!'

To tread deliberately on the cracks between paving stones would bring an accident and should two knives lie in a crossed position there would certainly be a row. A dropped spoon meant bad news or an unwelcome visitor, and at the first sign of a thunderstorm, Mum had taught us to cover up the looking-glass and the water jug with cloths, otherwise it was a direct invitation to have the house struck by lightning. Bad luck and tragedy had to be tidied up for our Mum by running in threes, whether it was another dreaded conception by one of her neighbours, the death of a public figure, a whitlow or a broken tea cup. The fates combined to keep her on tenterhooks until she had heard of a second and a third occurrence, no matter how coincidental or loosely related. 'Mark my words my ol' potherbs,' she said to us through a mouthful of hairpins as she stuffed them one by one into her thick plaits, 'I knew old Mrs Brimmer would pop off, she's the third,' and with utter conviction that death had finished with the neighbourhood for the time being, she was ready to start counting incidents for her next trio of events.

If we saw an ambulance or even heard its distant bell ring, we clawed dramatically at our throats, licked our fingers and touched the ground, gabbling, 'touch collar, never swaller, never get the fever.' Fever meant diphtheria, and it was not un-common. We knew two little boys who died of it, one of them a neighbour's child, and a girl in Lu's class at school lost her younger sister in the same way. 'The Town Hall men,' she whispered in a shocked voice, 'baked their rooms out.' Many children got scarlet fever, and Mum warned us that it was because they played around drainholes.

One day Mum had sent me down our street with a cup and a penny to get some mustard pickles from Mrs Daniels, to cheer up the dandy funk, and I tumbled down with a terrible belly ache and stayed bawling on the pavement outside the sweet shop. Lu carted me upstairs and I went on creating, lying on the floor with my knees bent up to my chest. We never had the doctor because he charged three and sixpence a visit and had to be paid on the dot, but the next day I was worse, so Mum got the district nurse. She gave me an enema and I brought the house down. As usual, Lu had to stop away from school to look after me, and when Mum came home from work Lu was beside herself with worry.

'Better get the pram out,' said Mum, and they pushed me to The Victoria Hospital for Children in Tite Street. They dealt with me straight away because I had acute appendicitis, and to add to Mum's anxiety asked her if I had been christened.

'What for?' asked Mum.

'Just in case.'

'She's called Rowie,' said Lu.

'Rose,' corrected Mum. So I was received into the Church of England, just in case, and was the only child in the family to be so distinguished.

When I came out of hospital Mum had a surprise for me. She had smuggled a doll home from the clinic jumble. I didn't much like dolls that had hats and hair and were dressed like ladies, but Bobby was made like a real baby. He had a stuffed cloth body, but his face and hands were made of shiny pink plaster. True, his face was a mosaic of fine cracks, and his mouth was broken where inconsiderate previous owners had stuffed his food, but to me he hadn't a single blemish. Lu and Dodie had made him a nightshirt and a coat and I took him into my bunk and cuddled his cold hard body until it was as warm as mine.

One day, I felt tired and droopy at school, and got told off for not paying attention, and when I went to fetch Joey I wanted to shut my eyes. We dawdled home and no one was in, so Joey went out to play by himself. I had a pain, somewhere in my neck and under my head, so I got Bobby and climbed on Lu and Dodie's bed and pulled the curtain. Lu came in first and immediately swung it back.

'What you up to?' She thought I was playing.

'I wanna lay down.'

'What you wanna do that for?'

'I'm tired.'

'Don' be daft. You can't lay down yet, it's tea time!'

'Lu, I got a pain.'

'Where?'

'Up 'ere.'

'Honest?'

'M'm.'

'Well, take your boots off.'

'I don' wanna sit up.' Lu looked more concerned and put her hand on my head, took off my boots and covered me with her coat. Then she pulled the curtain and left me. I lay in the green light that filtered through the bed curtain listening to the voices of the kids on the pavement outside the window, holding Bobby tightly to my chest. Then a clear sound threaded its way through the noise, drifted gently into the room and filled the space inside the curtain. It was a song, sad and haunting, and the voice held the notes and let them drift away at the end of each line. It was the lavender lady, and as she grew nearer I sang in my head with her. I knew what she looked like and could see her clearly as I listened, holding my breath in case I missed a moment as she filled the street with her glorious melancholy voice. She was not young and not old, upright and tall, and she wore black; a long black skirt that kicked gently at the back as she moved slowly along the centre of the road, gracefully turning first to one side and then to the other. A black shawl round her shoulders was hooked to her flat wide basket where a cloud of purple blue lavender drooped over the edge. She made the street sound lonely, and I lay enveloped in her song until I drifted into unconsciousness.

When Mum came home she had a look at me and decided to let me sleep, so it was with a lot of inconvenience that the rest of the family had their tea, as I was taking up the space where Georgie, Lu and Dodie usually sat to have their bread and jam. At bed time Mum bent over me to move me into my own bunk.

'Lu,' she cried, 'come and look at Rowie!'

'Oh Gawd Mum, she's dead.'

'Don't be silly. She's breathing.'

'What's the matter with her then?'

'I don't know. Oh Lu, I don't know.' Mum brushed her hands over my eyes, but I lay immobile with a fixed wide stare. Lu called: 'Rowie, come on love, Rowie.' I neither heard nor moved.

'Get the doctor Lu, quick.' Lu fled. Mum covered me up and took Bobby away and hurried down to Ethel.

'Can you lend me two bob?' she asked. 'It's Rowie. Something's happened to her and Lu's gone for Doctor 'Iggs. He's three an' six and I haven't enough.' Ethel came upstairs with Mum and peered down at me.

'Funny,' she said, ''as she 'ad a fit?'

'Never.'

''Ow long she bin like this then?'

'I just noticed.'

Yeah,' Ethel mused, 'I don't like the look of 'er. Is two bob enough, love?'

'Thanks,' Mum replied, 'we can manage the rest.' Mum and Dodie had to move my bunk and Joey's to make room for the doctor, and everyone had to stay dressed because when he arrived they all had to go down into the street to wait. He didn't stay long.

'Take her to Tite Street,' he said, 'immediately.' They wrapped me up and propped me in Ethel's push chair, Dodie pushing and Mum running beside her. They had to wait a long time until the matron came to see them. She rustled in stiff navy blue, with a long veil. She made a gentle face to Mum and smiled with a sideways nod of her head to Dodie.

'We can't tell you anything tonight,' she said quietly, 'come back in the morning,' and she touched Mum's hand, 'but Mrs Naylor, I have to tell you not to be too hopeful.'

'Why? What do you mean? What's the matter with her?'

'We think she may have meningitis.' They trundled the empty push chair home, hardly saying a word.

While I was in Tite Street Georgie became ill. He even stayed away from school, and after a couple of days he was flushed and in pain and obviously very sick. Dad was home with him and Georgie must have been bad because Dad went out at the last minute for the doctor and bang went another three and a tanner. With frantic urgency, Ethel produced her push chair again and Georgie lay back awkwardly on it, taking his weight on the foot rest. Dad pushed him, cursing and swearing all the way to Tite Street about the bloody state of the roads, because Georgie screamed each time the push chair hit a bump. Georgie had peritonitis.

So there we both were, Georgie and me, laid up in Tite Street.

Mum had to see the Lady Almoner about our finances and Lu was sent on the scooter three times a day to ask how we were, because visitors were only allowed on Sunday afternoon for half an hour.

The highly-polished waiting-room at the hospital had a display to keep visitors amused. It illustrated the story 'Who Killed Cock Robin?' made with real stuffed birds in a vast glass case, hardly a subject to lighten anxious feelings. The birds' feathers had long since faded to an overall dusty brown, and there was something sickening about their unnaturally frozen positions, glazed stares and dull, dead bodies. The grave-digging owl was there with his trowel and the rook with his parsony book, and robin himself, flat on his back, with spidery clenched claws. A number of other small birds were perched on the withered twigs of petrified bushes, their beaks pointing to the leading characters. Day after day Lu sat observing this dismal scene, waiting for messages from the wards upstairs about Georgie and me. She idly counted the birds and made the total thirty-one, and the messages came down, 'There is no change'.

Lu sped home with the news and returned in the evening. She counted the birds again, this time with intent. 'If it's the same number,' she said to herself, 'they're still all right. If there's more birds, they're better, and if there's less, they're worse.' She counted and only numbered thirty. 'They are going to be worse, I'll count again.' She did so, searching the leafless bushes for an extra bird. 'Twenty-nine, thirty, thirty-one. It's all right! They'll be all right, an' I didn't cheat.' Lu got just what she expected when the messages arrived, 'There is no change.'

I never saw Georgie in hospital, because I spent about a week in a comatose condition, my life ''angin' on a 'fread,' as Lu described it to her round-eyed mates at school. Eventually I re-entered the world as abruptly as I had left it, and little the worse. I soon sized up the ward and noticed that the long stay patients had things nicely organised and got the pick of the playthings. The nurses had boxes of toys which were put on the long table down the centre of the ward and those who could run about chose first. I strained to see what was going, and usually finished up with a flat box of stone building bricks, little pillars and triangles, cubes and oblongs, cold and smooth to touch. They were pastel-coloured, grey, pinky-red and slaty-blue, and there was nothing to build them on in bed but the lid of the box. The thing I wanted most was a black square of cardboard, punched with holes, and with it went a cotton bag of browny clay marbles, bearing traces here and there of paint, dots of gold and silver, crimson and blue. I turned them round to find the best coloured bits, licked them to make them shine and made patterns in the holes on the black board. This kept me quiet and content for hours.

When I was able to get up and join the foraging on the long table they dressed me in hospital frock and matching knickers. I was thrilled to bits and expected everyone to envy me, for the material was printed all over with buttercups, and the skirt stood out when I twisted round. The first thing I saw on the table was the farm, arranged on a green board and marked into fields by tiny white fences made of lead. Lead cows coloured white and brown bent to the painted grass, and fat lead sheep lay under two-dimensional trees. A brown carthorse stood with its head over a white gate and below it stood the pond. A rectangle of mirror made me a pond on which sat three white ducks, reflected upside down. I put my finger on one of the ducks and made it glide over the clear water. The scene opened before me and the farm was real.

'That's not for playing with,' interrupted a posh boy who knew everything.

'Sling yer 'ook,' I answered automatically, forgetful of the manners demanded by the buttercup frock.

For those of us who were dressed, tea was served on the long table, and on my first day up we each had a boiled egg with bread and butter. Most of the children's parents brought eggs for them on Sunday afternoon visiting and wrote their own child's name on each egg. Mine had 'Eileen' on it, so I turned it round. I knew all about boiled eggs and couldn't wait to get started. They cut the top off for us and my egg was good and runny, so I broke my slice of bread as best I could into fingers and dipped straight into the glorious gold. The yolk ran up the bread and cascaded over the egg and egg-cup, but I wiped my bit of bread round the outside and quickly bit off the yolky end. My mouth and fingers were eggy and I was blissfully enjoying every second, hurrying and swallowing, unaware of anybody else. A naggy sound penetrated my concentration and I looked up briefly to see every face turned towards me, and the lady in charge at the far end of the table leaning forwards, repeating my name.

'Rose,' she said loudly and crisply, 'we do not eat our eggs in that way.' She separated each word with a little pause, and went on, 'This is the way we eat our eggs,' and she nodded to everyone who took their spoons and dipped them gently into the shells. She held her own spoon out towards me, crooked her little finger and slowly and deliberately scooped a wee blob of egg on the tip of her spoon and put it into her wide open mouth, as if she were taking medicine.

I sat in a confused squirm of misery. We had boiled eggs at home, sometimes, and Mum always cut up fingers for us to dip. It was my first experience of being unprepared for the social niceties of life, and it was bitter. The girl next to me leaned over and whispered, 'You're a greedy pig!' Before I knew what I was doing I had bashed her in the face with my unused spoon, and she opened her mouth and let out a long piercing wail. I was quickly bundled back to bed and told that I was a nasty, spiteful girl.

I went home soon after that, and I'd never been so happy. Everyone was there, except Georgie. The first afternoon, before the others came home, I was sitting on my stool in front of the fire nursing Bobby and Dad asked me if I was all right. I nodded. Then he asked me if I wanted anything. I chanced my luck. 'Can I have a boiled egg,' I asked, 'with my name on it?' He went to Mrs Daniels and bought me a brown egg and wrote 'Rosie Naylor' on it, and boiled it. He cut up a slice of bread into dip-sized fingers and wrapped a paper bag round the egg and wedged it into the fish paste jar which we used as an egg-cup. Then he rolled himself a fag and watched me get all eggy on the floor, and never said a word. The only things I regretted were the white ducks and the buttercup frock.

The next day was raw and foggy and as soon as the others had gone back to work and school after dinner, I helped Dad wash-up. He looked at the sky out of the window, took his cap and muffler off the hook on the door and told me to find my scarf. Dodie had knitted it for me from many odd bits of wool. Every child in the street had a wide scarf which often substituted for a winter coat. Of course, some children had coats, but at best they were shoddy, and they usually wore a scarf in a special way on top. Dad wrapped mine round my shoulders, crossed it over my chest and grunted, 'turn round.' I did so, and he took the safety pin that was kept pinned in one end and anchored it firmly into the small of my back. Thus we were ready. We were going to Woolworth's in the North End Road to buy a sixpenny piece of leather to mend Mum's shoes. Dad had drawn round her shoe on a piece of newspaper, cut out the shape of the sole and it was in his pocket. We set off, Dad walking fast, and taking no notice of me, so I had to trot pretty smartly to keep up.

The street was as bleak as the weather. Doors and windows were tightly shut and no curtains moved. Blobs of soot had drifted on to the railings and the fog muffled the sound of our feet. The sky and the houses and the pavement had all turned the same wintry colour and my hands got cold and my fingers began to turn white. We got to the Fulham Road, and to my dismay turned into the cemetery where the rows of damp grey graves were gloomy with dead chrysanthemums, and the path between them went on and on, forever disappearing into the fog. I glanced at the graves and was startled to see the word 'Mother' engraved on a stone and felt a private stab that one day my Mum would die too. I looked up quickly at Dad, to see if he'd noticed, if he knew what I was thinking, but his face was fixed and stern and grey with cold, and his peaked cap, pressed low on his fore-head, stood out black against the low sky. Only his high nose jutted out beyond his cap and I watched a drip hang there. I wanted to talk, to say something, to hear Dad's voice. If only we could make a noise it would take away the closeness of the awful graves. But though he was so familiar to me, I couldn't take his hand, and I couldn't speak to him to let him know how much I was afraid. So I kept my eyes away from the gravestones and looked down instead and watched Dad's sharp knees dragging his trousers after them and saw how his boots were the shape of his feet with deep cracks where they bent in front.

At last his short cut ended and we got into the crowded road, bright with shops and buses, lamps hissing on the stalls and muck in the gutters and I felt excited. Woolworth's were getting ready for Christmas and chains of coloured paper and lanterns hung across the shop. I dawdled past the counters, my eyes on a level with the glittering displays. Dad went to the long counter covered with boot mending gear, heelball and boot thread with balls of beeswax, round black rubber heels and cards of steel tips and studs, bradawls, tingles and hobbing feet. Dad despised the ready cut leather soles, 'bloody pressed paper,' he muttered. Hanging on hooks above the counter were pieces of leather strung by a hole punched in one corner. He took out his pattern and began to measure it twice against each piece of leather with clumsy stiff hands, trying to get both soles out of one piece. When he found several pieces the right size he began to bend them between his hands to see if the leather cracked, taking no notice of the suspicious lady behind the counter.

I knew that I dare not keep Dad waiting, but while he was busy I had a quick look at the counters near him. One was crowded with boxes and piles of brilliant Christmas tree decorations, crimson balls and golden stars, strings of tinsel and tiny celluloid dolls with silver crowns. Then I saw the heap of blue candle holders, little tinny things made to hold a minute candle. The blue was rich and metallic and silvery all at the same time, and the colour went straight to my heart. I put my fingers up and touched one, and suddenly Dad was beside me. I had forgotten all about him. I had a familiar stab of panic, but he wasn't looking at me, he was picking up one of the candle holders, which looked even smaller away from all the others, especially between his horny finger and thumb. He handed it to the assistant with a penny and she put it into a little brown paper bag. He gave it to me and without a word walked quickly away out of the shop, and I nipped after him.

I stuffed my hand with the paper bag up my scarf, feeling the hard edges of the candle holder, and stumbled all the way home behind him. The fog had turned yellow and my toes had gone dead. I kept close to him as we climbed our stairs past Old Sacky for it was pitch dark. When we entered our room there was a glow of red from the banked-up fire and it shone orange on the line of the steel fender and picked up two sparkles from the lid of the tin kettle. The warmth and smell of the room wrapped itself round me and I was glad I lived there, that it was ours, and it was cosy and I was home. My fingers began to ache.

Dad unpinned my scarf, poked the fire, put the kettle on and lit the lamp. I took the blue candle holder out of the bag and put it on the table. 'I'll cut down a bit of candle to fit that,' he said to me. I smiled at him in reply. I didn't care whether it had a candle or not, I just desperately wanted to have the colour, but I couldn't tell him so. I kept the candle holder for years and it was put on the mantelpiece every Christmas. Dad never bought another present for anyone else, not even for Mum. He never seemed to have any money. Perhaps that was one of the reasons why he was always so angry.

I caught all the usual childish ailments, one after another, so I spent a lot of time at home on my own with Dad. He never made a fuss of me and rarely spoke, but we got along together so long as I could keep myself amused and not bother him. I began to notice that he seemed to be two separate people, because as soon as the others came home he wasn't glad to see them as I was. He changed from being my quiet companion into his usual irritable and bad-tempered self.

Mum was constantly worried by Joey's cough, and could never

get rid of it. He tossed about at night, hot and flushed, and every so often had to stay indoors with bronchitis. During the day Mum put him into Lu and Dodie's bed, and kept Lu away from school to look after him. Lu kept him amused, pulling the green curtain round the bed and pretending they were in a cave or on a boat, but sooner or later Joey's thoughts were for his pets. We couldn't have a dog or a cat, so Joey had collected a variety of beetles, grasshoppers and caterpillars from Putney Common and snails, leeches and shrimps from the bunches of watercress that we bought from old 'A'penny 'andful'. He kept them in jam jars with holes pierced in the lids which were banished to the shed in the backyard, because Dad said there was quite enough overcrowding in our room without Joey's bloody zoo.

One day in September, just before his birthday, Joey was sitting up in bed looking frail and bright-eyed. He stared hopefully up at Lu from under his ragged blonde fringe. 'Lu,' he said, 'could I go down an' juss 'ave a look at my snails for five minutes?'

'No you couldn't,' Lu answered. 'You gotta stay in bed, or you'll never get better.'

'I 'aven't seen my snails for a long time.'

'Oh yes you have, don't come it!' said Lu. 'You saw 'em yesterday.'

'That's a long time, innit?'

'See if you're better tomorrer.'

'Lu.'

'Now what?'

'Could you p'raps bring juss one jar upstairs?'

'No, p'raps I juss couldn't. Joey, you know Dad says they're not to come indoors! You get all wet when you have your snails an' you're in my bed.'

'I won't upset 'em.'

'No, an' that's final.'

'Lu. What about juss 'aving my beetle then? He ain't wet. Go on Lu, eh?'

'Oh Joey, I won't 'arf get told off. Five minutes then, an' that's all.' Joey beamed, and of course Lu went down to the yard. She brought back his jar of grasshoppers, the caterpillars and his treasured stag beetle. Joey was elated. He lifted out the shiny beetle and let it have a little walk up and down his knees and then opened the grasshoppers. They leapt in all directions, over the knitted squares of the blanket and up the curtain. Lu screamed and began jumping about after them and suddenly the caterpillars were free.

'Joey, what the 'ell you doin'?' shouted Lu.

Nuffing. I ain't doin' nuffing,' wailed Joey. 'I told 'em one at a time, an' they all got out. Where's my beetle?' He crawled about searching the bedclothes while Lu scrabbled underneath, and soon they were both scrambling on the floor after the hopping insects. Joey began to cough as Lu thought she heard footsteps on the stairs.

'Sh!' she breathed. 'Oh God, it's Dad!' She just had a second to bundle Joey into bed before Dad came into the room. He hung his cap behind the door and lit the primus stove. Joey and Lu watched his every move. As he poured water from the jug into the kettle a grasshopper pinged on to his hand. Joey's eyes were big as saucers. Dad opened the cupboard door and scrunched the stag beetle in the hinges. He turned a threatening face to Lu and Joey. Lu was standing by the bed, a protective arm round Joey who knelt up clutching an empty jam jar to his chest.

'What's going on?' demanded Dad.

'Nothin',' whispered Lu. She watched a caterpillar arch its way over Dad's boot.

'Nothing?' Dad roared. 'I'll bloody well give you two nothing!' Lu closed her eyes and Joey began to cough. 'Aren't there enough bugs in this house without you bringing in more? We'll have an end to it. You can get rid of the bloody lot, and you can do it now!' He turned off the primus stove and banged the door behind him. Lu and Joey kept still for a moment and then began to collect the corpses. When Georgie and I got home from school we helped. Lu was angry, but Joey didn't say anything.

A couple of days later Mum let him go back to school. At half-past-four he should have been waiting for me, but I couldn't find him, so I came home by myself. Joey hadn't arrived. By six o'clock we were all out looking for him. 'We got to find 'im,' Lu said in a panic, 'before Mum comes home.'

Georgie went down to the embankment where Joey spent a lot of time on the foreshore under Battersea Bridge, but he wasn't there. Lu went to Sloane Square, to the mews where there were rows of stables. She jumped up at each stable door to look over the top. She was trying to find a particular pony, a grey one with a white forehead called 'Starlight'. Starlight belonged to some posh kid, but he was Joey's favourite. We often went there on Sunday mornings to hold the horses and ponies while the riders mounted, and sometimes earned a few pennies. Lu found the stall and saw the pony, and in the far corner, crouching in the straw was Joey, his hands between his knees.

'Joey! Come outa' there! I bin looking everywhere for you,' called Lu.

'I've run away,' said Joey quietly.

'Well, I've found yer,' said Lu.

'Go 'ome, and tell 'em you 'aven't.'

'Oh come on Joey love, Mum'll be home when we get back.'

'I'm not comin'.'

'Everyone's lookin' for yer.'

'I don't care.'

'What you run away for?' Lu had heaved herself up and was hanging over the stable door.

''Cos I've lost all my things.'

'No you 'aven't,' said Lu. 'What about all your snails an' leeches an' shrimps from the watercress? They're still under the shed. Who's gonna look after them if you ain't there?' Joey didn't answer. 'I know somethin' else too,' Lu went on. 'If you go down Manor Gardens and stamp 'ard on the pavement, 'undreds of ants come pouring up outa' the cracks.'

'What for?' asked Joey.

'I dunno,' Lu answered.

'What colour are they?' Joey was interested.

'Black,' said Lu, hoping she was right. 'All ants is black,' she decided.

'No they ain't,' Joey looked thoughtful. 'I seen brown 'uns.'

'How about I take you there tomorrow then,' said Lu, 'an' you can see.' Slowly Joey got up, patted Starlight and climbed over the door. Lu grabbed his hand and together they scooted along the Kings Road.

'Lu,' Joey said, 'don't let Mum know I run away.'

'Course not,' Lu smiled. 'Tell you what.'

'What?'

'Georgie found one of your caterpillars and put it in Dad's 'at.'

'Serves 'im right,' squealed Joey. 'I 'ope he don't squash it.'

By the end of the week Joey was admitted into Tite Street. It seemed for a time that if it wasn't one of us it was another in and out of Tite Street, and this worried Mum and Lu because at the end of each visit came the interview with the Lady Almoner. Something had to be paid, even if it were only a few pence at the dispensary for ointment, where there was a notice saying, *Patients will bring their own bottles and gallipots.* Mum usually managed to give Lu a shilling for this. When we were a bit better off, we joined the Hospital Savings Association, but in the meantime Lu took the situation desperately to heart. She had been closely involved with the place, sitting three times a day in the waiting-room when Georgie and I were so ill, and then doing it all over again for Joey. She made wild promises to herself about her future conduct and good works, if only God and the hospital between them could make us all better. The outcome was that Lu and Dodie made up their minds to hold a concert in our backyard, and raise some money to send to Tite Street.

Dodie went through her books and decided on *Little Women*, and made up a muddled version of all the best bits. Lu, who was to play Jo, refused to call Dodie 'Marmee', because she said it would make the kids in the audience double up. Lu and Winnie went down Manor Gardens to practise a dance and kept it very secret, and Georgie was to sing and tell riddles. My part was to wear a bit of white cloth round my head like a nurse and take round the refreshments.

We swept the yard and tried to board up the chickens. Georgie and Lu humped the junk from the shed back to clear a space for the stage, and hung the green curtain from Lu's bed over a washing line in front of it. Ethel lent a couple of kitchen chairs in case there were any adults – everyone else would have to sit on the ground. Advertising was by word of mouth, with threatened bashings by Georgie and Lu if any of their own particular mates failed to turn up. But a concert was rare and our neighbours knew us, and they came. The yard was packed and some had to hang out of the scullery window.

The play was unrecognisable and the audience totally baffled by the plot, but it was all made worth while by the deathbed scene. Georgie winked and grinned at the audience from under a man's flat cap and sang music hall songs through a sooty moustache. He got through a chorus of 'Running up and down our stairs', and 'Skylark', then the audience took over, whistling and thumping the tunes. Lu and Winnie were a riot. They had each bought a penny bag of mixed beads and threaded them to hang round their heads and drape from their arms, and they tied coloured bits of cloth over their noses leaving their eyes peeping wickedly over the top, creating a remote whiff of the Arabian Nights. They performed to an adenoidal but suitably reedy chant. In the uproar that followed the chickens exploded into freedom.

Dodie finally established order by asking if anyone in the crowd would like to say a piece of poetry or sing. The response was chaos, everyone wanted to perform and there were more kids on the stage than out front. Georgie got rid of most of them by shouting, 'If you don't sit down, you'll get no grub!' I entered on cue. We had invested threepence on stale cakes and three-pence on lemonade crystals. The cakes were cut into quarters and spread out on our tin plates, and the lemonade was mixed in our washing water jug. We had only seven cups. I dipped the cups into the jug and handed them round, half full, and as I got a cup back I dipped it again. It hadn't occurred to us to make arrangements to wash the cups between use, but no one appeared to notice. As the lemonade got lower down the jug, Georgie just tipped more water in from the kettle, and when the cakes looked as if they wouldn't go round, Lu cut what was left into even smaller pieces. We charged a ha'penny to come into the concert and a ha'penny for the refreshments. Some of the grown-ups gave us a penny, and several gave twopence.

We counted the takings three times and finally made the grand total of seven shillings and twopence. Dodie swung me round and round and Lu couldn't wait for Monday. At dinner time she scooted up to Tite Street and waited once again to see the Lady Almoner. Strangely tongue tied, she placed the paper bag of pennies and halfpennies on the polished wooden desk and simply said, 'for the hospital.' The Lady Almoner thanked her gravely, and a couple of days later the postman brought a letter addressed to 'Miss Louise Naylor'. Lu carried the letter about with her for days, and then put it in her box under the bed with a rare sense of satisfaction.

SEVEN

Please give a Farthing

There was nothing more stirring to us as children than the sound and sight of a massed movement of ball-bearing scooters, every one home-made in our backyards. Some were naturally fast and smooth running, others, assembled in exactly the same way, were sluggish. We discussed the positioning of screw-eyes, size of wheels and treachery of axles, and consulted on plank angles with all the gravity of racing mechanics. The pattern was ortho-dox and simple, the problem was getting hold of the parts.

The first essential was two good planks of wood each about two and a half feet long by four to six inches wide and at least half an inch thick, one for the upright and one for the base. A new wood road block, usually pinched, was nailed to the base, and the two planks joined by four large screw-eyes, two into the upright and two into the road block, with a six-inch nail bent at the top, or preferably a bolt, slotted through the screw-eyes. This gave the upright a good swivel, for steering. The wheels were two ball-race bearings, greatly prized, and the highest cur-rency in our swap market. To seal a swap, particularly if you thought you had the best of the bargain, you hurriedly chanted: 'Touch teeth, touch leather, can't 'ave it back for ever an' ever'. The axles were the disaster area, particularly the one at the back. Slots were sawn, chiselled or scraped with penknives into the bottom of the upright front plank, as well as at the end of the base plank into which the wheels were inserted. Then a stick of firewood threaded the wheel, and was nailed on the underside of the planks. The space between the wheel and axle was filled with broken ends of firewood, hammered in until the slack was taken up. Many a time a scooter under full speed, and they could go, would swerve madly across the road or pavement without warning, shooting the rider off sideways, as the tread plank collapsed over the splinters of another busted back axle.

Getting hold of the wheels was the biggest problem, and having a spare one put you in the upper bracket. Our only source of supply was the motor works. Straight after school and all through Saturday mornings the boys hung about the open doors, cadging. Now and again an infuriated mechanic made a run at the door.

'Get out of it! Go on, sling your 'ooks!' and the boys scattered, edging back again one by one.

'Oi, mister! Gisser ball bearin', ay mister?'

Just once in a while their persistence got results when one of the mechanics rejected a ball-race bearing, and strode with it to the door, holding it above his head. Instant pandemonium broke out among the boys as they fought to reach it. He might hand it to the smallest boy who would dart off like a weasel until he was overtaken by the mob, or he might throw it into the road over their heads and sadistically stand back to watch the desperate scramble.

We shaped the handlebars from any bit of wood, preferably a sawn-off strip from the thick end of an apple box. The fashion was to have a second pair of racing handlebars, angled downwards half-way down the front plank, and this meant you had to scoot bent forwards with your head down. You didn't actually move any faster, but in a crouched position and with your hat on back to front, you gave the illusion of incredible speed. The idea was to copy the speedway riders on motor-bikes who were pulling in large crowds at Stamford Bridge. We decorated our scooters with bits of lino nailed to the foot plank, and a touch of class was added by nailing a shallow tobacco tin next to the road block, for tools. We made patterns on the front with drawing pins, or chalked the number of our house there, and bound the handlebars with string. Our scooter had a brass screw-eye in the front on which we hung the shopping bag. Apart from scooting errands and paper rounds, we rode them on collective charges round the streets, playing tag races and riding two up at a time. Your status fell if one member of the family couldn't produce a scooter.

We were lucky to be able to use the streets for everything we wanted to do. We used a sorbo ball for football and chalked out goalposts on blank walls. Every lamp-post had a wicket chalked on it too, and we tied lengths of greengrocer's sisal to the lamp lighter's bars for swings. We made a loop in the end of the rope and folded our coat into it then stuffed one arm through, right up to the armpit, and with a running jump swung outwards over the road, booting the lamp-post to send ourselves flying up and out into an arc, keeping the momentum going over and over again.

The sisal stretched and often broke and plenty of kids got hurt, and the lamp-posts took a terrible belting.

On summer evenings when everybody came out of doors, talking and sitting by their doorways, it was the long rope skipping season. Plenty of us had short bits of rope which we used for 'bumps' in the winter, but in the summer we knotted them together to make a long rope that stretched across the road from kerb to kerb. Two mums turned the ends and we played 'running-ins-and-outs', twenty or more of us, boys and girls, from those too small to skip right up to those who had started work but had not yet got too old for street games. We followed the leader, running up the rope, touching the ground, doing 'over the moon' and 'running through', the girls laughing and jeering at the hesitant boys who jumped with their feet pressed together, showing off, gliding casually into the rope, circling and twirling. When it was time to pack up, and some of us were called up for bed, we begged for another five minutes, until someone shouted 'all in together'. This was the recognised finale and everyone joined in, even some of the watching mums in their pinafores. We crowded, packed inside the rope, clutching hands until the turners shouted, 'Ready?' After many false starts we leaped unevenly over the rope as it turned and chanted:

'All in together,
This fine weather,
I-spy Peter,
'Angin' out the winder,
Shoot, bang, fire!'

On the word 'fire' everybody ran out of the rope, shouting goodnights, and leaving the owners of the ropes struggling to undo the scuffed-up knots. We went up to our room hot, tired and buoyantly happy. Dad said we were saluting the Peterloo massacre, though we never knew what he meant by that.

When we were home from school in August, the days were endless with hot summer pavements and bluebottles, dry dusty gutters that smelt of drains and the pungent darkness of the passage against the brightness outside. We wanted above all things to go swimming up the baths, so Lu decided to earn the twopence each to get in by making a grotto, which was a kind of home-made peep show. She nicked the orange box that was in the backyard waiting to be chopped up for firewood, and stood it on the pavement outside our house like a little stage, then sent me up Manor Gardens to pick the flowering pink weeds that grew there. She went indoors and borrowed Joey's woolly rabbit with pink eyes, ransacked Dodie's scrap basket and deliberately tore the cover off a *Picture Show* magazine that she and Dodie kept hidden under their mattress.

Sucking her bottom lip between her teeth, Lu set to work. She wound a little ball of red wool in and out of the open slats that made up the top of the box and tucked the already limp weeds under the wool so they dangled downwards. It looked quite nice, I thought. She placed the rabbit in the box and draped him with scraps of lace and ribbon.

'Stones, Rowie,' she said to me. 'Go and find some stones.' I ran off down the Grove and pottered about looking for special ones, and spat on them to make them shiny. When I got back the grotto was taking shape. She had threaded red wool in and out of the picture and tied it to one side so that a luscious-faced lady with black eyes and cupid lips smouldered menacingly at the innocent rabbit. Lu placed the stones creatively between them and stood back.

'We want some more colours,' she said. 'What we got with colours?'

'I dunno,' I said. I was fed up with being sent to look for things.

'Go indoors, an' 'ave a look round.' I climbed the stairs, hopped past Old Sacky's door and looked hopefully round our hot room. Everything was tidy and put away, nothing on the table or the bed or on Dad's chair. The shelves were high up, out of my reach. I opened the cupboard by the fire and got my stool. I never went to the cupboard on my own because a lot of the things on the top shelf were Mum's and Dad's. Nearly everything there was white and seemed to frown down on me as if I were looking at something private, and just as if I suddenly heard Dad's voice I jumped down and slammed the door shut quick. Then I remembered to look under the bed. I poked about among Lu's old rubbish and found a round tin crammed with wrinkled conkers and empty cotton reels with four little nails banged into the top for making woollen reins, a broken hair slide and a grubby paper bag. I tipped up the bag, and beads rolled all over the floorboards, and a lot of the little tiny ones, red and white, disappeared down the cracks. I picked up all I could find and put them back in the bag and put the bigger ones, brown and blue, into the lap of my frock, rolled it up to my waist and crept back to Lu.

'Where you bin all this time?' I thought she'd be pleased with what I'd found, so I didn't tell her about losing the little ones.

'Threadle 'em up,' she said, so I squatted down and sucked the wool and wormed it through the beads. Lu hung the string of brown and blue across the box which gave it a vague suggestion of theatre.

'Now,' said Lu, 'say this after me.

> "Please remember the grotto,
> Me father has run off to sea,
> Me mother's gone to fetch 'im back,
> So please give a farthin' to me!"

I said it, several times, until I knew it by heart, and then Lu sang it to a simple sing-song tune, until I could do it by myself.

With Joey in the pram, and the grotto balanced precariously on the end by the handlebars, facing away from Joey so he wouldn't be able to see his rabbit, we set off towards a big pub on the Embankment. We had quite a bit of trouble getting the pram up and down the kerbstones because the beads kept falling off. Eventually we found a doorway with a clean step, put the box down, rearranged the stones, hung the beads up again and stood back to look at the effect.

'We've forgotten a tin for the money!'

'What money?' I asked.

'Oh, Gawd, the farthings for the grotto, daft!' She darted at Joey, whisked off his knitted hat and placed it on the ground in front of the box.

'Now sit on the step,' she said, 'and sing.'

'I don't want to.'

'You wanna go up the baths don't you?' Lu said, getting cross.

'Yes.'

'Well, then!' She jiggled the pram to keep Joey amused, then pushed him up and down, getting further and further away from me. I sat on the warm step and started in a thin voice, 'Please remember the grotto,' looking back at Lu and getting louder as she shouted the words at me, 'me father has run off to sea.' A lady walked past and looked at me, so I stopped singing and pretended not to see her. She hesitated and then went on. 'Me mother's gone,' I wailed, 'to fetch him back,' a man was looking at the box.

'What's all this?'

'Our grotto.'

'What's it for?'

'To go swimmin'.' To my astonishment he put a halfpenny in Joey's hat. I felt a bit more perky after that and started up again, much louder. Lu raced the pram up to me.

'What'cher get?'

''Apn'y.'

'There y'are. Told yer!' Some more people were coming, so with a huge beam of encouragement Lu moved away and left me to it. I started again, but found I hadn't the nerve to sing when they stopped to look. They talked to each other and then went on, one of them looking back at me as if I was doing something wrong. I called to Lu.

'What's up now?' she shouted back.

'Them people.'

'Don't take no notice, and sing up!' A woman with a boy came by and he dragged at her sleeve to stop and look. The woman gave him something and he shyly put it on top of the box and hurried after her. It was a penny, so I treated them to a bit of the song as they left me. Nothing much happened after that. Several people glanced, but didn't stop. Then a man in shirtsleeves came out of a door next to my step and stood glaring down at me, so I started to sing.

'You with anyone?' I went on singing. 'And hold that bloody noise,' he shouted. 'Who's with you?'

'My sister, over there.'

'You'd better clear off,' he shouted, turning round to Lu. 'You're begging you are, and you'll get locked up!'

'No we ain't,' cried Lu indignantly, hurrying the pram across the road. 'We got something. We made something for them to look at!'

'Not 'ere you don't. Now I'm warning you. Clear out, an' take this rubbish with you.' I started crying. Pretty frightened herself, Lu heaved the box on the pram, and Joey immediately grabbed his rabbit, upsetting the stones and spoiling everything as Lu crammed his hat over his eyes. We ran the pram round the first corner.

'Let's go home, Lu,' I said.

'We 'aven't got enough money yet.'

'I don't care. I want to go 'ome.' Without another word Lu gave up and shoved the pram angrily towards our house, and I ran beside it, snivelling.

We dumped the grotto on to the baking pavement outside the house and I was smothered under a load of misery and failure. The little stage that had shone by the step on the embankment was now a splintery old box of rubbish. Lu was stiff and wouldn't say anything to me and my face felt puffy with dried salty tears. There was nothing to look forward to, it was all gone and I hadn't tried. Lu unstrapped Joey and took his hand as he climbed our dark stairs one at a time, still hugging his rabbit. I chucked the stones and weeds into the gutter, picked out the beads, a bit of lace and the crumpled picture and followed them indoors.

'Lu,' I said.

'What?'

'Talk to me.'

'I'm fed up.'

'Are we goin' to spend the three'apence?'

'No. We ain't.'

'What we goin' to do then? We can't go swimmin', can we?'

Lu poured some water into the bowl and wet the flannel. 'Hold your face up,' she said. She wiped my face over roughly, and suddenly bent down and kissed my forehead. 'It's all right,' she grinned, 'you can cheer up. I'm goin' to tell Dodie what we done. P'raps we can go with her on 'er 'alf-day.'

'Dodie doesn't never 'ave any money,' I said, through the flannel.

'I know. But she can ask Mum for us, can't she? Mum lets her 'ave a tanner now an' again, now she's workin', if she asks specially. We only want fourpence 'apenny an' we can all go.' Lu and Dodie whispered to each other that night, so that Mum shouldn't hear, and I saw Dodie telling Lu off. She said we were never to go begging again, no matter what we made for people to look at, because we'd get nicked.

The weather was still blazing hot on Thursday and we waited desperately for Dodie to come home from work. They always pinched a bit of her afternoon off. Mum had left her dinner on a tin plate on top of a saucepan of water over the primus and we fidgeted about impatiently until Dodie had shovelled it down.

''Ow much longer we gotta wait?' I asked Lu.

'Mum says she'll drown if we go swimmin' on top of 'er dinner.'

''Ow long then? We won't get in. There'll be 'undreds in the queue.'

'Give us a chance,' said Dodie. 'All that spud! I'll go straight to the bottom.'

'I'd better put Joey in 'is pram, better'n I,' said Lu, 'an' Georgie can cop an eye on 'im till we gets back.' While she was downstairs Dodie washed up her dinner things with the saucepan water and spread out our none too clean towel.

'We'll all have to make do with this,' she said. 'The clean one's in the cupboard an' we can't make 'em both wet.' She rolled our costumes and hats in the towel and counted out our sixpence in coppers.

'Right then,' she shouted. 'Who's going swimming?'

'We are!' I yelled, and I danced between Lu and Dodie, all the way up the shimmering street.

There were two baths, one for women and girls and next door one for men and boys. A white tiled passage between the pay boxes linked the two baths but this was vigilantly patrolled by the formidable superintendents. For me it was a vast echoing space, filled with watery danger and saturated with the smell of chloride. Our swimming costumes had to meet the required standard of respectability and no two-pieces were allowed. Dodie's came from a jumble sale and was very stylish. The lower bit was black with a modest skirt over the front of the legs that finished mid-way down her thighs, and the orange top was shapeless as a vest, to disguise any suggestion of a bosom. The classy touch was a white belt, slotted low on the hips. Hats were compulsory, and Dodie's was thick brown rubber with a raised seam over the top of her head, outside ear pieces, and a thick strap under her chin. With her long hair stuffed up inside it, she looked like Britannia. Lu's costume was on almost permanent loan from a girl at school. It was made of thin black cotton and was quite shapeless. The wide shoulders draped over her skinny arms, and it clung down to her knees flaring out into two un-evenly baggy legs, so she kept heaving up the wrinkles and tuck-ing them round her waist. My own costume was knitted from yellow wool, which doubled its size when wet and practically drowned me.

Lu and Dodie had learned to swim at school and they took it in turns to hold me up in the shallow end. There I was among the pouting-faced ladies who screwed up their noses as they gently glided forwards on pink water wings for a brief, single stroke. Other children clung shivering to the bar round the edge, with red-eyes and chattering jaws. After about twenty minutes one of the white-coated attendants would call us to come out. Once I remember she flung open a cubicle and grabbed a piece of clothing.

'Whose is this?'

It was Dodie's frock. I was sitting on the slippery wooden steps, too cold to get back into the water, and I could see it was Dodie's. The attendant stood on the very edge of the bath, waving it above her head.

'Come on,' she cried, 'whose is this?' I looked round and saw Lu swimming like mad up to the deep end. She didn't care. Dodie had her back to the attendant, pretending not to hear, although under that great walloping hat she probably couldn't. The attendant dangled the frock towards the water as a threat. 'You've had your time,' she called, 'out, out, out!'

I shouted out to Dodie. I wanted to get out anyway. I was shivering all over, my hands had gone all washerwoman's and my eyes felt inside out. Dodie led me creeping to our cubicle, my sagging costume dripping between my knees, and gave a convincing start of surprise as she met the attendant and claimed her frock.

'You know the rules,' she started on Dodie, 'you've had your half-hour.'

'Those kids were in here before us.'

'Who else is with you?'

'Only me and my little sister.' Dodie swept me into our box and rubbed me here and there and we dragged my clothes over the wet bits. I couldn't see out so I didn't know what Lu was doing, but Dodie was just getting dressed and standing in her bloomers when the curtain jerked aside and the attendant's angry face peered over the door. 'Hurry up!'

Dodie tried to pull the curtain back on our privacy but the attendant snatched it back.

'Whose shoes are those?' On the floor under the bench were Dodie's shoes and Lu's boots. 'I knew there was someone else with you, where is she?' Dodie looked over the door and saw Lu doing a neat little flip off the springboard, and nodded to her. The attendant strode warily along the wet red tiles between the cubicles and the bath and in no time Lu squeezed in, dripping cold water all over us.

'Innit good,' she beamed, 'we n'arf 'ad a long time.'

'Didn't you see her with my frock?'

'Yeh,' grinned Lu, 'an' I didn't n'arf get told off. Wait for me.'

'Rowie's cold,' said Dodie, 'I'm taking her outside.' We left Lu to get dressed and I clung to Dodie's hand, treading gingerly along the edge of the great slopping bath of blue water. As we went through the door we heard the attendant having a go at someone else.

'Whose is this? Out, out, out!'

'Cor, what a job!' said Dodie.

Sometimes, in the summer, we got the urge to run about on a bit of grass, not the coarse yellowing spaces trodden flat by dogs and people in Hyde or Battersea Park, but a private green bit we knew about. It was hidden down the Old Man's, which was our name for the Royal Hospital, fully enclosed inside iron railings and portered at the gate by uniformed Chelsea Pensioners. There was a list of strict regulations stuck up on a green post, which we never read. Nursemaids in grey and navy-blue outfits pushed elegant perambulators with fringed canopies and the children with them had velvet collars on their coats – they got through the gate easily. We knew that ragamuffins got scrutinised, so Lu tidied us up and shoved our pram with her nose in the air, talking posh in a loud voice.

Once we got inside Lu made us keep to the middle of the path and we walked properly in a tidy procession, holding on to the sides of the pram and taking small, careful steps. As soon as we were round the bend and out of sight of the gate, we whooped over the low hooped wire and up the grass slope between the bushes, all shoving the pram, until we stood on the perimeter of a small dell. A semicircle of gently sloping grassy banks dipped before us, green and secret. We tipped the pram over the edge and charged down the slope, rolling over and over until we landed in a glorious struggling heap, sprawled out in the dappled sunshine. Sometimes other girls with their little brothers and sisters to mind came with us. The dell was a natural stage, so we danced, taking it in turns. We did cartwheels and the splits, and flung ourselves madly up and down the slopes and then lay breathless, digging our fingers and pressing our faces into the grass.

They chucked out at half-past four and one of the Pensioners tottered along the neat paths crying 'All out, all out!' and ringing a handbell. We collected at the rim of the dell and nipped between the bushes, waiting until the coast was clear, then skittered over the 'keep off the grass', lifted the pram over the low rail and swaggered, red-faced and untidy, to the gate, free from caring whether we were posh or not, until the next time.

All the boys who lived around us wore boots, small replicas of those made for men with steel rims round the heels. Girls had both shoes and boots, though some of them squelched throughout the year in threadbare plimsolls. Girls' boots were laced all the way up to the top, fitted closely and finished about two inches below the knees. They were inelegant, practical and invariably black, and were identical to those worn by lady policemen. But there was one girl in my class who wore a pair of shiny patent leather ankle strap shoes that fastened in front with a single button. I used to watch her feet with a strange feeling of pleasure until I was almost convinced they were my own, and then I looked down at my own thick socks and scuffed boots and came to with a bump. I often found myself pretending that I was some-one else, and I was certain that if I could wish hard enough and believe hard enough I could be magically pretty and have patent leather ankle strap shoes.

Every so often Dad had to repair our boots, and the couple of hours banging didn't go down very well with the neighbours. So on a Sunday morning, if the weather was fine, we all trailed off to Hyde Park with the snobbing gear. Dad put his hammer and hobbing foot into the pram with a tin of brads, pincers, a knife and whetstone and bits of cut up machine belting. The belting was about six inches wide and came in two varieties, equally infuriating. One was made of thick layers of grey woven cotton pressed together with a rubbery solution, and the other was bright yellow and looked like solid sorbo. Dodie sat Joey on the top of the gear and gave him our bucket to hold, and we set off, with Dad walking some distance in front of us, pretending we weren't with him.

Exhibition Road was a long shove up and as soon as we got into the park we made straight for Rotten Row, where Dad settled under a tree with his back to the pram and surrounded himself with the gear and our boots. We took off our socks and ran on to the coarse brown sand, falling about and swinging on the black painted rail at first, and then choosing a place to build a sandcastle. Lu and Georgie went down to the Serpentine to fill our bucket with water, slopping it back over the grass, and we tipped it into the sand to make a muddy patch, pressing our feet into it and squirming the dirty grit between our toes. Kneeling in the muck we dug with our hands and piled up mounds, smooth-ing and rounding them and sticking stones and leaves in the top for flags and windows. Georgie burrowed a moat and we ran and ran with bucket after bucket of water to pour it along the channel, bunking up the sides and screaming as it disappeared.

All the time we played, the horses trotted and cantered out in the middle of the Row, and we squatted back now and again to watch them, especially if the riders were children. They were wholly absorbed with themselves and looked neither to the right or left, certainly not at us. They made a bright and endless pro-cession, jingling by, and to them we were invisible. The fun started when some of the riders came along the edge of the Row, and groups of them trod right through our game. Their horses came straight at us and we scrambled out of the way, looking up at the vast brown bellies and shining straps and boots.

''Ere mister! Look what your 'orse's done!' shouted Georgie at the jogging backsides of one lot.

'Get orf an' push it!' screamed Lu, showing she was just as brave as Georgie. If one of them had stopped, or if they had simply glanced down at us we would have run, but they didn't, and we got out of hand, shouting cheeky remarks louder and louder, throwing ourselves on the sand with the sheer luxury of bawling at the nobs. When some bowler-hatted ladies rode by, Lu yelled, 'Old rotten 'ats,' and Georgie topped her by calling out: 'Old fat bums. Bum, bum, bum!' at a couple of gents on great rumpy chargers.

When a shower of dung fell within feet of us it was the last straw, and we doubled up with hysterics as Lu cried: 'Go 'ome missis, an' get yer shovel!'

When we'd had enough we usually wandered about under the trees, and if the horse chestnut flowers had fallen we picked them up and sucked the ends, finding a trace of sweetness. By this time we were listening for Dad, who called us as soon as he was finished. We tidied our clothes and presented ourselves obediently, eyeing our boots. Yellow this time, black boots with bright yellow clumpy soles. If it had occurred to Dad to expect a word of thanks he never got it. Glumly we covered our dirty feet with our socks and pushed them into our boots, which had assumed the usual curious shape after being mended. Dad stretched the belting so tightly over the sole and instep and nailed it on so hard it caused the boot to arch downwards, so that the toe pointed fiercely to the ground. The fine heads of the brads sank into the soft rubber and the new sole sprang outwards away from the boot, making a round yellow bulge underneath, so when we walked about we rolled on the bulgy balls of our feet, and it took some getting used to. The cotton webbing he used on some occasions did at least stay flat, but it frayed, especially when it got wet, and our boots then developed a grey fringe all round the outside.

We bounced home in our repaired boots, keeping pretty quiet, and all the way I dreamed of a pair of patent leather ankle strap shoes.

Two days stood out in our year above all others. We talked about them, whispered in bed, anticipated and counted, until the bust-ing excitement of the day itself actually came. One was the second Monday in August when Mum was on her week's holiday, and she took us to the cheap day at Regent's Park Zoo, and the other was Boxing Day, when we went to the panto at the Chelsea Palace.

The zoo day began as usual, but we were fidgety and dying to start getting ready and Mum moved cautiously through the routine to see that nothing upset Dad. When the beds were cleared away we got down to it, packing the primus stove with a medicine bottle of meths, matches, cups, tinned milk with matchsticks stuck in the openings, spoon and sugar, the kettle and teapot with the tea already in it, and paper bags of bread and jam. Once Dodie had started work, Mum shared out the shopping bags between herself, Georgie and Lu, and Joey carried his rabbit. We walked to Hyde Park Corner and waited excitedly for the 74 bus, for the journey itself was an occasion and we exploited it to the full. Mum let us ride upstairs on the open top and we heaved ourselves up the winding steps and made a fuss about where to sit, which side, front or back? The front was best, over the driver. The seats were slatted and curved at the top and there was a tarpaulin lap cover rolled up behind the seat in front, fastened with a little strap. The first thing we did was unroll the tarpaulin, drape it over our seat and crawl underneath, making it into a tent. Eventually we sat properly, riding high above the streets, looking down on the busy people and working traffic, with that deliciously superior air that comes of being on holiday. London from the top of an open bus was nothing less than spectacular, and we savoured every moment. At last the green haze of Regent's Park clouded between the buildings and we got odd glimpses of wire netting and tall grey birds between the railings. At the zoo stop the bus emptied and we joined the long queue to get in, keeping together and shuffling slowly forward until the almost painfully exquisite bit when you passed through the iron turnstile. Mum came through last, and we smiled triumphantly at each other for a brief moment, we were in!

We didn't mess about with the owls and pheasants, we had come to see lions and tigers, elephants and monkeys, and watch the keeper chucking herrings to the sea lions, although we had to let Joey have a little while being lifted up to stare solemnly into minute glass cases of insects. We could never make Joey out.

On this particular day it was raining steadily by dinner time but Mum insisted that we had it somewhere nice. 'How people can eat,' she said, 'with the smell of lion's pee in their sandwiches, I can't think.' We settled in a row of dripping iron chairs in front of an impeccable outdoor aviary, with flat yellow sand ironed between fringy pools, watching the dapper birds dipping and flitting, living their clean lives behind the wires.

'Much more healthy, this is,' said Mum, as she pumped the primus. 'Eat your bread, Joey, don't poke it all in the cage, and Georgie, come down here and hold your coat open, the wind's blowing the flame out.'

'Better than hafting to go to the caff, innit Mum?' said Lu, her hair plastered against her wet face. 'All them tables piled up with other people's grub.'

We saved monkey hill until last. It was our favourite place in the whole zoo, where a circular granite wall protected the open rocky habitat for a colony of baboons. We went there to see the fights and waited patiently until they happened. A great dominant male displayed all the overbearing bad-temper required, and we watched entranced as he snarled at the smaller animals, sending the slender females scampering and screaming with babies clinging perilously under their bellies. We knew all about this. To see something of our own situation so vividly displayed gave us an added fearsome pleasure. Although we never admitted our thoughts to each other, we must have been the most sympathetic onlookers that monkey hill ever entertained.

Christmas was a long, long wait after the summer, but as the evenings drew in we made paper chains with flour and water paste and saved up our ha'pennies and farthings in a cocoa tin. Excitement built up until it was almost unbearable, for we believed desperately in Santa Claus and there was no knowing what he might take into his head to bring us. Even Dad made an effort for Christmas. During the night of Christmas Eve he transformed the mantelpiece into a snow scene, with cotton wool on the alarm clock and a blue and white cardboard picture of mountains and snowy trees. We hung our socks up in a row, and I got a little bag of gold-covered chocolate coins and a packet of real coloured chalks. We had boiled belly of pork for dinner and huge helpings of currant duff for afters, with custard.

After the wonder of Christmas Day came the final treat, the pantomime. As soon as tea was over on Boxing night, we went up our street in the crackling cold to get into the front of the queue for the gallery. The Chelsea Palace glowed red and yellow lights all over the road, and people spilled in and out of all its doors. There was music from the buskers and cries from the pedlars, hot chestnuts, peanuts-all-roasted, hot taters and toffee apples. Great posters lit with spotlights showed the fairy queen and the long-legged principal boy, shining and glittering above the crowds. We dragged Mum across the Kings Road in a panic that we shouldn't get in, and joined our queue that huddled in the darkness of Sydney Street, willing the doors to open. At the squeak of the crash barrier we edged forward and the queue began to move until we caught the airless smell of the grey stone stairs. Up and up we went, Mum breathing heavily, and Lu and Georgie racing ahead to grab our places.

The first sight of the gods was a shock, for the steepness of the seating took your breath away. There were no real seats, just slightly curved layers of stone, each covered with a strip of thin matting. People squeezed up together and leaned back on the feet and knees of those squashed in behind them. We bounded down the tiers to the iron bar, filled in with wire mesh, that separated us in the gallery from the proper red seats of the upper circle, and sat on our folded coats so that we could see over the top. The stage was covered by a shiny stiff curtain painted all over with advertisements, and we twisted round to watch the crowd pouring in and filling every space, pleased and excited that we were in the front. There was such a noise with everyone talking and moving about and kids running up and down to the lav, not using the stairs but pushing between the seated people. Lu pointed out the bald heads bobbing in the orchestra pit, and families settled in the gold boxes each side of the stage. One large lady sat prominently forward displaying a sparkling necklace.

'Diamonds,' hissed Dodie. I stared at the sumptuous box, red curtains glowing in the golden light, and I saw the glittering jewels. It was all marvellous and magic, and there we were in the same place as a lady wearing diamonds.

Immediately below us the upper circle was packed full, and further down were even more sweeping curves of people in the dress circle. We could just see the first few rows of the stalls behind the curtain of the orchestra pit. People began to clap when the conductor suddenly appeared. He nodded his head to them over his shoulder and held up his arms. I clutched Dodie's hot hand and leaned forwards, pressing my head to the wire mesh. The orchestra burst into a jiggy tune, making a thin loud noise so that you could hear every instrument. The advertisements disappeared upwards and the great, gold-fringed curtains took their place. Softly, slowly the lights dimmed, the people grew very still, the footlights sprang into a line. Like lightning the red curtains flew away and I almost fell on to the great open stage, brilliant with light and colour, painted trees and cottage, and awhirl with identically dressed dancing villagers in tap shoes. The panto had begun, and I was already intoxicated.

We learned to shout 'Allo Willie!' every time the fat funny man came on stage, and we sang a song about a 'Whatnot', reading the words from a printed screen. We boo-ed the wicked baron and shouted warnings to the buxom Idle Jack, but my passionate attention was devoted to the chorus girls, for Lu and I were determined to go on the stage, and our ambition was to wear red tap shoes with bows on top. I watched every routine, hummed every song and picked out the best and the worst dancers.

For weeks after the pantomime we practised down the cul-de-sac in Manor Gardens, Lu and me, Winnie, Elsie, Cissie and Reen, 'Ilda and Dolly, with any other straggler we could entice. We stood in a row, arms along each other's shoulders, gasping a tune as we bent in the middle trying to kick in unison. It was all awful and hopeless and we went on and on. Enthusiasm was beginning to peter out and Lu was having difficulty in keeping up the attendance, when one Saturday afternoon she came flying down the middle of the road, jumping every few steps, waving her arms.

'Come on you lot!' she cried. 'I found it!'

'Found what?'

'A place where they do dancin'.'

'Where?'

'Come on!' We pelted after her, up to the Kings Road and down Flood Street until she stopped by a white-painted building which was a sort of garage. A flight of wooden stairs went up the front of the wall and at the top was an open door. Lu crept up the steps on all fours, mouthing at us to keep quiet, and one by one we followed her and crowded at the top. She gently pushed the door further open so we could all see, and then the music started. Someone was playing a piano, slow and soft.

The room was bare, without any colour, and the floor was just wooden boards, and there were lots of girls with nothing on their feet or legs. They all wore yellow frocks, short ones, with floppy bodices and bare arms, but the most startling thing about them, which made them look dressed-up and foreign, was the yellow band of ribbon tied straight across their foreheads. They stood anywhere, facing all over the place, listening to the music and then, together, they raised themselves upwards on one foot and slowly lifted one arm, palm upwards. I had never seen anything so graceful and simple, and I felt a jump of breath. We watched the girls having their lesson and I know they saw us. When Lu judged it was time for us to go, we backed clumsily down the steps and I was surprised for a minute to see what a lot of clothes we all wore.

'Well?' Lu beamed. 'What about that?'

'Funny, innit?' Cissie was undecided.

'I reckon it was lovely,' said Dolly, all smiles.

'Potty if you ask me. All that floppin' about, they never done one splits.' Elsie was fat, and rotten at dancing.

'You're not supposed to,' explained Lu. 'That's real dancin' that is, not like up the Palace. Anyway,' she said firmly, 'it's what we're goin' to do from now on. We're comin' up 'ere every week an' learn.' Thus the dancing class found us on their doorstep, and never once told us to go away.

Down the cul-de-sac we tried, we tried so hard, but it was chaos without any music. Lu counted, 'one and, two and,' and sang vague bits of some of the tunes, and after a while some of us got the general idea. We all cottoned on to the fact that it was serious stuff and set our faces into suitably glum expressions. Slowly our exertions began to satisfy Lu, and to keep up our spirits she said we were ready to give a performance. This was dynamite.

'We ain't got nuffing to wear,' Cissie started moaning, 'an' I'll tell yer somethin' an' all Luli Nayler, I ain't goin' to take me shoes off, not for you nor no one.'

'You got to!' exploded Lu, 'proper dancin' is in yer feet!'

'I ain't.'

'You saw them girls, they don't 'ave no shoes on!'

'They don't dance in the road do they? Look at them stones!'

Cissie had struck a blow, and meant it. Lu had no words. She couldn't explain that if they were really dancing properly they'd hardly notice the stones, and she couldn't understand why Cissie didn't share her feelings. Dolly sided with Cissie, so Lu had to compromise.

'Ow, awright then,' she said, 'but I ain't 'avin' no boots nor shoes. You'll have to get 'old of somethin' else, slippers or drill shoes,' and she left them to it to solve their problems as best they could.

'I 'aven't got a yeller frock.' Reen was always ready to have a go at Lu, whom she thought was too bossy by half.

'A' course you 'aven't. Nor 'ave I. Course none of us 'ave, 'ave we?' Lu was exasperated. Why couldn't some of them use their loaf? 'Go 'ome, an' ask for somethin' for dressin' up.'

The following week we turned up with nothing more than rags. Eagerly, Lu told everyone to spread them on the road, and we sorted them out. In no time we realised that it wasn't any good, and nobody had brought anything that was remotely like the baggy bodices and short skirts of the girls at the dancing class. There was a man's waistcoat with the buttons cut off, a faded beige chenille tablecloth with bobbles, two cloche hats in mauve straw, a long brown skirt and a grubby piece of lace curtain.

'We can't do it, can we?' said 'Ilda miserably, 'not with them ol' things.'

'We gotta think of something,' Lu answered fiercely. 'I know what! What you got on underneath? Go on 'Ilda, show us your bloomers.'

'I ain't,' screamed 'Ilda.

'Don't be daft.' Lu was on to the solution. 'I seen girls doin' sports in their vests an' bloomers. I seen their photo in the paper.'

'Well I ain't! You're dirty, you are, Luli Nayler, an' I'm tellin' my mum.' 'Ilda was indignant.

'I got navy ones,' said Win.

'Mine's white, an' I got a petticoat an' all,' joined in Dolly.

'Rowie, off your jersey,' commanded Lu. She yanked my jersey over my head and I stood proudly in the liberty bodice. 'Dance around a bit.' I capered up and down, holding my palms upwards under their critical stares. 'That's all right innit?' Lu was charged with enthusiasm.

'We can cut the bobbles off the tablecloth an' put 'em round our 'eads.' The excitement in Winnie's voice was catching. Dolly took her frock off and displayed a high-necked flannel petticoat.

'Feels lovely,' she said, 'juss like 'avin' a summer frock on.'

We all took off our top clothes and scampered about in shabby vests with missing neck strings and drawers with the elastic gone in one leg. Lu tore feverishly at the lace curtain and handed strips round. With the band of cotton twisted round our foreheads we were transformed. We felt like the girls in the yellow frocks and the performance was on.

'I betcha no one comes,' Cissie started again.

'Course they will.' Winnie was dead keen.

'Go on then, tell us, who's comin'?'

'You've all got to tell your mums, an' next door, an' everyone down your street,' said Lu, 'an' I'm goin' up the dancin' class to tell the lady up there.'

'Oh Lu, you ain't.'

'Yes I am! We can do it as good as them.'

A few people did come to watch us, pushing prams and carrying babies. It was a chilly afternoon and they stood in a thin circle in the road as we ran into our places, leaving our clothes in little piles against the wall. We danced, and we accompanied ourselves breathlessly with the now familiar bits of tune and the discerning listener might have recognised a brief moment of Brahms. We finished with a panting tableau, unfortunately only too reminiscent of the Chelsea Palace, and waited for the applause. We smiled selfconsciously when it came, sparsely enough, but sufficient for Lu to leap to her feet and walk round with a cardboard box. A couple of coppers rattled in it as she stopped before the one well-dressed lady.

'Did we do it right?' she asked. 'Did you like it?'

'Indeed I did, very much,' smiled the dancing teacher as she put her hand into the box and gently dropped a half-crown.

We went to the dancing school to watch several times after that, but the great moment had passed and the incentive melted away. We were on to something new. We began to make up plays, or dramers, as Lu called them.

EIGHT

We Go West

There was nothing gradual about growing up. As long as you were at school you looked like a child in short trousers and frocks, and you were treated like one, but when you left school at the end of the term after your fourteenth birthday, childhood ended. It was abrupt and final, and your life changed overnight.

The boys were expected to appear straight away in long trousers. If their mothers belonged to a clothing club there was a fair chance of a new pair ready and waiting, but more often their first pair were cut-downs, the slack folded into a belt and the crutch half-way down their thighs. They slicked their hair with water into a quiff above their foreheads and half a comb stuck out of the top pocket of every jacket. They had finished forever with street games, barrers and scooters, but they still hung about the lamp-posts and street corners. We knew them, of course we did, but we all recognised the change that had taken place and the old familiarity had gone with it. When it grew dark and we had to go indoors, they sauntered off towards the Kings Road, smoking openly with fag ends cupped in their fingers.

After a month or so, they had become absorbed into the grown-up world, and came and went like any other adult. As soon as they began to earn, remnants of junk-yard bicycles dotted the street on Sunday mornings. Old frames stood upside down in the gutter outside their houses, and they were absorbed with wheel hubs and punctures, broken chains and battered mudguards. There was a flourish of little hard whiskery brushes as they daubed rusty handlebars and pitted wheel rims.

The girls cut themselves off completely. It was not considered decent for them to hang about the street once they had left school. Old Reen was only recognisable by her familiar short school coat. She flitted by, wearing it over a long heavy skirt cut on the cross which was barely three inches above her ankles. But her hair! It was short at the back and pressed into corrugated waves against one side of her face. The other was hidden beneath a bright green beret, flat against her sulky cheek.

''Allo Reen,' we said as she swept past us.

''Allo,' was all she answered, without stopping, and she pattered up the street and out of our lives. Old Reen, who had danced with us in her bloomers and pinched tar blocks!

'She's got stockings on,' Lu said to Hilda.

'Yeh, lisle. Like my mum's best ones.'

'Reen got a job?' Lu asked.

'Yeh,' said Hilda. 'Up the ABC caff.'

'Posh.'

'Not 'arf, an' when she's old enough she's gonna be a waitress.'

'Yeh?' Lu was impressed.

'Yeh. Her mum told my mum. She said Reen's goin' to get on.'

Lucky old Reen, to have prospects! For most kids any kind of job was a job, and there was little fuss about talents or training or choice. Many of the boys started off as errand boys, riding heavy trade bicycles with a whacking great basket over the front wheel, hoping to progress into the back of a delivery van. With a bit of luck, there might be a chance to get into Philip Mills in Battersea baling up the waste paper. Small and shaky back-street service firms occasionally had an opening for a boy, but few of them ever resulted in learning a trade. The girls went into laundry work, where there was a constant demand for labour for sorting and hand finishing. A few got into shops, and some went into small factories in Battersea. They were worth from eight to ten shillings a week to their families, and scrambled for anything local.

Lu did none of these things. When she was fourteen she just stopped going to school. Her attendance had become so irregular that the School Gawd man must have thrown up his hands in delight when she came of age, which is more than the family did. She was so small and looked such a ragamuffin that no one would believe she was grown up. She stayed just as she was with short straight hair which Dad cut into clumpy ends every fortnight. We waited for her to blossom out.

'What you goin' to be?' Georgie eventually asked her.

'I'm goin' in a shop,' Lu answered, 'an' I'll 'ave a black frock an' wavy 'air.'

'When you goin' to start then?'

'Soon as I can get fixed up,' said Lu. She tried, but her appearance indicated nothing of her energy and ability, and she never got as far as an interview. Each night she told Mum and Dodie what had been happening to her.

'I seen some rotten ol' stuck up cat,' said Lu.

'Who?' asked Dodie.

'Some woman in charge up Clapham Junction.'

'You bin right over there love?' asked Mum.

'Yeh. Lily Browning told me there was a job goin' in 'aberdashery, you know, cotton an' buttons. Well, this ol' girl looked me over an' she said, "not with them 'ands". Honest Mum,' said Lu, 'I give 'em a good scrub, but the dirt's wore in!'

'Never mind,' Dodie began.

'I wouldn't, I wouldn't have minded,' said Lu, 'but she never even asked me my name.'

'Look Lu,' said Mum gently, 'sit down love, and let's face facts.' Lu perched on the edge of the bed and looked expectantly at Mum, certain that she was going to produce a smart outfit and an idea for a job out of thin air. 'Now then,' Mum sat in Dad's chair and smoothed her pinny over her knees. She always did this when she had something difficult to say. 'There's one thing you can do, Lu, and do well. You're a good little cleaner, none better. I've been thinking, if we worked up a few hourly and daily jobs for you and fixed the times just right, we could sort it out so that you were home in time when Rowie and Joey comes in from school. The pay's not bad, you could get up to fourpence an hour.'

Lu leapt to her feet then flung herself on the bed. 'Oh no, Mum! I done with that! Please Mum, I don't wanna be a char!'

'Maybe you'd better start where you can, Lu, an' we'll try and get together something better for you to wear, then you'll have a better chance to get into a shop.'

'No!' yelled Lu. 'Oh Mum, no!'

'Couldn't Lu have a bit more time to look around?' asked Dodie.

'Your father is already asking when Lu is going to make a start, and I can't for the life of me see anything else she can do,' said Mum.

'It's all right 'im askin' about me,' Lu smeared her rare tears on the back of her hand. 'When's 'e gonna bring somethin' in?'

'That's enough Lu,' said Mum sharply.

'Well, I ain't goin' charrin' for 'im,' Lu screamed. 'Not for bloody 'im!'

'Lu,' Mum shouted, 'I said that's enough! You won't be doing it for him, it's for me. For me, love. I've been thinkin' how we should manage after you left school, and it would help me an' stop me worrying if I knew you were here when the kids come home. Rowie is old enough now to bring Joey home, but I'd be easier in my mind if I knew you were here when they get in. Georgie's got his paper round, an' besides he won't know how to look after them if they come home wet.' Lu sat miserably scuffing her boots and twisting her grimy hands.

'Promise me then, Mum,' she said. 'Promise me that as soon as the kids are old enough, I can start in a shop.'

Lu's future was settled. Mum put the word round at the clinic, and within a couple of days two of the ladies there gave her the addresses of friends who needed domestic help. A doctor's surgery was added to her list and in no time Lu was up to her ears in work, with fifteen different jobs each week. She scrubbed four flights of stone stairs and landings every week in a block of service flats in Fulham, and rushed to Earls Court to wash-up and tidy for a business lady. Next she walked to Pont Street to clean and polish, hang up dresses and put away a scatter of pretty shoes, marvelling at the things that other people ate and owned and wore, and her real education began. Dodie made her a sacking apron for scrubbing and Mum cut down a crossover pinny to wear under her coat.

One of the jobs that Lu liked best was at Miss Harberry's which was a first-floor flat in a tall Edwardian house just past the Worlds End. She lit Miss Harberry's gas cooker, jumping backwards every time the flame exploded round the ring and turned on the wheezy gas geyser over the sink, holding her fingers unbelievingly under the instant hot water. She sat in Miss Harberry's chintz-covered armchair, crossing one leg over the other, holding an empty blue porcelain cup above its matching saucer with carefully crooked fingers. We had no saucers at home so Lu practised being refined at Miss Harberry's expense. She wound up the gramophone and danced as she dusted to Miss Harberry's records.

On her way to Miss Harberry's home, Lu had to pass a massive building site where four blocks of flats were nearing completion. It was an uncommon sight, and she often stopped for a moment to loiter on the edge of the crowd of unemployed men and boys who hung around to watch. Listening to the talk she found out that the builders were not putting up blocks of flats, but 'buildings'. There was an enormous difference. Everyone knew that posh people lived in flats, but 'buildings' were something that we could hope for. 'Why not?' said Lu to herself. 'What's to stop us?' She felt her heart hammering at the cheek of the idea. 'I don't care what no one says,' and she took a deep breath as she gazed up at the scaffolding, 'I'm goin' to get us into them buildings.'

She whispered her discovery to Dodie, and Dodie helped her to convince Mum. Mum had to speak to Dad about it, she just had to. There would be no worry about the rent, Lu promised she would take on extra work, evenings, weekends, anything, if only Mum would speak to Dad. Days went by, but Mum couldn't find the right moment to mention it. Things were not good with him, and Mum said there was no point in asking for trouble. Lu became furious and then desperate, convinced that all the flats would be taken and that there would be no room for us. She could hardly bear to walk past the building site, but one morning she saw a man in a proper suit talking officiously to some of the painters. Without thinking what she was doing, she ran through the gates and interrupted him. 'Please mister,' she said, 'my Mum wants to live in these buildings.'

'Nothing to do with me,' he said, 'tell your mother to go to the Town Hall,' and he shouted over his shoulder: 'George, keep these blasted kids out!' Miss Harberry got nothing done that day. Lu fled straight to the Town Hall with no idea who to ask for or what to say. 'We got to go in the buildings,' she repeated to herself all the way, 'or I'll die, I'll die, I'll *die.*' A clerk took Lu into an office, put a white form into an envelope and wrote Dad's name on the outside. It was so simple. There was nothing more Lu could do, from now on it was all up to Mum.

Mum dithered. For a few days the form lay hidden in her corset box under the bed like a packet of dynamite. She knew perfectly well that we could not go on living in one room much longer, for we were growing up. She decided to show the form to Dad on Saturday afternoon, when Dodie would be at work and Lu could keep the rest of us out of the way. Lu took us to Battersea Park, and we got home in time to see Dad having stewed eels for his tea. Nothing was said to us, but Lu kept looking at the envelope propped up against the clock and raising her eyebrows at Mum. Dodie came home from work, but we still had to wait until Dad had gone out to the pub before Lu pounced on the envelope. 'Come on Dodie,' she cried. 'Read it!'

The application form was for a three-bedroomed flat in the buildings and Dad had signed it. Lu yelled, and flung herself into Mum's arms, while Dodie went on to read all the twiddly bits. Dad had described himself as wharfinger and licensed waterman. 'What's a wharfinger?' asked Georgie.

'Well, I dunno really,' said Mum, 'but around the beginning of the war he used to be in charge of the stevedores who loaded the ships. That's when he had a good job, we were all right then. P'raps that's what it is.'

'But he hasn't done that for years!' said Dodie.

'If it's too posh we won't get in the buildings,' Lu shouted. 'What's he wanna show off for?'

'He wasn't always like he is now,' Mum answered.

''E ain't a licensed waterman, is 'e?' asked Georgie.

'He says he is,' answered Mum doubtfully.

'It's no good! He's goin' to muck it all up!' Lu was almost in despair. 'If 'e says 'e's all them things, they'll tell us we can afford to live in our own house. You gotta be 'ard up to get in the buildings.'

'We are, ain't we?' asked Georgie.

'Course we are,' said Dodie.

'I'll tell you somethin' Mum,' said Lu, with the conviction of sheer desperation in her voice. 'If they think we're too well off, we won't stand a chance to get into them buildin's!'

Mum looked thoughtful. 'Dodie,' she said, 'you can write best. Just you write the word 'unemployed' where Dad's described what he is, and then I'll stick down the envelope and he'll never know.'

Lu beamed with relief but Dodie drew in her breath. 'I couldn't.'

'Don't be so bloody daft,' shouted Lu. 'Course you could!'

'Here's his pen,' said Mum. 'Go on Dodie, do what I tell you.'

Dodie dipped the pen and was suddenly afraid of the immaculate copperplate that she had to copy. 'I can't Mum,' she said. 'I can't.'

'Think of it Dodie,' whispered Lu. 'Our own bedroom, just you, me an' Rowie, all on our own.' That did it. Carefully, Dodie made the thick downstrokes and thin upstrokes.

'Lovely, Dodie,' Mum smiled at her. 'You've done it lovely! Now, behind the clock with it, wipe the pen, and Lu, get it out of this house first thing in the morning. I shan't sleep a wink till it's gone!'

For the next few days Lu was ecstatic and buoyantly waited for a reply from the Town Hall, but two weeks went by and we heard nothing. Mum said it was too soon to worry, and that no news was good news. Lu said it was nothing of the kind and we were too late, and she had given the form to the wrong person and no one knew that we wanted to move. By the end of a month we all had the miseries, and Lu hardly spoke to anyone. She made desperate bets with herself by racing vans to street corners, convinced that if she got there first we should go into the buildings, but sometimes the van won. At Miss Harberry's she wiped up the frugal breakfast things and hung the blue porcelain cup on its hook where it swung gently to and fro. As she watched the tiny movement her lips formed the words: 'We are, we ain't, we are, we ain't, we are. We are!' Lifted just for the moment, she rushed round the flat, tidying and polishing, until the full weight of her anxiety overwhelmed her, and she fell into the chintz armchair, buried her head in her arms, and sobbed.

Then someone started the rumour in the street. A whisper that everything was to be knocked down and we were all to be chucked out.

'About bloody time,' said Ginger's dad. We were sitting on the kerb with our feet in the gutter playing fivestones and listening to the crowd outside the butcher's.

'They say,' said Ivy Trotter, 'that we shall be offered flats in the new Guinness buildings.'

'I ain't goin' into no buildin's.' Mrs Bellew lifted her bosom up on to her folded arms. 'I lived in my 'ouse all me married life, Christ 'elp me, an' no one's tellin' me what to do.'

'What about the gas? They're gonna 'ave gas,' said Hilda's mum.

'It ain't free is it? You gotta pay for gas 'aven't yer?' Mrs Bellew glared at her audience. 'I does all right with wood up me copper, an' never paid 'apenny. My Charlie,' she added proudly, 'brings it 'ome.'

'There's rules in the buildin's.' Mr Dandy was determined to stir the old girls up.

'What jer mean, rules?' asked Reen's mum.

'No knees-up after ten o'clock for a start,' he began to count on his fingers. 'No wallpaper, no kids playin' in the yard after dark, no 'ammerin' nails in no walls, no pets nor animals. Cor, I could go on all day.'

'Ain't it fair!' Mrs Bellew appealed to her audience. 'Ain't it marvellous! Look what we come to! No one ain't tellin' me what to do in me own place, an' you can all take that for gospel.'

'The rents,' said Reen's mum, 'is goin' to be somethin' terrible.'

'Yeh, but they got baths ain't they?' put in Mrs Brimmer.

'What the 'ell difference does that make?' Mrs Bellew raised her eyes with contempt. 'Honest,' she said, 'can you credit some people. We 'aven't 'ad a bath these thirty years an' never missed it! 'Ow much do you reckon to fork out every week then, for a bath? Gawd, give me strength! 'Ere, come on Bill, I needs me stout before I falls over.' Mr Dandy escorted her across the road and the door of the *Bricklayers* closed behind them.

The worrying and the speculation continued. The women talked in doorways and in Mrs Daniel's shop and the men argued in the pub. The kids picked up the restless mood, knowing that something was going to happen that would make everything different, but nobody could tell what it was going to be like.

Our letter telling us that we had a flat in the buildings arrived in February. It was addressed to Dad, of course, and straight away he took charge, giving orders and making decisions. He didn't bat an eyelid at the rent, which was sixteen-and-six a week, plus fourpence for the shed, a mere nine shillings and tenpence more than Mum paid Ethel for our room. We were not going to move on a barrow. The Naylor family, for once in its career, had a legitimate reason for changing residences, and we were to do it in style. With supreme disregard for the cost, Dad knocked up old Duffy Fairchild and arranged to borrow his bony horse and coster cart for two bob an hour, 'Or part,' said Duffy, 'thereof.'

'To think of it,' Dad exploded, 'it's taken a brewer, and an Irish one at that, to put a roof over our heads that doesn't bloody well leak!' We accepted this outburst without understanding one word of it, and it never occurred to us that if anyone was responsible for providing us with a roof it was Dad himself. He announced that we were taking no old lumber with us, and he had Mum, Lu and Dodie on their knees dragging the boxes from under the bed, clearing out the cupboards and shelves, and sorting the drawers under the table. His temper flared as the muddle spread all over the room and our last few days were a misery of treading over boxes and looking for things that had already been packed. We were drenched in Lysol, because Mum sprinkled it over everything in case our bugs decided to come with us.

By now Lu and Dodie had lost their enthusiasm. Each of them had secret and dreadful doubts about going to the buildings. Lu was frightened by the colossal amount of the new rent. She thought that she alone had committed us, and that her wild promises to find the extra money would now have to be met. Dodie also knew that we could not afford to move, and thought she was being punished for altering the application form.

'Do you realise, Lu,' said Dodie, 'that we've no furniture to take with us?'

'Course we have.' Lu assumed her old confidence. 'We got Dad's chair, the table, Georgie's bunk, the stools and the chairs for Joey.'

'How far to you think that lot will go in a living-room and three bedrooms? And what are we going to sleep on? Mum's bed belongs to Ethel, and so does ours.'

'The kids will be all right,' said Lu. 'We can fix up their bunks same as we do here, and we can sleep on the floor.'

'Joey is far too big for the two chairs. Honestly Lu, it's time he had a proper bed. And what about Mum! I don't care where we live, but I'm not having Mum sleep on the floor.' Dodie fell silent and looked miserably at Lu. Lu slowly closed her fingers and clenched her teeth. She wanted to scream, to scream and swear out loud. She had tried so hard to make things come good for us, but we needed too much.

'You know there's only one way out, don't you,' said Lu. 'We shall have to get a few things on the never.'

'Oh Lu, you're worse than Dad. Where *is* the money to come from?'

'Us,' said Lu. 'I told Mum I'd take on evening jobs didn't I, and it's time you asked for a rise.'

'Right then.' Dodie was relieved that Lu had produced some sort of solution. 'We'd better tell Mum.'

'Don't you think she's already thought about it?' said Lu.

Mum had thought about it. She listened to Dodie and Lu and made a cupper, just for the three of them. 'Now look here my potherbs,' she said, 'when you get a bit of luck just you go ahead and make it last. If you stop in the middle and start worrying about what might happen, you'll finish up with nothing. Now then, we've got the best chance we've ever had, and we're going to take it. It'll be a struggle to start with and God only knows how we shall manage, but we've been far worse off before. Now drink your tea, and perk up the two of you. It's not like you to get the 'ump Lu, and Dodie, rub up Dad's collar. I can tell you now that your father and me are goin' to Drages tomorrow, and if his collar's grubby we'll start off with a row before we get there.'

I had never seen my Mum and Dad going out together before. As we watched them walk up the street on that Saturday after-noon, I understood for the first time that she belonged to him as well as us. Mum was wearing her straw beehive hat that rose up into a point above her head and the brim dipped down on each side of her face. Dad's collar had passed inspection and he had clipped on his large bow tie. Otherwise, he looked the same in his flat cap, shiny trousers and slightly too large jacket that hung as if there was nobody inside it. As if to compensate for his appearance, Dad gave Drages the full force of his contempt for their furniture. He bullied the salesman, found fault with the workmanship, criticised the quality, deplored the prices and gave one hell of a performance. With sparkling eyes, and knowing that she was being wickedly imprudent, Mum enjoyed herself equally as well as Dad. She trailed behind him, making up her own mind about what they were going to buy. She knew to a penny how much they could spend because the deposit lay in her purse, the exact amount that she had received from uncle when she popped Dad's suit.

The great trek to the west started early on a raw foggy morning. Between thirty and forty families were migrating, and there had been a fierce scramble to hire and share coster barrows and ponies and carts. Every front door stood wide open and a stream of women and kids went in and out, carrying buckets and boxes and bundles and dumping them in shabby heaps on the kerbside. The men cussed as they shuffled backwards with pianos and iron bedsteads. They swore as they stacked and rearranged the overloaded carts, and blinded as the ungainly piles swayed and threatened to topple. Kids were sent climbing and perching among the rolls of lino and brass fenders to catch the ropes and pass them over chair legs and bird cages, mattresses and mangles. At last the men crouched between the shafts and staggered as they took the weight, straining forwards to get the barrows moving. The procession limped along the Kings Road accompanied by a small armada of old prams. Some families had to make three trips, and the last of them ran their empty barrows back after nightfall. Ivy Trotter didn't come with us, she wouldn't leave her cat.

Joey and I were sent to school as usual that day, but Georgie was kept home to help. He said we were late getting away because Old Duffy needed his cart first thing to fetch his fruit and veg from Covent Garden. Dad loaded our entire home on the little cart, including our barrer and two bags of coke. Lu came to the school at dinner-time and we sat on the bench under the shed and ate the cheese sandwiches she brought us, and had a drink of water from under the spout. She told us to wait for her at half-past four, because she was coming to fetch us. As we sat side by side after school, Joey said, 'Why ain't we goin' home?'

'We're never going home any more,' I said. 'We've moved.'

Lu took us down Danvers Street, along the Embankment and

up the Worlds End Passage, past the shops in the Kings Road until we stood looking up at the immaculate buildings in the February dusk. There was a wide pavement with a row of tall brown and yellow patched plane trees, with bobbles hanging from leafless branches. Tall black railings ran along a low cement wall to a pair of wide iron gates. The buildings were made of pinky red brick and the hundreds of windows each had a black decorated iron guard on the sill, where there would be window boxes. We walked close together across the great open space of the yard into the white-tiled entrance of the block. Everything was big and cold, and it felt like a new school.

'We're lucky' said Lu. 'We live right up the top. Go on, up you go!' We climbed the grey stone stairs, stopping on each landing to look over the black iron banisters at the frightening drop in the gloomy light. On the top floor Lu took us to one of four big brown doors. 'Now shut your eyes,' she commanded, 'you gotta have a surprise.' We held on to her through a short passage and then she shouted, 'Now!' For a moment I was dazzled by the brilliant light all over the clean white ceiling and bare yellow walls. This light was streaming from a round glass bowl that hung from the centre of the ceiling.

'That's gas,' said Dodie. 'Isn't it lovely!' Joey went to the window and Lu lifted him up. We were taller than anything. Stretching away as far as ever were dim rooftops and chimneys, poking into the smoky sky, and tiny lights stood out in squares that were other people's windows. We had no curtains, but we had a proper floor, all over the same with no cracks. Mum had bought plain brown lino.

'Take your fingers off!' Dodie grabbed my hand as I touched the shining square of polished wood that was our new table. It had twisted legs that were joined underneath and there were four brown seated chairs with twisted legs to match. We had a sideboard, shining brown, smothered with beading and little handles and drawers. The fireplace was a bright black range, the fire already lit with coke on one side and an oven on the other. Our old fender was on the floor with a new little brown and orange mat. On the fire side of the range stood a brand-new wooden armchair with two stiff brown cushions.

'That's for Dad,' said Lu, warning me off. The old alarm clock lay on its face in the centre of the mantelpiece and our snuff box, the candlestick and the pen and ink were there too.

'Where's Mum?' asked Joey.

'Come on,' said Dodie, 'there's lots more.' She laughed at Lu.

They were so happy. They had forgotten, for the moment, all about the rent, and they didn't care that only twenty-five bob's worth of the new furniture belonged to us. Mum was in the kitchen with Georgie, and the gaslight in there was brighter than sunshine. We crowded excitedly round the tiny black cast-iron gas stove, turned on the tap over the white sink and pulled the chain in the lav. Next to the draining board was a large, flat, wooden board that looked like a table. Georgie lifted it and swung it upwards on a hinge and hooked it to the white tiled wall. We stared incredulously into a bath, clean and white and brand new. Between the end of the bath and the wall was a gas copper with the trademark *Hurry* raised in metal. Mum said it meant that we would have to hurry up and put pennies into the gas meter when we used it.

'Bedrooms,' shouted Lu. She lit the candle and we trailed behind her.

'Won't we have gas in the bedrooms?' I asked.

'Yeh,' said Georgie. 'But Mum says we got to use candles.' The largest was for Mum and Dad, and it was almost filled by a built-in brown cupboard and a huge double bed. It was covered with a cheap gold taffeta bedspread, embroidered in the centre with gaudy orange flowers. In the candlelight it glowed with a rich and sumptuous sheen. The unexpected vision of such luxury made an immediate and lasting impression on me. With a feeling of overwhelming embarrassment I backed out of the room, and for weeks afterwards I could talk only in whispers in Mum's room, because of the bedspread.

The other two bedrooms felt more like us. There were no curtains and nothing on the plain custard walls or bare floors, which were made of a greyish yellow cement. Our voices echoed although the rooms were so small. Georgie's rotten old bunk was made up ready for him and its rapier leg was standing safely in an empty tin. In the opposite corner stood Joey's bed, still made of our two plywood seated chairs and the washing board. It looked so small in the bare room, and when I saw his red woolly slippers with the heels trodden down on the floor underneath one of the chairs, I suddenly felt sorry for Joey, but he didn't seem to mind at all. My armchair bunk was in the next room but there was no bed for Dodie and Lu, so they had spread their bedclothes on the gritty floor. Just as in Mum's room we also had a large built-in cupboard in each of our rooms, and Lu said that Dad was going to put hooks and shelves in them so we left our things in boxes.

Lu showed us how to pull out the table extensions and Dodie threw a sheet over it and began to lay out places. We were going to have our first meal all sitting down together. Dad came up from the shed in the yard and sat with his armchair twisted round to the table. Lu, Dodie, Georgie and Mum had the new chairs, and Joey and I were perched at one end on upturned boxes. We had penny bloaters with their heads on. Dad read his paper while we were eating, as if the occasion was quite usual, but although we did not talk, we grinned and made faces at each other. Joey concentrated on his fish, and shot sideways glances at me, and Mum sat on her own at the top of the table and didn't eat anything. She just watched us and kept on cutting bread.

Dad went out as usual, and Dodie washed Joey and me in the kitchen, sitting us on the lid of the bath. The bath was to be kept for Saturdays, and now we had a proper place she said we were to have toothbrushes, as soon as she could afford it. 'It's funny,' she said to Mum, 'what a lot more things you want when you've got room for them.' Lu tucked me up in my bunk and put a nightlight on my old stool next to me. I lay and watched the light run across the ceiling whenever I heard a car go by in the road far below. I could make out the shape of the cupboard door, and it grew and grew in the dark, and I knew it was going to open. I felt myself turning cold with fear, but I went on looking at it. Where was everybody? Why was I all by myself? I shouted: 'Mum, Mum, Lu!' The door opened and the yellow gas light flooded round Lu's head, but I couldn't see her face properly.

'What's up?' she asked.

'When you comin' to bed?'

'Not yet.'

'When?'

'Not yet. We don't all have to go to bed at the same time now. I'm gonna have a talk to Mum.'

'Why can't I?'

'Because you're not old enough. It's past eight, now go to sleep.'

'I'm cold.'

'Yeh,' said Lu, 'it's freezin' in 'ere. I'll get you Mum's coat.' She left the door open, hurried back and hugged me as she put it over me.

'Lu,' I murmured from underneath Mum's collar, 'will you look in the cupboard?'

'What for?'

'There's someone in there.'

'Oh Rowie, don't be daft! There's no one 'ere but us.'

'I don't like it Lu. I want to be with everyone.'

'Now look 'ere,' said Lu crossly. 'We're livin' proper now, and proper people sleep in bedrooms. We've 'ad a terrible job gettin' in 'ere, an' you've got to like it. Joey's not making all this fuss.' She went out and once more I was alone in the strange empty room. I thought about Joey and banged on the wall. After a few seconds two bangs came back, and I knew that old Joey was next door and I wondered if he was frightened of his cupboard.

For the next few months Dad was busy making furniture. We haunted the grocers, Perksies, Frosties and the Co-op for tea chests, and the greengrocers for apple boxes. He took them to pieces and after school we had to help him by holding the flat iron against the wood while he banged in the nails. We had to know the difference between a bradawl and a gimlet or he chucked the wrong one back at us, and we had to tread carefully to avoid taking the shavings and sawdust out of the kitchen. He sent us to the oil shop with jam jars to buy two penn'orth of brunswick black for staining and a penn'orth of light spirit varnish for the shine. He made a long narrow stool for Joey and me to share when we sat up at the table which tipped if we did not sit down or get up at precisely the same moment. The coke bucket was disguised under a varnished box with a transfer of two birds sitting on a spray of apple blossom on the lid, and he made each of us a locker with a shelf which were put into the bedrooms. Over the mantelpiece he built a plywood backing with the shelves edged in beading on which we displayed Mum's 'pieces', a glass vase, a china shoe and a frosty-looking old-fashioned lady with a china head and torso and a puffy skirt made of blue satin and white lace.

On the wall at the side of the chimney Dad put up the bookshelves which Dodie began to fill with second-hand penny books. Over the years we had Conrad and Wodehouse, Eric Linklater and Geoffrey Farnol, Edgar Wallace, Jane Austen, Thomas Hardy, Mark Twain, Arnold Bennett, Robert Louis Stevenson, John Buchan and a host of others, good, bad and awful, and we read the lot, some of them over and over.

Lu and Dodie were mad to have a bed and curtains. Our regular weekly income from Mum and the two girls amounted to around two pounds and twelve shillings, and Georgie was good for at least five shillings. The rent and repayments to Drages totalled twenty-one and tenpence, without allowing for the gas meter, so Mum had a bit under thirty-five bob a week to keep us all. The great thing was to keep ten shillings intact to start off on Monday morning, then we could get through the week. Now and again Dad got a casual day's work off the pier and he picked up a bit of carpentry and occasionally addressed wrappers and envelopes. When the extra came in, Mum got everything out of pawn, which she said was like having money in the bank. That summer Dad got three months' regular work sitting in a rowing boat on the Serpentine waiting for someone to drown, and that's when we got the second-hand beds. Dodie bought thin cotton dress material printed with tiny pink flowers at fourpence three-farthings a yard, and made curtains for our room.

Soon after we moved into the buildings I was on the list to see the school doctor. An empty classroom was used, and sitting at the table with the doctor was a posh lady in a hat and fur coat. She watched the doctor briefly look down my throat with a thin stick of wood, and then she spoke to me. 'I understand that your family has moved into a new flat.' I nodded. 'And how many rooms have you now?' I thought, and counted on my fingers. There's the passage, and the kitchen, the lav, and the bit in the kitchen behind the larder where you go into the lav that's got its own little window, and the living-room, and the bit between the bedroom doors and the bookshelves, and three bedrooms and the shed in the yard.

'Ten,' I said. She raised her eyebrows and looked sharply at a piece of paper. I was a bit worried about it for the rest of the day. Perhaps I should have explained how I got it to ten, but she had the sort of face that you couldn't talk to. I kept wondering if I could try and find her and go into a little more detail, but by then I was back in my classroom. I decided not to tell anyone what I'd said, in case we got chucked out of the buildings for having too many rooms.

Being chucked out was a threat that hung over us. It happened if you didn't pay the rent on the dot, and if you didn't keep the stairs and the landing window clean. We were also afraid of com-plaints from our neighbours, because another rule stated that no noise was permitted after ten o'clock and our rows continued. I had thought everything would be different now we were in the buildings, but I found Dad didn't change. In fact things were worse because we were now in separate rooms, and when he started on Mum at night we got out of bed and stood listening at the doors, wondering whether to go out and help her. Lu and Dodie and sometimes Georgie left their rooms, and the noise was dreadful. When we lived over Ethel we didn't worry too much because she knew all about us, but it was different in the buildings. A lady whom we didn't really know lived underneath us and she spoke nicely and her husband was a chauffeur. When I met her on the stairs after one of our rows I always wanted to apologise or say something, but I never knew how to begin, so I was always specially polite to her. I asked Lu if she would complain to the superintendent about us, and if so what would happen. Lu said it was better to leave it to Mum to explain to the lady underneath, and if she was a decent sort she would not get us into trouble. She never did, and the people each side of us were sympathetic too, because Mum had a way of making people like her, without trying. But it worried me.

I was glad we had moved into the buildings and within a couple of weeks I wouldn't have lived anywhere else. The reason was the yard. The bare concrete squares bordered by our black railings suddenly became a vivid and exciting world, exclusive to children. It developed its own codes and had but one rule, never *ever* to complain to our parents about anything that happened there. There were times when a girl went whining up the stairs, turning on the tears, and once or twice a serious fight stirred up a row among the adults, but for the most part we kept our secrets to ourselves and suffered miseries rather than use the threat that we would 'tell our mums'. The yard overflowed with children. There were close friends and loose groups, gangs with their hangers-on, loners and outcasts, but everyone came under the protection of 'the buildings' if they were attacked or threatened by kids living in the streets outside.

As soon as I had finished my jobs indoors, I used to jump down the first flight of stairs and look down on to the yard from the high landing window, to see what was going on and who was out to play. The formula for joining a game was to approach anyone who was already playing and say, 'Gisser game.'

The orthodox reply would be: 'T'ain't my game.'

'Who's game is it?' you had to ask.

'Alfie's.' This meant that Alfie had suggested, or as we said 'got up' the game, and had dipped up for sides with one of the other kids. So you had to approach Alfie, and await Alfie's convenience.

'Gisser game Alfie.' If he wanted you on his side, he said so, otherwise you were lumped together with all the other kids he hadn't chosen. Until you became known to everyone, you were addressed as, ''ere, you girl!' or, ''ere, you boy!'

By the simple means of changing our vocabulary, the spaces

between the brick blocks of flats became battlefields for English against the Germans, back alleys crammed with cops and robbers, or hideouts for cowboys and Indians. Because I was a girl and on the small side, I was always one of the losers, in turn a German, a robber and an Indian. I was frequently shot, hand-cuffed with string, and dragged around on the end of a rope.

The seasons merged and changed with the wealth of remem-bered and passed-on games like warney-echo, whips and tops, tin-can-warney and peashooters. There was a time for conkers, fivestones and chip'ems. This was played with a piece of cord, a long-pegged top and a crown cap from a beer bottle. The best tops were made from creamy-coloured boxwood, hard as stone and called 'boxers'. We threw the top spinning into the air and caught it on the palm of our hand, and while it was still spinning chipped it down on to the metal cap, whizzing it along the ground. We played in partners, each chipping the bottle top in opposite directions.

We lost and won fag-cards from each other at 'lick'ems', propping half a dozen cards against the wall and knocking them down by flicking another card at them. The game got its name because we ran the edge of each card down our tongues, certain that our spit would increase its speed and improve our aim. The same action was used for 'kiss'ems', a lick, then a jerk with our fingers to send the card spinning to the wall, until one dropped on top of another to decide the winner. We got most of our fag-cards from the football crowds that passed the buildings on the way to the game at Stamford Bridge on Saturday afternoons. We hung about outside our gate crying, 'Giss a fag-card mister.' Some men stopped and opened their fag packets and handed us a brand-new card. Others had to be pestered, and we ran along-side them begging, 'Go on mister, giss one, ay mister?' Some-times they took a swipe at us, and we ducked and dodged among the crowd, but persistence often paid off and we all got some.

Our clay marbles were fragile and crumbled to a powdery dust if trodden on. The posh glass ones were called 'alleys', but there were very few about. As well as the usual marble games, we rolled them at numbered holes cut in a cardboard box. One enterprising boy made himself such a box and began to win all our marbles. When it was rumbled that the winning holes in his box were too small to allow our marbles to pass through, we ganged up on him and chased him and broke his box up. He kept our marbles, but no one would play with him and he had to mooch about on his own. 'Cheats never prosper' we shouted at him whenever he appeared, and it was months before he was reinstated.

A set of fivestones cost a halfpenny at the sweet shop. We played a strict game with different actions for pecksie, bushels, clawsie, Marble Arch and Nelson's Column. Some of us could go through a whole game without dropping a stone, so we made it a fault if we spoke or laughed.

For warney-echo we only needed a wall. We dipped up sides and one half made a chain of backs that stood out from the wall, where one boy braced himself. The other side took it in turns to drag themselves bodily across the kids on the chain who bobbed and bucked, trying to shake them off. The object was to reach the boy against the wall, bang him on the head and shout, 'Warney-echo one, two, three, all over, all over!' The chain often collapsed under the weight and frantic scrambling of the kids on their backs. There were plenty of bruises and torn clothes, yells and threats, because you could get your own back if you had a grudge by digging your fingers into a kid you disliked, and giving him a good booting as you dragged yourself over his back.

No team games involving a ball were allowed to be played in the yard and the porter made sure that we obeyed. If we wanted a game of football or cricket we had to clear out and play in the street, which we did, chalking the wicket on a lamp-post. We could play 'tuchicunder', an abbreviation for 'tuck the stick under', which was almost like cricket, but played with bits of wood and chalk circles for the wickets.

We copied our putting green from the real one in Battersea Park. We chalked numbers for the holes by the drains at the bottom of every down pipe, and drove off in pairs from the iron sewer covers, using old tennis balls and bits of wood. The concrete squares outlined our hand tennis courts. Nobody had a bat, but we biffed the ball with the flat of our hands and did some very fancy overarm services. The squares were also the edges of our hopscotches. We had no time for the silly little things that we saw on the pavements outside. Ours were huge, and we used bits of broken glazed tile which we called a 'licker', to slide into the numbered squares. We spat on it for luck, then whizzed it over the concrete. We also made circular hopscotches, drawing them from wall to wall across the yard. The hops were marked out over three feet across, so to hop to the centre and back again on one foot was a tremendous achievement.

For certain games there was an accepted separation of the sexes. The girls played intricate ball games against the wall, onesy, sixy and sevensy, patting and bouncing, under your leg, round your back and twisters. We used two balls, juggling with one hand and repeating the learned routines with stiffsy, dumbsy, one-leg, jiggety-jig and clapsy. The even brick walls were just right for these games and the balls bounced true on the concrete ground. One old girl used to tell us off, sticking her head out of her window to shout at us because the rhythmic thump of the balls against her living-room wall knocked her budgie off his perch.

Sometimes we formed into two huge groups and whooped into the rough and intense game of 'releaso', with no holds barred between the sexes, attacking in fierce mobs and flinging the captives into bedlam. Bedlam was the huge communal dustbin that served forty families. We didn't put anyone in the dustbin, but used the square in front of it which was pretty stinking during the summer and crawled with maggots from pea-shucks. The dustbin commanded a view straight down the middle of the yard and was perfect for tin-can-warney, as it had a sewer cover let into the concrete just in front of it, which was our base for 'home'. One boy or girl was chosen for 'warney', and the rest of us were against him. The game began by throwing an old tin can as far from 'home' as possible. While 'warney' ran to fetch the can, the rest of us bunked in all directions and hid, up the stairs, over the railings, behind jutting walls or sprawled beneath the suffering privet. 'Warney' had to put the tin on the sewer cover and try to find us. It was easy to spot someone's head peeping from a landing window, and 'warney' rushed to the tin, banged it on the sewer cover and shouted, 'I spy Jimmy, one, two, three. All over, All over! Come on out Jim, I seen yer, 'angin' out the winder!' Jimmy was caught, and had to stand by the dustbin. So it went on until 'warney' had bagged several kids. The fun came when a bunch of us in hiding decided to make a rush at 'warney', smothering him under the weight of numbers while he frantically banged the tin, crying out the names of those who had charged him. If only one of us could reach the tin before our name was called, we grabbed the tin, flung it up the yard again and everybody was free to hide once more. The game made a shocking row and we banged the tins completely flat.

Squabbles between us sometimes turned into scraps, and now and again a serious fight was arranged. A circle of onlookers would stand round watching intently until someone gave a shove to one of the opponents in the centre of the ring, to get things started. We all enjoyed a good fight and you knew where you stood in the order of things according to whom you had beaten.

The girls chopped and changed their close friends, quarrelling, not speaking, then making up with little fingers entwined. Here and there on the brickwork we chalked that someone loved someone else, using their initials. The girls took it very seriously, hotly denying the libel. There was always something going on in the yard, either a huge game that swept you up, one more making no difference, or knots and groups of kids dotted all over the place, talking and swapping, arguing and cadging, boasting and lying.

When it was wet and cold we crowded into one of the block entrances and sprawled on the muddy stone floor to listen to the 'Colonel', who was an enormously fat boy with a gentle, humorous face, and a strangely adult air. He also held our respect because he was the only boy in the yard who had money in his pocket, every day, sixpences and shillings. He went to the pictures two or three times a week and re-lived all the films he saw by telling their stories to us. When he lowered himself to the floor on his beautiful outstretched hands, we knew we were in for a treat, and crowded round him waiting for him to begin. When he did Laurel and Hardy we yelled with laughter, punching and shoving each other, and shouted at him to do it again. To show that he was ready to continue he knocked the kid nearest to him flat with a casual swipe of his vast forearm. The 'Colonel' rarely joined in our games but often watched, and acted as a referee giving impartial judgements, which we always accepted. The yard was incomplete without him, and I was always disappointed when he wasn't there.

Soon after dark in the winter and at eight o'clock in the summer the porter cleared the yard of kids, blowing a whistle and shouting, 'Upstairs – or out of it!' Some of the older kids went 'out of it', that meant messing about outside the gate, and that is where the flirting and getting-off started. As Joey and I had to have our supper, get washed and be in bed before Dad came in, we had to go straight upstairs, so it took us much longer to discover the secrets that many of the others shared.

After chucking out time, we made appointments with each other to meet on the stairs to swap comics. This was a serious and intimate business as we squatted close together in the dim-lit vastness of the silent flights of stairs, and it often led to whispered confidences. One night I arranged to meet Winders, whose red-rimmed eyes watered behind thick lenses. 'I gotta 'urry up,' said Winders, ''cos my gran's comin'.'

'Does she give you anythin'?' I asked. I was curious to know of the advantages of having relations, and was frankly jealous of kids with uncles and grans, who appeared to shell out pennies in a very liberal way.

'Nah,' Winders turned down his mouth. 'She only comes for what my mum gives 'er. My dad 'ates my gran.'

'Yeh?' I asked, interested. 'What for?'

''Cos 'er false teeth clicks when she 'as 'er tea.'

'My mum's got false teeth,' I said, 'an' 'ers don't click.'

'Well my gran's does,' explained Winders, 'an' my dad sez it puts 'im off 'is grub.'

'Does your dad shout?' I asked. I knew that some kids liked their dads, and even sat on their laps, and I searched among all my mates to see if there was another dad like ours.

'Yeh,' said Winders. 'But only after my gran's gone 'ome, then my mum don't arf cop it.' That cheered me up no end.

Winders had a pile of twopenny books and I prayed he would find something he wanted among my frowzy collection of penny comics. He shoved them aside, one by one, 'Chips', 'Comic Cuts', 'Funny Wonder' and 'Butterfly'. I waited patiently until he thought he'd found two that he hadn't read and then it was my turn. The rate was two comics for one book, and before old Winders could change his mind I rummaged through the 'Hotspurs', 'Rovers' and 'Wizards' until I found what I was looking for, 'The Triumph'. Leaving Winders to gather up his belongings I snatched up my comics and ran upstairs. I could just see myself, in bed, candle alight and all by myself to be carried away by 'Dane, the Dog Detective'.

NINE

No Miracles for Me

I was now fully independent of Lu. I was in the junior school and responsible for taking Joey to and from school, and if Dad was not at home when we came in I made our cup of tea. The only way to stop Joey dawdling was to 'bus-up'. All the little kids did it. We crossed our arms behind our backs and held each other's hands, pretending we were bus horses. We trotted most of the way and had to hold our breath when we passed the undertakers, because Georgie told us that if you breathed in the undertaker's smell, you'd catch your death. The undertaker made coffins in the yard behind his premises and the acrid smell that wafted up the alley from the yard was from the elm sawdust, but to us that alley was the jaws of hell. Georgie also told us that you could be pinched, poisoned and planted in the space of a hundred yards in the Kings Road, referring to the police station, the pease puddin' and faggot shop and the undertaker.

When Joey and I arrived at the school gates we joined the crowd of eager cadgers outside Ma Phoene's, hoping to catch one of our mates coming down the steps from her tiny sweet shop. Ma Phoene was like a scraggy little bird. She was wafer thin and encased in a dark, tight-fitting old-fashioned dress with a high-boned collar. Her thin white hair was piled up above her brown wrinkled face and she darted suspicious glances over her steel-rimmed glasses. She defied shoplifting by barricading her counter behind chicken wire, leaving a mousehole at the bottom just big enough to squeeze a hap'orth of sweets through, and she armed herself with a sharp little toffee hammer. If you poked your fingers through the hole in honest antici-pation of your purchase, the hammer whacked down on them like a bird of prey, and Ma Phoene rarely missed. Disputes about the value of a coin were always settled in advance. If anyone had a whole penny, he never pushed it through the mousehole until he had said, 'a ha'porth of sweets, – and a ha'penny change!' I liked her cough candy best, and I always hoped someone would buy some. It was bright orange and tasted of paregoric and pear drops.

It appeared that the sole purpose of the Junior School was to prepare us for the Junior County examination when we were eleven, and the school ran like clockwork. On the first day of term the headmaster came into our classroom and wrote the alphabet in large and small letters on the grey slate that was fixed to the wall. We absorbed his effortless rhythm and heard the smooth sound of the chalk as he made the perfect copperplate shapes. He finished with a flourish, glared at us over his glasses, pointed to his handiwork and left. There was no need for words. For the remainder of the year his example was before us, and we looked at it every day.

Equal emphasis was given to reading, arithmetic, spelling and writing. Ink monitors were chosen, and the two envied and heavily-stained boys mixed ink powder into jugs in the cloakroom sink and filled a shallow tray of white china inkwells with the pale, watery results. They backed round the class, dishing them out, while two girls distributed half sheets of lined paper and varnished wooden penholders with long thin nibs fitted into strong metal collars, which were well made and intended to last. We had to sit upright, point our pens towards our right shoulders and copy from a single sentence stuck on a narrow cardboard strip. The sentences contained good moral advice, which I suppose it was hoped we would absorb while we practised our joins and loops. My first teacher had grey shingled hair and a face like a sweet Worcester apple. She kept her watch on the end of a long chain which hung round her neck and disappeared down her bosom into a pocket at the bottom of her petticoat. When it was nearly time for the bell, she raised her long skirt, which never failed to rivet our interest, and fished out her watch. Her petticoat was always mauve.

My next class was with Daddy Macko from Mespot. He had been an officer in the army during the war, and had fought in a place called Mesopotamia, and I think he wished that he was still there. He often talked about his soldiers and his war and his command in Mespot. in a way that made us feel that we were not good enough for him. He was daft about music, and although we spent the whole morning on sums and tables, composition and spelling, he occasionally took us into the hall in the afternoon and made us stand at ease, all spaced out. He put a yellowing roll of tonic solfa music over the blackboard and played the notes and shouted their names. Painstakingly we began to learn how music went up and down. We had to close our eyes and put our fingers in the air, and as the notes went higher we raised our hands and lowered them as the notes fell, tracing the shape in the air. In no time we began to sight read fairly well.

When we sang songs he taught us the words and music line by

line. When we knew the song he left the piano and conducted us unaccompanied, swaying in front of us, fanatically raising his arms and making us hold on to notes by lifting his head and disappearing his eyebrows. He enjoyed himself so much we did our best to please him. We sang the *Faerie Song* from *The Immortal Hour, Ye Banks and Braes*, and a jolly little tune about 'opening wide our lattices, letting in the laughing breeze'. It says something for his teaching that we threw back our heads and gave it real feeling, considering half the kids thought the word was 'lettuce' and the others didn't care what it was. Old Macko was hot on poetry too, and he wrote verse after verse on the blackboard, and we learned them by heart. He must have had a particularly depressed view of life because the poems were tragic and sad. There was drowned *Mary on the Sands of Dee*, and the *Fishers who sailed away to the west, and the harbour bar be moaning*. I had never seen a harbour and I couldn't make it out. I visualised a sort of bridge across the Thames where all the people lined up and moaned. That was the pattern between us and our teachers, you never asked questions, you just did what they said and hoped that enlightenment would come.

Miss Trimble grabbed our hand and beat it down hard on the desk over a blot or a mistake, and it hurt. Daddy Macko had a tin ruler. He hit the boys on the hand with it and whacked it against the calves of the girls' legs. We didn't resent it because we liked him.

One day he caught me talking and I had to spend the remainder of the lesson standing on the bench of my desk. There was I, towering above the class, when the headmaster came into the room. The whole class shot to its feet and I felt the chill of his glance. He handed a small pot, in which a single white hyacinth was growing, to Daddy Macko, swept the class with a fierce look, and disappeared out of the door held open in readiness for him by a smarmy short-sighted kid in the front row. 'Ah! Now! Attention!' We were all ears to the welcome interruption, as Macko addressed us. 'It would appear that between us we have produced this intelligent flower, that even now awaits entry for the Chelsea Schools Flower Show at the Town Hall, this very day. Who more suitable to bear it than our own fair Rose?' Fair Rose indeed, with my stringy hair hooked behind my ears, steel-rimmed dark glasses with the nose piece bound in white darning wool and my socks asleep in my boots. But that was what I liked about Old Macko. A lady teacher would have added that as I was in disgrace I could not go, but Macko bore no grudges. In a gentlemanly way he assisted me down from the bench, and I would cheerfully have died for him at that moment, although the class sniggered. He placed the little pot into my grubby hands and told me to 'be off, and luck attend me.' In his ordinary voice he added that I need not come back to school until after dinner.

In common with all the other kids I held the Town Hall in no less awe than Buckingham Palace. I cautiously entered the main doors, and as I walked slowly into the main hall carrying our pot, I was hit in the face by a great gust of perfume. There were rows of trestle tables covered with pots of growing flowers, daffodils and narcissus, jonquils and hyacinths. They made a fragile pattern of trembling yellows and greens wherever I looked. I had seen things that excited me and heard things that moved me, but I had never before cried because of a smell. I gave our pot to a fat lady. She stuck a little bit of card into the dirt and it was soon lost among the sumptuous entries from other schools.

Regularly, the Junior School had visits from the nurse, Nitty Nora, and we queued up to see her in an empty classroom. She parted and lifted our hair with a metal comb which she dipped into a white enamel bowl of disinfectant after perusing each child. Then she turned down the front of our clothes at our necks and behind our collars. Several kids got a card from her and had to go off to the cleansing station. One girl in my class had ringworm in her head and they shaved off all her hair. She came to school wearing a tight round cotton cap. Nobody took any notice, it was just like seeing a bandage on her knee.

I was sorry to leave Daddy Macko and envied the new kids who moved up into his class. I went into the scholarship class with Fatty Topham, whose German haircut, rolls of neck over his collar and steel glasses filled me with dread. He held us in the palm of his hand and to disobey was unthinkable. He bullied the boys, and his voice alone was sufficient to stun the girls. When he taught us new sums, I stared at him so hard, to convince him of my full attention, that I never took in a word he said. In the afternoons, the girls from my class swapped with the boys from the lady teacher next door. We learned to knit with stringy brown thread on slippery steel needles with no knobs. We never made anything, but learned how to do plain and purl, moss stitch and ribbing. I rarely got further than casting on, and spent most of my time holding a handful of loose stitches, grovelling on the floorboards for my dropped needle, and trying to thread it back into the muddle. At the end of the lesson the crinkly thread was rewound into iron tight little balls. We also learned how to sew on small pieces of thin flimsy paper, tacking, running and hemming. Eventually we progressed to real material and I took a whole term to hem two sides of a tea towel. Those who were better at sewing than I made embroidered chair backs with crinoline ladies in chain stitch. For years I had a deep sense of failure at never having achieved a crinoline lady, until I was taught at my next school that they were in very poor taste. I don't know what the boys were doing while we were so busily employed, but I sometimes saw them putting chipped plaster casts of cones and cubes into the corridor cupboard, and there were drawings on the blackboard in our class, which looked even more difficult than chain stitch.

Our ignorance of history and geography continued, but there was a memorable occasion when nature study was introduced by a student who showed us how to grow a single broad bean on a piece of blotting paper. Twice a week we read the Bible. The monitor placed one between the two of us in each desk. Only two chapters appealed to Fatty, Luke and Isaiah. We read a verse each round the class, and then learned it by heart. There were no explanations or discussions, but I liked the feel of the thin paper. I believed in God, largely because there had to be someone to ask to make things happen when it was no good asking Mum.

I had never been to church, but I had two friends, Maureen and Doris who were sisters, and they were sent every week because they were Roman Catholics. One Sunday I went with them. The church felt just like being up the museums and it smelt as if something was scorching. I followed them into a corner where there was a stone sink and I quite enjoyed making a cross on myself. Over the heads of all the kneeling people the stage was burning bright with hundreds of candles and it filled me with expectation. Like Maur and Dol, I did ever such a big kneel before I went with them into our bench, but from then on I was thoroughly disappointed and bewildered. They kept standing up and sitting down without telling me when, and then a little bell began to tinkle and everyone started walking about. I couldn't understand any of the words, and worst of all, I couldn't see what was happening on the stage. I looked at the pictures and statues around the walls, but they reminded me of the angels on the graves in the cemetery and I didn't like them much. When we came out I expected to feel different, and I didn't. I hadn't seen God and I didn't see how He could know I'd been there.

'Maur, I don't think I'll be a Catholic,' I said.

'You can't be one,' Maureen answered. 'You have to be born like it.'

'Well, I'm glad I wasn't,' I said.

Doris was shocked, and took a step backwards with her mouth hanging open. 'You mean you ain't one?' she asked in an unbelieving voice. 'You mean you bin in our church an' you've touched our 'oly water, an' you ain't a Catholic?'

'No,' I shouted back at her, a bit frightened, 'I ain't.'

'Then you'll get struck down dead,' pronounced Doris unshakably. 'God'll strike you down dead, an' serves you right.' I stuck my tongue out at them both, as far as it would go, and fled. I ran all the way home.

Mum was dishing up Sunday dinner and Lu and Dodie had just finished the weekly sweep and dust round the bedrooms. Everything was ordinary and normal and reassuring, steam on the windows and the smell of greens. I ate my dinner and waited for the blow. In the afternoon Dad went for his lay down and Mum moved into his armchair with the darning, her feet to the fire. Dodie began to read to us and Lu and Joey were drawing pictures. 'You all right love?' Mum asked me a couple of times. I sat at the table doing nothing, until I could hold my secret no longer and to their astonishment I poured out my crime and the threatened punishment.

'Oh Rowie, come here love,' said Mum, putting down a sock. I fell on to the mat and snuffled into her knees. 'You silly,' she said. 'You shouldn't take any notice of what that Doris says! She ought to have her bottom smacked! God won't do any such thing, love, 'E don't go around strikin' people down. Now blow your nose, that's right. I shouldn't wonder,' she went on, 'if some of them Catholics don't get on God's nerves, never giving 'Im five minutes peace. Now then,' and she looked at Lu and Dodie, 'who's goin' to pop the kettle on?'

On Saturday mornings, the children who lived in the buildings had plenty to do. There were errands to run, and the stairs and landings to be washed in turn with other families on the same floor. Many of us went to the Gas Works to buy coke, while others struggled with the bag-wash. Customers at the bag-wash shop were supplied with roughly woven sacks the colour of cooked porridge, which deposited a mat of immovable fluff on everything they touched. They were identified by unevenly daubed painted letters and were filled with about twenty pounds weight of washing. The washing was never removed from the sack, it was simply dunked in suitably prepared water by the laundry operators and returned damp to the shop. My mum would not use the bag-wash. She thought there was something sinister in not scrubbing every single item of our washing, and she didn't fancy her stuff bouncing up and down in the same water as some people's she could mention, and God only knew what went into some of them sacks.

It was Georgie who initiated Joey and me into the coke run. We earned a little by bringing back a sack for some of our neighbours, for which we charged a penny. One of the worst runs to the coke factory was on the day I forgot the string. Everything went wrong. It was a raw, grey Saturday when we dumped Joey on top of the empty sacks in our barrer and ran it along in the road, keeping close to the kerb. Georgie heaved on the rope in front while I pushed at the back. The coppers chucked us out of the road when they caught us, but we chanced it because it was a hard job to get the barrow up and down the kerbstones, especially when it was loaded with coke. The gas works were in Fulham, and I felt nervous once we had crossed Stanley Bridge. I kept an eye open for other kids from the buildings to back us up in case we came across a gang of Fulhamites.

The colourless streets surrounding the gas works had a frightening air of waiting for doom. Georgie said that if anyone struck a match inside the gas works the whole place would blow up, and I believed him, so I braced myself for the great explosion and remained in a state of suppressed panic all the time I was there. The tall dirty buildings towered over us and huge pipes snorting steam crouched against the walls. We rattled our barrer through the gates and Georgie queued up at the pay window to buy three pale-mauve tickets from a grey-faced man in a cloth cap. The price was fourpence for twenty-eight pounds of coke.

Anxious to get away as quickly as I could, I pushed hard, and forced Georgie to run deep into the gas works to the tall, pointed coke hills. Perched at the top of one of them were a couple of men with a weighing machine. A little group of kids and men stood around them waiting to be served, and others were slithering downwards, dragging and heaving their filled sacks. Leaving Joey on the roadway with our barrer, Georgie and I trudged up the coke hill and waited our turn. I could see Joey's blonde fringe peeping over the top of our barrer, and all around him prams, carts and barrers were being loaded. Some were jolting on buckled wheels with kids staggering sideways holding the sacks upright. One had sagged over a broken axle and was surrounded by a fiercely arguing mob, and others, loaded up, were heading madly for the gates like triumphant chariots, the kids shouting as they ran.

Georgie handed our first sack, which wasn't a real sack at all but an old and filthy army kitbag, to one of the men. He held the bag open and tipped the coke into it, filling it to the brim. With one heave he swung it out of the way and while his mate was shovelling more coke on the weighing machine he said to us, 'Give us yer string, an' I'll tie yer bag up for yer.' I waited for Georgie to give him our string but Georgie was staring expectantly at me.

'I ain't got none,' I said.

'Come on, come on,' the man bawled at us, 'I ain't got all day.' By this time the second sack was filled, and the man swung it next to the kitbag.

'I told you to bring the string,' Georgie shouted at me.

'No you never!' I yelled back.

'Out the bloody way,' the man ordered as he dumped our third sack, 'you're 'oldin' everybody up. Who's next?' Half a dozen kids clutching grimy sacks held up their mauve tickets and shouted to be served.

'It's no good you shoutin' at me Georgie,' I said. 'I ain't got any. What we goin' to do?'

'What the 'ell can we do?' Georgie glared at me and at out three gaping sacks. Then I had a flash of inspiration.

'S'all right, we can take out our laces.'

'What? No bloody fear, not me! It's your fault, take your'n out.'

I gave Georgie my laces and he tied up two of the sacks and began to drag them behind him down the coke hill, leaving me with the open kitbag. I gathered it up at the neck and took a step downwards and stumbled. Both my feet sank into the coke and my boots gaped open. I tried to get down sideways, burying my boots into the coke and trying to drag the kitbag with me without spilling any. Every yard I stopped to hook little sharp bits out of my boots. Once the kitbag took over and I stumbled after it, finishing up on my bum. When I reached the bottom in a shower of loose coke I was filthy and angry, and ready to bash Georgie, but Joey saved the situation. He was pink and breathless with laughing. 'You ought to see yourself Rowie,' he said, 'you n'arf look funny.' Georgie started grinning at me and I looked down at my collapsed boots, and we all got the giggles.

My boots slopped as I ran so I tried to curl my toes under to keep them on, and we were soon jogging out on the main road going home.

'Watch out for a copper, Joey,' Georgie warned, as we were

shoving up Stanley Bridge with our heads down. Almost as he spoke a strolling policeman was coming up the other side of the bridge. He stepped off the pavement and took Georgie's arm.

'Now then sonnie,' he said 'You know you shouldn't be in the road with this thing.'

I wouldn't have had the nerve to talk to a copper, but Georgie had. 'We can't get it up an' down the kerbs mister,' he said, 'not with all this coke.'

'I'm sick of telling you kids not to put so much in your barrows,' said the copper. 'Now I'm warning you lad, get it off the road, now!' He towered over us for a moment and as I looked up at the law his helmet blotted out the sky like the side of a bus. Having dealt with us the policeman paced majestically on his way.

'Aow! Get the bloody coke out,' grumbled Georgie. Joey climbed off the sacks and together we lifted out the two which were tied with my laces and dragged them on to the pavement. Then I trod on the sides of my boots, stumbled, and let the kitbag tilt and coke shot all over the road. 'Gawd! Now look what you've done,' Georgie shouted at me. 'That blasted copper! We'd be nearly 'ome by now.' We squatted in the road shovelling coke into the kitbag with our hands as the traffic swerved round us.

'Stop playing, Joey,' I said angrily, 'and help.' Joey always forgot what he was supposed to be doing and was carefully poking little bits of coke down a drainhole in the gutter. I was really frightened when the policeman came back. I thought we were going to be nicked.

'You kids mucking me about?' he said, in a very nasty voice.

'No, we ain't!' Georgie was just about to lose his temper, and we must have looked a pathetic trio.

'Mind out the way,' ordered the copper, and with one heave he dumped our barrer on the pavement, put our three sacks in it and sat a very bewildered Joey on top. 'Now,' said the copper, 'get!' Leaving a lot of our coke in the road, we fled. When we got home we ran the barrer straight to our shed, tipped what was left in the kitbag into an empty sack and flogged it to the lady who lived next door to us for the full price.

On Saturday afternoons most of us had earned a penny or more to spend. If there was a chance of getting in, some of the kids went to the pictures and practically everyone else went to the sweet shop. We were all desperate gamblers and demanded 'ha'penny-half-ounce' from the shopkeeper, known as Cods'ead on account of the set of his features. He had an expressionless face, as well he might, for he gave nothing, absolutely nothing away.

First he took our halfpenny then slapped a grubby shoe box, well filled with dog-eared envelopes, on the counter. Inside the flap of each envelope old Cods'ead had written a number. The majority of them read 'half ounce'. A very few were marked 'one ounce', a precious one or two bore the winning remark 'two ounces', and there was just one legendary envelope with the dazzling amount of 'four ounces' written inside. Most of the cheap sweets sold by old Cods'ead were priced at halfpenny for one ounce, so we might just as well have got the full weight for our money by simply buying a ha'porth of sweets, but the lure of the two and four ounce envelopes was too much for the best of us. You never knew, some day you might hand over a halfpenny and pick out the two ounce envelope, the equivalent of a whole penn'orth of sweets! We never even thought about the four ounces. It was so rare that most of us disbelieved in its very existence, and anyway it was considered bad luck to expect to win.

I nearly always took Joey with me to the sweet shop on Saturdays and I usually let him have first go. 'A'penny arf ounce,' said Joey. Quick as a flash the shoe box appeared in front of him, old Cods'ead standing behind the sticky counter with as little sympathy as the earache. Joey closed his eyes and let his fingers hover over the line of envelopes as he concentrated on his own magic words, 'ta tiddely a ta, jam puff!' When he lifted the flap of the envelope he had chosen to see what was written there, he always did it very slowly and deliberately, and each time I saw the disappointment on his face I could have cheerfully murdered old Cods'ead. Why couldn't he let our Joey win, just once?

'Well, what you got son?' old Cods'ead always asked, with pretended surprise in his voice.

''Arf ounce, like I always get,' whispered Joey each time as Cods'ead diddled him just as often out of a farthing.

Occasionally someone opened an envelope marked 'one ounce', and old Cods'ead behaved as if they had won a fortune instead of merely getting their moneysworth. There was even one jubilant day when the 'four ounces' did come up. Kids ran shouting along the Kings Road and the buzz went round the buildings. Everyone stopped what they were doing and belted to the sweet shop to stare in the door and surround the lucky winner. He chose a bar of chocolate and had to dart home and stop indoors until he'd eaten it.

There was another sweet shop up the Kings Road where they

had a twopenny lending library. I went there one Saturday with Clara, to get a quarter of boiled sweets with jam in the middle for her gran. While Clara was being served, I looked at the books and was surprised to see one that looked familiar. Embossed on the green spine was a silver girl in a filmy dress, poised like a fairy. We had one just like it at home and to show off my knowledge to Clara I took it down and opened it. Stuck inside the front cover was a school prize label: *Dora Naylor, for progress and conduct*. It was our book. I had such a shock I nearly dropped it and found myself blindly pushing it back into its place. I recognised more of our books, among them one of my own, the book I liked best, Ernest Thompson Seton's *Two Little Savages*. Mum had brought it home for me, and it was all about how to be a real Red Indian, and track animals and live in a wigwam. I forgot about Clara and I forgot all about cadging one of her gran's sweets. I had to go home.

Dad was sitting in his armchair by the fire reading the paper. I walked quietly past him and stood in the corner to look at our bookshelves, they were half empty. I knew that something was terribly wrong, and I knew instinctively that I must not say anything, so I went down into the yard to look for Joey. I found him on his knees looking for ants in the solid bit of dirt by the dustbin where a couple of privet bushes fought for life. I flung myself down next to him and poured out my story. Nothing disturbed Joey, he just sat back on his heels in the dirt and looked thoughtfully at me.

'I expect it's Dad,' he said.

'He can't,' I cried. 'They're not his, he didn't ask!'

'He don't have to,' Joey said simply. 'He's Dad.' Looking at Joey with his small serious face and grubby knees I felt he was far older and wiser than I, and I calmed down.

'What can I do, Joey?' I asked. 'I want my book.'

'The lady in the shop might sell it back to you.'

'I dunno how much it would cost. I know, suppose I joined her library and borrowed it, an' never took it back? I would only have to pay tuppence for that. I could get tuppence easy.'

'They wouldn't let you. You have to be grown-up.'

'I want it back,' I shouted. I felt a wave of helpless hatred for Dad and the red-haired pointed-faced woman in the sweet shop, with her daft frilly blouses and dangling ear-rings. 'I'll never go in that shop again, nor see my book, nor that woman!'

'That's silly,' said Joey. 'It's not her fault. She didn't know it was your book.' I was getting nowhere with Joey, he was too reasonable.

I nursed my anger and resentment all day, and when Dad had gone out that night I told Lu what had happened. She already knew because she had been trying to calm Dodie down, and couldn't wait to explode her wrath on Mum. Mum listened to us with an anxious face, pleating her pinny between her fingers. She was sorry, ever so sorry about our books, but said that we must say nothing about them in front of Dad. What was done was done, and we must put up with it. There was not going to be a row about the books and that was her last word, and she meant it. For the next few days I stared sulkily at Dad whenever I happened to be near him, hoping that he would read my thoughts, but he didn't show any signs of doing so.

During the long school holidays an air of restlessness crept into the yard. A couple of families went to pick hops in Kent, but the majority of us had never been away on holiday. There was a common urge to do something that would take us out of the buildings, even though it was only for a day. On sunny mornings we took lemonade bottles filled with cold tea and paper bags of bread and jam to Battersea Park, and ate the lot almost as soon as we arrived, so that we were starving for the remainder of the day. There wasn't much to do at the park, apart from rolling around on the flat grass. We watched the tennis and the putting and looked at the deer doing nothing behind their railings, and stood by the lake to see the rowing boats, but most of the time we roamed around in an untidy gang hoping that something would happen. The best part of going to the park was the enthusiasm with which we set off.

Sometimes we decided to go to the museums for the sole purpose of playing at which of us would be the last to get chucked out. The museum attendants were a suspicious lot, and their jobs were easier if they could rid themselves of as many unaccompanied kids as possible. We pushed all the knobs and buttons in the Science Museum, slid along their long polished benches and rode in the lift, if we could squeeze in unnoticed. We saved the Victoria and Albert museum until last so that we could have a look at David. We had never heard of Michelangelo. Without a glance at any of the exhibits, we made straight for the cluttered gallery where he towered above everything. A hostile attendant usually hovered in our wake and it was with some difficulty that we pretended an interest in the foreign statuary while stealing furtive peeps at David's tiddler. I was always surprised that it was so small. We were familiar with nude statues. There was a greeny-bronze lady in the open air among the bushes and railings on the embankment. Once we got used to her bosoms we scarcely noticed her, but David was indoors, and that made his nudity quite shocking.

When we didn't know what to do we went out of the gate and walked in any direction, turning corners and crossing roads, getting further and further away until we were lost which was a very enjoyable feeling. Mysteries and adventures happened all the time to kids in books and comics, and this was our way of inviting one to happen to us. Sometimes we had to ask the way home, and once an old girl forked out a penny to each of us to ride home on a bus. We spent the pennies on sweets, and walked, pleased as punch with ourselves. That was about the most exciting thing that happened, but we continued to hope.

The Round Pond gave us plenty of entertainment. It was a sight to see the varnished model yachts crossing the dancing water, attended by puffing old men in deerstalker hats and baggy plus fours. Perfect reproductions of *Shamrock* and *Britannia*, the yachts glided to the shallow edge of the pond and I longed to touch one, to turn it round and send it out again on its next voyage. The owner always arrived just in time, legging it surprisingly fast on spindly ankles, mouthing at us to stand back and waving us away with his bamboo pole. We got our own back, though, when we had a go at the posh kids. The grass round the pond was thick with nannies and nice children in floppy white cotton sun-hats. Many of them had fishing nets and little jars with string round the top to hold their catch of tiny gasping fish. We created deliberate havoc by running round the pond and sliding their jars into the water with a flip of our boots, leaving a trail of tears and flapping nursemaids behind us.

When we had lived in the buildings for a couple of years we had another shake up in our fortunes. Mum had to give up her job at the clinic and Georgie started work. Mum had been poorly for a long time and eventually had to go into hospital. When she came out she had to look about for something easier, and managed to find a job in a factory canteen with a nice bit of easy office cleaning in the evening with no scrubbing. We managed to pay the rent while Mum was laid up, but got behind with the furniture repayments. Dad had to write one of his stylish letters explaining that we were temporarily unable to meet our commitments and assuring them that they had no cause to doubt that we would shortly resume our regular payments, and you couldn't blame the firm for believing him.

Mum had only been working in the canteen for a few weeks

when she told Lu that there was a vacancy, and that she was to present herself on Monday morning for an interview. It took Lu all day Sunday to get herself ready. In the morning she and Dodie went through everything they possessed to decide what Lu was to wear, and in the afternoon they shut themselves in our bedroom and tried to make a brassière out of a nice white bit of pillow slip. Dodie cut the material on the cross and they darted and tacked, the two triangles becoming smaller and rounder until they looked like a couple of tiny tea cosies. They made the straps and the fastening at the back out of bloomer elastic and pulled it so tightly that the straps bit into Lu's shoulders. She didn't care, and said it felt marvellous. She washed her hair and rinsed it with vinegar in the water and went to bed with her whole head screwed in paper crackers. In the morning she tugged it out into a frizz like a halo all round her face, and she looked quite different, pretty in a funny sort of way. With her bosom high up on her chest and her hair done, she was a lady, and I couldn't understand where the old Lu had gone. She sailed into the job and released herself for ever from charring, but she did stop behind to give Mum a hand with the offices in the evenings, which wasn't the same thing at all.

Georgie had joined the sea cadets and was so completely absorbed by their old converted barge on the Thames that we rarely saw him at home. His whole interest was in ships and the river and his few books were about whaling and voyages. It must have been disappointing for him at the age of fourteen to have to earn his living by riding a delivery bike for a high-class grocers, standing up on the pedals to ease the crop of adolescent boils on his backside. He earned ten shillings for a fifty-six hour week, coming home after nine o'clock on Saturday nights too tired to eat his supper after scrubbing out the shop. Mum worried about him, but Georgie was biding his time until he was old enough to go to sea.

The routine after dinner on schooldays was for Dad to give me a penny to buy an evening newspaper for him on my way home. Each day I wrapped the penny in a piece of paper and put it up my bloomer leg. At frequent intervals during the afternoon I would assure myself that it was still safely there, but one day I couldn't find it. I fidgeted and worried until the bell ran at half-past four and rushed to the lav. I had lost it! Joey was waiting for me, and I told him what had happened.

'We'd better go home then and tell Dad,' he said.

'I can't. I can't go 'ome without the paper!'

'Where we goin' to get another penny from?' asked Joey.

'I dunno.'

'There you are then! Come on Rowie, we'd better get a move on, it's ever so late.' To Joey the situation was perfectly simple. He would have gone home, told Dad he had lost the penny, accepted his telling off, and everything would have been settled. I did not share Joey's courage, but had to contrive a way to get out of trouble. While we were talking we had left the playground and we were approaching Poultons Square when I saw Alfie in front of us. He lived in Blantyre Street, quite close to us, and seeing him gave me an idea.

'Quick Joey,' I said. 'Let's catch up Alfie.' Alfie Wilson was a dull and lonely little boy, and he must have been surprised at my enthusiastic greeting. ''Allo Alfie,' I cried. 'Going 'ome?'

'Yes,' he answered, in his usual quiet way.

'You're late, ain'tcher?'

'Yes,' replied Alfie.

'Is your mum in when you get 'ome?' I asked.

'Yes,' said Alfie. This was just what I wanted to know, and I nudged Joey so hard that he bumped sideways into Alfie.

'Go on,' I hissed at Joey. 'You know him, he's in your class, ask him.'

'Ask him what?' said Joey in a perfectly clear voice.

'Oh for Gawd's sake Joey! If 'e can get a penny off 'is mum an' lend us,' I muttered through my teeth. Joey began to tell Alfie about the newspaper as we crowded each side of the poor little kid, and I joined in to exaggerate the bashing I would get for losing the penny. We promised that we would give the penny back to him the very next day because we would tell our Mum and she would give us one. Carried away with the impression I thought we were making on Alfie, I even said we would be his friends and let him play with us at playtime. Alfie remained quiet and non-committal and I couldn't think of any other enticements to get him to agree to help us.

When we reached Alfie's house Joey and I hung on to the railings outside while Alfie knocked on the front door. It had barely opened six inches before he scuttled inside without saying a word to us, and there was a horrible finality about the way in which it closed behind him. Hopefully we waited and waited, until I looked at Joey and he lifted his shoulders. 'It n'arf gettin' late,' I said. 'I'm gonna knock.' None too loudly I lifted Alfie's door knocker and almost immediately the door was jerked open by Alfie's mum.

'Yes?' she snapped.

'Is Alfie comin' out?' I asked, taking a couple of steps backwards.

'No, 'e's not!' She slammed the door.

'Mouldy little tyke,' I said to Joey. 'I bet 'e's too windy to ask 'is Mum. I'll knock 's rotten 'ead off tomorrer.' For a moment I was so angry with Alfie's treachery that I had forgotten all about the penny.

'We're sunk all right now,' said Joey. 'Let's buss-up.' We held each other's hands behind our backs and made our way up to the Worlds End, and ran slap into Dad. He grabbed each of us and marched us home, his hands heavy on our shoulders. I saw nothing but the paving stones running beneath my feet.

We scrambled up the stairs, racing ahead of Dad, and waited for him in the living-room. He was terribly angry and made a dreadful noise, shouting at us demanding to know where we had been. Joey sat on one of the chairs, his feet not reaching the floor, and Dad pulled him roughly off it to stand up when he was being spoken to. Joey fell against the table and banged his head and was sick on the floor. I started crying and poured out a torrent of words about losing the penny, and it wasn't Joey's fault. Dad cleaned Joey up, sat him in the armchair and made a cup of tea. He sent me into the kitchen where I got a good telling off, not for losing the paper money, but for coming home late. Then he did an extraordinary thing, he gave Joey a ha'penny and sent him out to buy himself some sweets. From that day onwards Dad never gave us the penny to take to school. One of us was sent out to buy the paper after we had come home. Alfie and Joey struck up a strange friendship, saying little to each other and pottering around together, but Alfie kept well clear of me.

I had hardly recovered from one financial catastrophe before I was up to my neck in another. A lady came into our classroom one morning and told us all about the Country Holiday Fund. She held up a little card and said if we could save up until we had ten shillings entered on it, we could go away to the country for a fortnight. I had no doubt or hesitation and shot my hand straight up to say I would join. I was so carried away, seeing myself among the buttercups and daisies at last, that I never listened to another word she said. No power on earth would prevent me from going to the country, and the first week I scraped up three ha'pence. I hid my card in my locker in the bedroom, and gloated over it at night after Lu had lit my candle and gone out of the room. The following week I only paid in a penny. It never occurred to me that at this rate I should be saving for about two years, but like Mum I believed that if I wanted to do something badly enough I could make it happen.

When I had tenpence on my card authority took over. Someone official sent a letter to Dad, pointing out that they had not yet received his consent and that my contributions were far from adequate. That evening, when I came up from the yard, Mum and Dad were in the living-room with the letter on the table. 'What,' said Dad, 'do you think you're up to?' I wondered what I had been up to for I knew nothing about the letter. I looked at Mum for help, but for once she seemed to be on Dad's side. I hadn't nicked anything or bashed anyone, so I kept quiet. 'This holiday lark,' Dad went on. 'Why didn't you tell your mother?' I knew perfectly well why I hadn't told Mum or anyone else, because I couldn't face the thought that I might not be allowed to go. I had planned to save up the ten shillings first, and then ask, and when Mum knew that no money was involved, she might agree.

'I was going to tell you,' I said to Dad, 'but I wanted to pay for myself.'

'Didn't they say that you had to ask your parents for permission?' Dad's voice was getting loud, and I knew I was in for it. 'Didn't they tell you that you had to take a letter from me, agreeing that you could go away on this business?'

I stared back at him, trying to remember what had been said. All I could recall was the feeling I had about going to the country, I had heard nothing of the conditions. I avoided Dad's eye and spoke directly to Mum. 'I want to go, Mum,' I said.

Mum pursed her lips in a bit of a smile at me and looked at Dad. 'It won't do her no harm,' she said. 'She's never been out of London.'

The next Monday I paid in three sixpences, one each from Georgie, Lu and Dodie, and the following week Mum gave me a shilling. By the time the summer came, I had paid the whole ten shillings, and on a warm misty morning Lu took me to the station. I stood with her on the bewildering platform clutching the string of a blue cotton bag which Dodie had made to carry my things, fingering the buff-coloured label round my neck, and shivering with fear and excitement. Mum had given me a shilling to spend and two postcards addressed home with the penny stamps already stuck on. The fund was sending me to a village in Shropshire, just outside Ironbridge.

I adored every second of my fortnight. I was lodged in a

rambling old cottage that finished up in a muddle of sheds and lean-tos with bits of brick and old stone floors. It had a huge sloping garden, untidy and weedy except for the vegetables that grew like soldiers, with a dear little wooden hut bang in the middle which turned out to be a very smelly lav, with no chain. My landlady was small and comfy and fat, and at first I couldn't understand a word she said. She had five huge sons who picked me up and chucked me from one to the other and went off to work in the mornings before I woke up. The ceiling of my tiny bedroom sloped down to the floor and I had to kneel down to look out of the window. The room was papered with a rosy pattern and smelt of clean washing, and there was a pot under my bed. Every night I had supper with the family. We sat at a big wooden table in the kitchen, fiery hot from the old iron stove, and crammed with shelves of china and great black saucepans. We ate thick rashers of bacon and fried potatoes and Mrs Peg-mill in a clean white pinny poured rich transparent bacon fat all over our blue-edged plates, and called it liquor.

Two of the brothers took me over the fields with them on my first Sunday morning to the farm where they worked, and showed me the cows and hens, and I came home to an enormous Sunday dinner with my arms full of long white daisies. I fell down the garden slope and discovered the needle stings and white lumps that come from stinging nettles. I fought in the woods, which I learned to call the copse, with the village kids, and dug up spuds, shouting when I found the little ones in the soft soil with my fingers. On Saturday afternoon Mrs Pegmill took me to see the Iron Bridge and we stayed to wander round the market where I bought a glass butter dish for sixpence for my Mum. I was spoilt, entertained, fed, scrubbed, tucked into bed, and told I was a funny little Cockney beggar. I gathered pink flowers from the hedges and smelt honeysuckle. I poked my fingers into a foxglove and squelched beside the muddy pond to watch the green dragonfly.

When they put me on the train I cried, and when I arrived home I found the two unused postcards in my bag. I stood by myself at our bedroom window in the pink light of the red setting sun which lit the clouds behind the bottling plant and the furniture depository. 'When I grow up,' I said aloud, 'and I am rich and famous, I am going to live in the country.' Then I spat on my fingers and crossed my heart, to seal my promise.

Dodie, Lu and Georgie were now grown-up and had endured their stint of Dad's own peculiar ideas of education. Now that

Joey and I were old enough to stand its rigours, our turn had come. We began with London, to be exact the City. Dad had a deep feeling for London and knew it well, particularly the old and unvisited corners. On Sunday mornings he made us get up early and we walked for hours, trying to keep up with him and listening to his tales of kings and charters, famous mayors and judges. We went into the Wren churches and stood outside all the livery halls and the Hudson Bay Company building, and tried to imagine the search for the passage through the ice. We saw Dr Johnson's house off the Strand and the Roman Bath, and went to Smithfield to see where the peasants faced the king. We shivered on London Bridge while Dad described all the ships in the Pool of London and told us what they carried and where they were bound. We did not have any background knowledge to relate to the wordy information poured out by Dad, and every Sunday morning meant a long and dismal walk through empty grey streets with Dad telling us to pick our feet up, and wipe our noses.

Sometimes he took us to Club Row and Petticoat Lane. The roadway between the stalls was always jammed with people and we had to squeeze and push to keep close to Dad, who didn't wait for us. It was noisy and lively, and when Dad stopped to look at a stall we wormed our way to the front to stare at the caged birds, or the puppies, or the goldfish. There were stalls of clothes, new and secondhand, which we didn't bother to look at, but we lingered round the food sellers, holding our noses and giggling at the unusual smell of the open barrels of oily fish. There were clocks and toys, tablecloths and jellied eels, second-hand bikes and tortoises. We never bought anything, but we liked going there.

In the autumn we walked to Putney Common to fill paper bags with woody little blackberries, and we searched for and Dad dug up wild horseradish. Joey used to slope off whenever he could to find beetles and caterpillars which he hid in matchboxes in his pocket. Dad could always get his hands on a boat and we had to learn to handle a dinghy on the Thames. We soon discovered that Dad would never tell us anything twice, and if he noticed anyone watching us he shouted at us to 'smarten up'. We learned to row and to scull with one oar from the stern. We had to slog to turn the boat into the fierce tide when we came alongside the pier, and ship the oars, lifting them blade forwards into the bow without swiping or wetting Dad, and nipping out with a rope in one hand while fending off with the other. Learning to handle a boat with Dad was no fun, it was more like earning your living. Sometimes he rigged a short mast and got the rag up, and with neither a keel nor a centre-board we could only flop along with the wind behind us, rolling about under bridges trying to keep under the centre of the arches, knowing that we would have to pull the boat all the way back to the pier under oars. We learned the signals of the tugs' hoots and knew enough to keep clear of each end of a lighter. My hands soon blistered and I got no sympathy. 'I've told you the right way to hold the bloody oars,' Dad said, utterly unconcerned. As soon as we could escape back to the yard we shed everything he had told us and thankfully embraced our own affairs.

At that time everyone was talking about Annie Conway's Sunday School class. She said the Sunday School gave away sweets for nothing. Some of us decided to put this to the test, so the following week we toiled all the way to Earls Court, and arrived late. A cheerful noise of kids shouting, rather than singing, met us as we followed Annie down the steps and through the swing doors. We entered a low-ceilinged hall and were hustled into a circle of chairs near the door, which was the bottom class, while the school rounded off *Fishers of Men* just in front of the harmonium. I don't know what denomination of Sunday school it was, but once the uproar had died down, our teacher tried to hold our attention by teaching us the names of the books of the Old Testament. She was an earnest little wisp of a thing and we quite liked getting our tongues round 'Leviticus'. 'Deuteronomy' was beyond us, and we soon lost interest in her efforts and turned round to size up the kids in the other circles and wonder when they were going to dish out the sweets. When it was time to go home we queued up at the swing doors where the Rev. Holly stood benignly to pat the odd child on the head and slip each of us two sugared almonds, and small ones at that.

The following week only three of us turned up from the buildings, which wasn't surprising. We got there in time to join in *Fishers of Men*, and when the stamping died down the Rev. called our attention to the platform. He told us that there was to be a prize for the best composition, and it was to be called 'Why I believe in God'. With nothing but the prize in mind, I decided to enter the competition.

I told Mum about it and she gave me a ha'penny to buy two sheets of foolscap paper from the newspaper shop. The paper had a margin on one side and red ruled lines on the other for pounds, shillings and pence. I didn't mind this, because it left very little space for writing in between, so I could fill up the pages more quickly. My problem was to get hold of the pen and ink. We had several pencils, but Joey was determined that I should not write about God in pencil, He'd got to have ink. By Saturday I still hadn't written my composition, so Mum said if I hurried up I could use Dad's pen when he went out. With a whole newspaper spread out under the bottle in case I knocked it over, I sat in my nightie and expounded my belief in God in my best writing.

I was getting fed up with Sunday school, the lure of the sweets was proving an exaggeration, but I went with Annie to find out who had won the prize. The old Rev. spread his arms joyfully at the noisy circles of kids and addressed us. 'Boys and girls. I was so pleased with all your compositions, it was difficult to decide who should be the winner, but we have agreed to give the prize to R. Naylor. Is R. Naylor here?' For a second there was absolute quiet, and then all the chairs scraped as the kids twisted and turned. Annie gave me a shove. 'Come along, R. Naylor,' coaxed the Rev. I don't think my teacher knew my name because when Annie pushed me forward and I stood up, she got quite excited.

'Oh my goodness,' she flustered. 'I do believe it's one of my class, Reverend. Come along dear.' Every bit as surprised as I was, she led me to the platform.

The Rev. looked doubtful, and in a very different voice he said to me sharply: 'What's your name?'

'Rosie Naylor,' I answered.

'Did you write this?' He bent down to me so that I looked straight into his big black moustache. He thrust the composition at me and I saw my pounds, shillings and pence paper. I nodded. He put his arm round me and turned me to face the crowd. 'And here is her prize,' he said, in his happy Reverend Holly voice. 'Well done,' and he gave me a book.

Mum was ever so pleased that I had won, and we all had a look at the book and didn't think it was much cop. It was some sort of biblical analysis, full of references to chapters and verses and way above my head, and Mum's too. I was pleased it had a lot of pictures although they were only black and white drawings, so one wet Sunday evening Joey and I took it in turns to colour most of them with a couple of greasy crayons.

I had become quite friendly with Annie and she invited me to her birthday party, but I was a bit put out when I was told by some of the other girls that I would have to take Annie a present. I didn't know what to do about this, so I kept putting it out of my mind until it was too late, and on the Saturday afternoon of the party I had nothing for her. Lu was home from work and she had never failed to help me.

'Lu, I gotta take Annie a present,' I said.

'It's no good asking me,' Lu answered, 'I haven't got anything. You should have asked Dodie.'

'She won't be home till after six, an' that's too late.'

'Oh Rowie,' Lu said angrily, 'why do you have to leave everything until the last minute? It's your own fault, and you'll have to go through your things and find her something.'

Mum told me to have a wash and then she tied a bow of creased white ribbon on my flat hair. 'My gawd Rowie,' she said. 'You don't look much like a party.' I didn't feel like a party as I tried to find something for Annie among my bits and pieces. Then I thought of the bible book and regretted colouring the pictures, because the book itself looked almost new. I decided it would have to be the book because there was nothing else. I shut my eyes and had an urgent word with God, asking Him if He couldn't remove the crayon or at least not let Annie open it until after the party. Convinced that He and I shared a special interest in the book, and that I no longer had anything to worry about, I went to Annie Conway's.

All dressed up, Annie was surrounded by girls from the buildings who were giving her their presents. She had handkerchiefs and a puzzle and a bar of chocolate, all of them new. I gave her my book, unwrapped. We had tea in her mum's kitchen and then played oranges and lemons. We were all standing around, just talking, when I suddenly realised that I was all by myself and that the others were crowded about Annie, and she was showing them my book. I could just see one of Joey's scribbly pictures all over the edges. I had a terrible feeling of shame, and I rushed into the kitchen where Mrs Conway was washing up, thanked her for having me and said I had to go home.

When I got indoors Joey was standing on a stool at the sink giving his tadpoles a swim. His jersey was soaking wet. 'You ain't been long,' he said, not turning to look at me. 'What was it like?'

'Rotten,' I answered.

'What did you 'ave for tea?'

'White blamonge, paste samwiges an' cake. 'Ere Joey, do you believe in God?'

'Yeh,' said Joey.

'Miracles an' all?'

'Yeh.'

'Well I don't,' I said. 'I'm fed up with God an' 'E don't do no miracles, specially not for me.'

'Ain't you goin' to Sunday School no more then?' asked Joey, peering into the sink.

'No I ain't!' I said. 'I got that rotten book from Sunday School, an' I wish I'd never seen it.' Joey didn't answer, and as I watched him, totally absorbed, I began to understand that Joey did exactly what he wanted to. He never got into muddles by showing off and wanting to be included in everything. He lived in his own quiet reflective world, and his way was happy.

'Come an' look at my tadpoles,' said Joey. 'They suddenly got legs.'

The next week I sat for the preliminary examination for the Junior County Scholarship. There was a paper on sums and one on English, and I passed, which entitled me to sit for the second stage. The arithmetic paper was composed of problems, and I couldn't do any of them, because I could never find the sum hidden among all the words. I had a vivid picture of three funny men running up and down the stairs with buckets of water, filling a bath, and someone else pulling the plug out while they weren't looking, but it was beyond me to express the situation in terms of figures. Nobody from my school won the scholarship, so there would be no name on the board of honour in the hall for yet another year. Just before the end of the term I was given the chance to sit for a special place at a private school, where they had an arrangement to receive a few scholarship girls. I had a long interview and did some sums and writing, and Dad received a letter to say that I had been accepted. He was quite proud of me and generously gave his consent, landing Mum with the problem of fitting me out.

Lu came with Mum and me to the school where the uniform was displayed in a room, crowded with other girls and their parents. We were handed lists of the necessary clothing and began to wander round the exhibits. I had never heard of indoor shoes as well as outdoor, and lisle stockings were for ladies. The gymslip alone cost more than Mum's wages for a week, and the overcoat and blazer were out of the question. I tried on a black velour hat, disappearing under the brim, and fingered its bright encrusted badge. There were knickers and blouses, gym shoes and a cotton overall dress with gathers low on the hips. Mum hung about on the end of the queue, reluctant to let the school tailor get his tape on me, and not wanting the other parents to hear her questions. We held a whispered conference in the corner.

'I never seen anything like it,' Lu muttered.

'Sh! Lu! Keep your voice down! I wonder how much of this stuff we could buy outside?' said Mum.

'The shoes, stockings and the bloomers for a start,' answered Lu. 'I should reckon Dodie could copy that frock out of cheaper material and one navy coat looks like any other. I mean, honestly Mum, four quid for a kid's coat! We'd have to buy the hat band and the badges 'ere though, and probably the blouse too. She won't need the blazer, not yet. They only wear blazers in the summer don't they?' Lu was running down the list and deciding what we could buy elsewhere at half the price. I began to cheer up, I knew old Lu and Mum would find a way to get me to the school. 'There's another thing Mum,' Lu went on, 'if she only has one of everything and we rinse it out overnight, we might manage. Blimey Rowie,' she said to me, 'you 'aven't 'arf landed us in it this time.'

'Sh! Lu!' Mum mouthed at her, shaking her head. We waited until everyone else had finished with the tailor, then Mum placed our modest order. One hatband and badge, and one blouse. The tailor looked somewhat surprised.

The following Saturday afternoon Mum took me to dear old Blakie. Mr Blake ran a cheap little shoe shop in the Kings Road, where Mum bought our boots and plimsolls, Dad's socks, and stockings for Lu and Dodie. Over the years she had become friendly with him, and bit by bit he had learned a good deal about us. He was the one to help us now. Mum took the school list to him and explained our difficulty. Straightaway he fitted me with black lace-up shoes, cheap strap ward shoes and drill shoes. He found a pair of stockings only a little bit too big for me, and asked Mum how much money she needed for the remainder of my things. 'A good ten quid,' Mum answered.

'Right,' said Blakie, 'get on with it. I can get you the coat and drillslip wholesale, you sort out the rest.' They decided that Mum should pay off my debt at five shillings a week.

'Now,' said Lu to me, 'perhaps you'll learn to look after your things.'

I started at my new school in September. I was neither a fee-paying pupil nor a scholarship girl, but a 'special placer', which, in my class of thirty-six, put me in a minority of two, and made me well aware of my station.

TEN

French with Tears

I was really excited about the idea of being at a posh school, but I didn't want the day ever to come when I should have to go there. Everything smelt new as I dressed on that bright September morning. Dodie had sewn two wide elastic garters to hold up my stockings, and Dad had put a heavy clump of leather on my new shoes to save wear on the original soles. The square-necked blouse and navy drillslip were a good size too big, to allow for growing, and I felt all lost inside them. Dodie put my ward shoes and drill shoes in my case with a clean handkerchief, and folded up my blue dress in newspaper to save it from creasing.

'What you putting that in for?' asked Lu. 'She wears that in the summer.'

'It's on the list,' Dodie answered. 'I think it's supposed to be some sort of overall. She'd better take it with her the first day.'

Mum and Georgie had already gone to work, and Dad was shouting at Joey to get up. There was a tray on the living-room table with cups of tea already poured out and stirred, which Dad made every morning. We stood up to drink our tea, for we had not changed our custom of not having breakfast. Lu smiled at me over the top of her cup. 'Cheer up, Rowie love,' she said. 'You ain't goin' to a funeral.'

'Get your coat on quick,' said Dodie, 'an' I'll come with you to the bus.' My thick velour hat brim was turned up at the back and rubbed against the nap collar of my new coat and with the unbendable shoes as well I walked stiff-necked and flat-footed. Old Blakie's overcoat buttoned up all right, but the cheap-jack cutter had made no allowance for an overlap, so the front sprang away from the bottom button.

'I got the wind up, Dodie,' I admitted, as we waited for the bus. Dodie carried my case and held my hand, as if I were going to school for the first time.

You'll be all right once you get there,' she said. 'Don't say anything, but watch the other girls and do what they do.' With this excellent advice in my empty head I clambered up the winding stair at the back of the bus, lugging my fibre attaché case, and to my delight the first person I saw was Tina, the other free placer from my old school. I plonked myself thankfully next to her and the burden of my anxiety simply melted away.

'Where's your dress?' she asked, staring at my drillslip as my coat opened when I sat down.

'In my case,' I answered.

'Why haven't you got it on?' She opened her coat and I saw the bright blue dress with the black bow pinned at the bottom of the open neck, which revealed her school blouse.

'I thought we just wore our drillslip. All school uniforms are drillslips.'

'At our school we wear them underneath,' said Tina. 'You put your dress on over the top in the winter terms.'

'All the time?'

'Yes, except when we have drill and games.'

'Oh damn!' I said. 'Ne'mind, I can nip in the lav as soon as I get there an' put it on.'

'I don't think you'd better swear any more, not at this school,' Tina remarked in a serious voice, peering at me through her glasses, 'and another thing, I am going to use my proper name, which is Ernestine.'

'Yeh,' I said, 'I know it is, but that's only when they call the register.'

'Well, my mother says I should be Ernestine all the time now.'

Blimey, I thought, this is a fine start! I paid my fare and slumped in my seat, my hat nudged over my eyes. Tina turned round from looking out of the window. 'And there's another thing I ought to tell you,' she said. I wondered what was coming next. 'You know my father is an inspector on the buses?'

'Yeh,' I answered, 'course I do.' We all knew that Tina's father had a good regular job, and that she was an only child – she was always talking about her holiday at Lee-on-Solent, wherever that was.

'Well,' she went on, 'if I am asked, I intend to say that he is an official of the London Transport Board.' I could find no answer to this brilliant bit of thinking and I got the message all right, but it opened up a problem for me. What was I going to say if anyone asked me what my Dad did? My immediate thought was to say that I hadn't got one, but then maybe the teachers would get to hear about it and would know I'd told a lie. I'd better stick to what Dad said on the paper when we went into the buildings, and I would say he was a wharfinger, and I wondered whether or not to pronounce the 'h'. Anyway, nobody would have any idea what it meant, so sucks in the eye to them. When we got off the bus I was more reluctant than ever. I had got the wrong clothes on, Tina had turned into a very self-assured Ernestine, I was ashamed of Dad, and I hadn't even got inside the gates.

The school was a graceful Georgian house set behind a small semi-circular drive with trees and shrubs. A modern extension in the same architectural style had been added on one side, fronting the road. A series of buildings which included the assembly hall and gymnasium extended behind the house into the long garden. The interior was confusing at first. Classrooms were linked by passageways and steps, with odd lavatories and cloakrooms popped into corners that looked like cupboards. I followed Tina into our classroom and we were taken with the other new girls and allocated places in our cloakroom. Hurriedly I began to scramble into my dress and slide my feet into my indoor shoes, keeping everyone waiting. 'Who is that girl who is taking so long?' said a crisp voice with a peg on its nose.

'Please, it's Rose Naylor.' They trooped off, and when I eventually crept into the right room all the desks were taken except one almost in the back row, and I was far too self-conscious to say that I could not see the blackboard properly. I was pleased about my desk. At least I had a real one where I could keep all my things, but when I sat down I had a feeling of isolation that I was not used to. There was something comforting about the old two-seater desks in the junior school, even if you didn't like the kid you shared it with.

Prayers were no longer a gasping hymn and a gabbled Lord's Prayer. We sat cross-legged on the hall floor to listen to music, stood for the hymn, which we sang from hymn books, then said the Creed, which I didn't know, knelt down for prayers, and then sat again to listen to the lesson. This was read from a lectern by a beautiful long-skirted sixth former, who instantly became my ideal.

When we were back in class we were given a form to fill in, for which I had to borrow a pencil. It asked where I went to church and for the name of the vicar. This was a right turn up for the book! I sucked the pencil and looked round. Everyone was writing, including Tina, and I had no idea what to put down. It never occured to me to tell the truth and say I didn't go to church, instead I wrote 'Salvation Army' in big letters to take up all the space. Well, I had been there a couple of times and there was such a crowd of kids no one would ever know if I was there or not. The next question asked how much money I would give each term to the school mission. After another suck I wrote down 'six pence'. Added to this expense I had to find three and six for my school hymn book, and I now knew that we had to supply our own pen, pencil, ruler and geometry set, and everyone had a pencil box on their desk filled with coloured pencils. I imagined Lu and Dodie's faces when I took that lot of news home! At playtime, which I had to remember to call break, I found my way to the cloakroom, changed my shoes and wandered out into the garden. There was a hard netball court at the bottom and I watched the girls practising shooting. Others were walking round and round with their arms linked, talking with their heads together. I didn't know what to do, and wished I were back in the old school with all the kids I knew.

Our first night's homework was to cover our textbooks in brown paper and learn the collect. Nobody asked what the collect was, so I thought I'd better keep quiet and find out for myself. I went home on the bus to dinner, which was a lot cheaper than staying at school as the meal cost a shilling. On the bus I asked Tina about the collect. She turned a contemptuous pair of eyes on me. 'It's in the Prayer Book,' she said. I only had about twenty minutes indoors to eat my dinner which Dad dished up. Just as I was rushing back to catch the bus I met Dodie coming across the yard, and I asked her if she could find me some brown paper. That night Lu and Dodie showed me how to put the paper round my books. We used Dad's solid carpenters' glue to stick down the corners, which we had to warm up over a saucepan of water on the gas stove. Mum made us open the windows to get rid of the smell. Just as we were finishing, I asked them where I could borrow a Prayer Book.

'How many more things are you going to want?' asked Dodie.

'There's a collect in it.'

'A what?' asked Lu.

'Something I got to learn by tomorrow.'

'If she's got to learn it tonight, we'd better find 'er one,' said Lu.

'I know,' said Dodie. 'Next door, Rowie. Mrs Gardner'll have one. I've seen her carrying a book when she goes to church to see her Ernie at church parade.'

'You go, Dodie,' I said.

'Certainly not. It's high time you did something for yourself.'

I tapped on Mrs Gardner's door. She was a nice old girl, a bit deaf, and barmy about her soppy great son who was something in the Scouts. I told her what I had to do and she sat me down on her brown shabby sofa, put on her glasses and fetched a tiny little book with a gold cross on the front.

'Now then, Rosie love,' she said, sitting down next to me. 'You'll need to know your way through this,' and for the next hour I discovered where to find the collects and the Creed, and how you got married and buried. 'Take it with you,' said Mrs Gardner kindly, 'until you can get hold of one of your own.' All this, I thought, has been going on all this time, and I never knew anything about it!

The days went by and we settled down to a routine timetable and the structure of a variety of subjects was carefully introduced by specialist teachers. We had to move about the school for some of the lessons which meant remembering to take the necessary books. Somehow, my desk was always in a muddle and I never allowed enough time to be in the right shoes, and I often arrived at class both late, improperly dressed and without the correct books. With all the good intentions in the world I soon ran into difficulties with French. I told myself that we were all starting at the beginning and that nobody knew any more about it than I did. I was going to listen and keep up with the others and try. I did, but my teacher assumed that I knew things which I did not. She kept talking about some people but never explained who they were. There was this first person who was single, and another lot who were called plural and had numbers. I learned the verbs like anything, saying them over and over to myself in bed and on the bus, but 'to be' and 'am' and 'was' were totally unrelated to each other, and futures and pasts were taken for granted and I was in no position to grant anything.

I had not been accustomed to an all-female establishment and it soon began to dawn on me that I did not know much about being a girl. Somehow I had missed out on all the things that my class mates considered important. Until now I had settled most of my differences and held my place among other kids with my wits and fists, with nothing to choose between boys and girls. I did not know how to react to a snub. I had no interest in my appearance, but I began to be aware that some of the girls were pretty, and I wondered how they did it. I couldn't wait to rush home and tell Lu when I discovered that some of them had their hair cut at a real hairdressers. I learned that they used scented soap and noticed they did not shout, and disliked getting their hands dirty. They talked a lot about clothes, planning a new

Sunday coat and knowing exactly which shoes they wanted to go with it. I never had the least inclination to read a girl's book, particularly those sissy things about boarding school, and I could not understand the rapture and hugs that went on when someone found an Angela Brazil that the others hadn't read. They invited each other to tea and showed each other their bedrooms. I wanted to be like the girls in my class when I was with them, but I honestly had to admit that I enjoyed myself much more back in the yard.

Early in my first term I was out shopping with Mum on a Saturday afternoon when I saw a girl with a lady standing at the counter in the Co-op. I left Mum's side and darted back to call through the open shop door: 'Coo-eee! 'Allo Lizzie!' I waved to her and then ran to catch Mum up, telling her ever so excitedly that I had seen a girl from my school. The following Monday at morning break she came towards me with two of her friends. She was a good bit taller than I and she looked down at me from half-closed eyes.

'Should you meet me again in the company of my mother,' she began, rolling her jaw all over the place as she spoke, 'would you kindly not refer to me as Beth, Betty, Liza or Lizzie, because my mother does not happen to approve of those, or any other abbreviations.' She punctuated 'abbreviations' with sharp little stabs in her voice. Before I could think of anything to say they had gone, three blue figures walking away from me with arms entwined. When I got home that evening I went straight into our bedroom and changed out of my uniform. I hated it, and all it stood for, and I slung my blue dress in a fury of temper on my bed. I went over the scene again and again, thinking of the replies I could have made, but I knew deep down that faced with the same situation again I would have been just as daft. I was fed up and miserable when we had our supper but no one seemed to notice, and I couldn't have explained why I was so upset about a few words. But it wasn't the *words*, it was not being able to think of something to say back. Only a short while ago the solution would have been simple. I would have sloshed her. I made up my mind to try not to do or say anything that would land me in such a mess again.

Most of the girls in my class who had come up from the kindergarten were rotten at arithmetic and did not know their tables. The girls from the elementary schools were far ahead of them, and this gave me my first feeling of being able to cope. I began to relax and even enjoy the skill with which the maths teacher handled us. My toils at copying the strips of writing in the junior school also bore fruit, for I had no difficulty in dropping the copperplate loops for the quicker italic style, and I took pleasure in presenting my written work. Gradually the rawness and anxieties of being new wore away, and I started to make friends.

As soon as I arrived home in the evening, Dad gave me a cup of tea and I was free to join Joey in the yard until Mum came home, when we went upstairs for supper. After we had eaten I had to stop indoors and the table was cleared for my homework. In my old clothes I continued to play all the yard games, mixing happily with the 'colonel' and Winders and all my old mates, who were not in the least interested in my new school. I took good care, though, not to use any of the new pronunciation I was learning. I now had three lives to live, one in the yard, one at home and one at school. Each was completely separate from the other. A constant fear was that I should meet one of my new school friends when I was pushing the coke barrer on Saturday morning. Another was trying to keep my parents in ignorance of the well-meaning Parent-Teacher Association. One day I was given a note to take home, addressed to Mum and Dad, and our teacher said it was to ask them to come to the school in the evening. I had quite enough trouble coping there myself, and I could just imagine what would happen if I let Dad loose among them. I took the note home, hid it in the bedroom and told Lu about it.

'What does it say?' Lu asked.

'I dunno, but it's for Mum an' Dad to talk to my teachers.'

'What about?' Lu looked worried. In our experience a parent only went up to the school to have a row, and that was rare.

'P'raps they want to chuck me out,' I said.

'Let's 'ave a look', said Lu, and opened the envelope. We read the letter together. It was an invitation to spend an evening at the school to meet the staff. It did not specifically mention me. 'I shouldn't worry,' said Lu, putting her arm round me. 'It's just some daft idea.'

'I don't fancy Dad goin' up there Lu,' I said. 'Some of them are ever so posh. Supposin' he starts rollin' a fag.'

'Gawd!' Lu closed her eyes, then laughed. 'He'd probably flog 'em their own doormat.'

'They don't have to go, do they Lu?'

'No,' she said, 'not if they don't know about it.'

'What do you mean?'

'We can chuck the letter away,' Lu answered.

'I can't do that! I gotta take back an answer.'

'All right then,' and Lu rose to the occasion. 'I'll write you one.'

I couldn't believe it. I just couldn't believe that Lu would do something so daring for me. 'What you gonna say?'

'Give us a minute, I'll 'ave to think. Yeh, I know. I'll make out I'm Mum an' I'll put that me an' Mr Naylor can't come because . . .'

'Because what?' I interrupted.

'Oh Rowie, 'ang on! It's not convenient. That's it! Me and Mr Naylor can't come because it's not convenient. We don't have to make any excuse if we say it like that.'

'It's marvellous Lu,' I said with a feeling of indescribable relief. 'When you goin' to do it?'

'Stop worrying. I'll nick a bit of Dad's paper and an envelope as soon as he goes out, an' you can take the answer back tomorrer.'

'Ta, Lu,' I said, and I meant it. ''Ere, what do you reckon the idea is, to 'ave parents messin' about up the school?'

'Search me,' Lu answered.

'It's hard enough as it is,' I said and flopped down on our bed.

'What's 'ard?' asked Lu. 'The lessons?'

'Well, yeh,' I admitted. 'But it's not only that. I have a job makin' out we're not hard up.'

'Then don't take no notice Rowie! Juss learn your lessons and sod the others.'

'I only wish I could,' I mumbled, thinking of Elizabeth and her abbreviations.

I could not conceal my report. It was in the form of a fools-cap-sized book and it was presented and sealed in a buff envelope. I slid it to Mum after Dad had gone out. Against most of the subjects my various teachers had written things like 'a fair beginning', but it was the comment from my form teacher that stung. She wrote, 'Rose must learn to mind her own business'.

'What she on about?' asked Lu indignantly.

'I don't think she likes me,' I said, 'an' anyway, how do I know what to do if I don't ask?'

Quite by chance Dodie stumbled across an opportunity that was to change her job and her life and have a lasting influence on the whole family. She had asked for a rise at the greengrocer's when we moved into the buildings, and had not had any luck. Her wages were only eighteen-and-six a week, all of which she gave to Mum, and her prospects seemed unpromising to say the least. One afternoon she was sitting on a sack of spuds with her mug of tea chatting to Billy the errand boy. 'I'm goin' in the army,' Billy confided in her.

'What on earth do you want to do that for?' asked Dodie.

'I ain't stickin' 'ere pushin' a bike for ever,' said Billy. 'I'm knocking' twenty an' I can't leave 'ome on what I earn. I bin lookin' for another job for munce, but there ain't nothin' doin'. Me an' my dad reckons the army's the only answer for me.'

'I know what you mean,' Dodie nodded. 'There's no work about. Did you see the picture in the paper of all those unemployed blokes marching to Hyde Park? Some of them came all the way from Wales. I wish I could make a move.'

'You wanna stay in a shop?' asked Billy.

'Yes,' said Dodie, 'if I can.'

'I know somewhere,' said Billy, 'where my gran does the cleanin'.'

'Where's that?'

'Some place off Sloane Street.'

'That's not far from here. What sort of shop is it?' Dodie was interested.

'I dunno really,' said Billy vaguely. 'My gran sez there's all posh stuff up there.'

'Oh Billy,' Dodie wanted to shake him. 'What sort of stuff?'

'I tell yer I dunno, but my gran sez they want someone.'

'When do you see your gran?' asked Dodie.

'She lives wiv us. I see 'er tonight.'

'Then you ask her,' said Dodie firmly, 'where this shop is.'

Two days later Dodie did not come home to dinner. She went instead to the shop off Sloane Street and applied for the job of assistant. It was not an ordinary shop. In the first place there was practically nothing in the windows and inside there was no counter. It had a quiet, cool interior and suggested a beautiful room rather than a shop. Dodie was only too well aware of her unsuitable appearance in such surroundings, but her experience in the greengrocer's had given her some self-assurance and her determination to make a move kept up her courage. In some undefinable way the two lady partners who owned and ran the shop sensed Dodie's potential, and gave her the job. With breathless joy, Dodie rushed home from work that night with the news that she was leaving the greengrocer to start in a posh shop at twenty-seven-and-six a week, a jump of nine bob in her wages.

The shop was called 'The Little Gallery', and it sold the work of artists who were also superb craftsmen. After a short time a second assistant was needed and Dodie successfully introduced Lu. Together they became absorbed in the shop, each finding their own particular interest. Slowly, under the guidance of their employers they gained confidence, and their speech and assurance developed with everyday use.

The shop sold pottery by Bernard Leech and the now world-acclaimed Hamada, unglazed fine work by the partners Braden and Pleydell-Bouverie, and slipware by Michael Cardew. The fabrics were designed and hand-block printed by Phyllis Barron and Dorothy Larcher with indigo and other natural dyes. There was silverware by Catherine Cockerell and marbled papers by her father Douglas, the master bookbinder. Sometimes exhibitions of weaving or Victorian patchwork quilts or embroidery were held. The partners sold glassware from Sweden which was engraved by a hunched little old man who had a workshop off the Tottenham Court Road, and a range of superb china. Japanese red lacquer bowls and wood kitchenware from Finland were displayed with simple Chinese peasant bowls in delicious celadon green, and rough toffee-coloured salt glaze pots from France. Natural-coloured village rugs with bold simple designs came from Mexico, and there was English furniture made by Edward Gardiner from smooth untreated ash wood with rush-seated chairs. One of the partners travelled widely and selected her imported goods from items in daily use in the countries she visited. Because they were designed to function, and were made from locally available materials, they had each achieved a traditional shape which was simple, and in its own way beautiful. Poplin was sent to the wives of coal miners in South Wales and Durham. They used the wool from local sheep to stuff the poplin, and then hand sewed exquisite quilts in patterns traditional to their villages. Lu became an expert in this part of the business and took measurements and orders, often illustrating a customer's choice of the basic patterns in her correspondence with the needlewomen. At Christmas time there were painted angels and horses from Czechoslovakia, woven straw birds and decorations and deutsch dolls with wooden faces.

Lu and Dodie were sent to the Wynchcombe pottery to see how the slipware was made, and they printed lengths of material for themselves in Painswick. They tried their hands at marbling paper and learned how the things that they sold were made.

They had not been at the shop for more than a few months when it came up in conversation that neither of them had seen the sea. The astonished owners responded at once. They produced the fares and the next morning Lu and Dodie went to Victoria Station to spend their unexpected day off at Brighton. The late October morning was chilly, but as soon as they arrived they found their way to the beach and spent exhilarating hours paddling, two lonely figures in the gloomy grey sea. The following summer one of the partners took them for a weekend to a hot sandy beach on the north coast of France, to make up for the pebbles.

One of the first things Dodie did was to put down a shilling at the bicycle shop next door to 'The Little Gallery', and began the hire purchase of a second-hand Raleigh bicycle. It had tall old-fashioned handlebars, an oil lamp and thick green cord threaded from the rear mudguard to prevent her skirt from becoming entangled in the wheel. The price of the bike was nine shillings and sixpence. Lu went the whole hog. She paid one and six a week off a brand-new Rudge Whitworth, with racing handlebars and toe clips on the pedals. The price of Lu's bike was an astronomical three pounds nineteen-and-six! They bought carriers to fix over the back wheels of their bikes, so that Dodie could carry me and Lu take Joey, and the four of us sped on wheels to Battersea Park. Things had decidedly taken a turn for the better.

I soon became involved with the shop and began to earn a few shillings. On Wednesday afternoons – a holiday for the lower school – I delivered parcels. On Sunday afternoons I decorated sheets of paper with potato cuts and these were put on sale with the more elegant efforts from professional artists like Edward Bawden. I had a page in the ledger, and my papers were on sale or return at a price of one and threepence each less one third. In the winter evenings Dodie brought home square and circular cellophane boxes. I decorated them with gummed stars and spots, instinctively never using more than two colours and sticking them on like stamps, picking up the stars on my finger, dabbing them on my tongue and slapping them straight on to the cellophane. It reminded me of the clay marble patterns I had made years ago in hospital. They were sold at Christmas time as gift boxes.

One day Lu and Dodie came home in a dither of excitement. Queen Mary had visited the shop. They had seen her quite close and described her hat and shoes and cream silk umbrella. They had stood breathless in the background and bobbed a curtsy. 'And you'll never guess what, Rowie,' Lu was all smiles and big eyes.

'Go on then, what?' I asked.

'Your spit's gone to Buckingham Palace!'

'She never!' I gasped, my hand over my mouth.

'She did!' Lu flung her arms round me as Dodie said, 'Queen Mary bought one of your boxes!' I clamoured for every single bit of information. Had she said anything? Which one did she choose? I thought I would bust with sheer pleasure.

'Rowie love,' said Mum, smiling all over her face, 'I am glad!'

The rich and famous jostled in 'The Little Gallery', including actors, writers and titled people. The nicest of all that I saw was Charles Laughton, who often dropped in at tea time. He invited us all to see him play Captain Hook in *Peter Pan*, and he took Joey and me on stage after the performance to see how they made people fly.

Unconsciously we all began to absorb the values of the shop, and to distinguish between shapes and colours, patterns and fuss, simplicity and clutter. We began to relax and speak unself-consciously to posh people, and learned how to handle a saucer at tea time.

Soon after Lu and Dodie were established at the shop, Georgie made his move. He got a job on a Thames sailing barge called the *Monarch* and at last began his career. Joey and I were so proud of him when he came home in a blue jersey, carrying a grubby kit-bag. We used to sit in his bedroom and listen while he described every bit of the river to us, and explained how they drove the barge under the bridges with nothing but the tide and a great sweep. We learned the names of the sails and why barges had leeboards instead of keels, and felt what it was like to sail silently into the pearly estuary at dawn. Bargeing sound a fine life to us, and Georgie was happy, but one terrible day he had an accident. He fell from a hatch beam into the hold of an empty barge and seriously injured his back. When he came home from hospital he was cased in plaster from his neck to his hips and he could not work. He continued to knock about along the river and he came upon a wreck.

It had been a heavily-built four-oared skiff, which had started life as tender to a London County Council fire float. When she was replaced, she was sold to a dredging company who used her for positioning the four massive anchors which held the dredger fast while she was working. One night one of the anchors was dropped into the boat, breaking her middle thwart and causing her to spread and sink. After a couple of days she was lifted, full of mud, and dumped out of the way on a nearby wharf, past repair and written off. Georgie had all the time in the world and much in common with the old boat, so he began to scull around for bits of timber to repair her. Joey and I went to watch him rig a tackle round her and wind and lash a stout spar of wood, making a Spanish windlass, to bring her sprung planks together. Over the unemployed months, Georgie worked on rebuilding the boat, scrounging his needs in return for odd jobs, until the wharf manager complained that it was in the way. He agreed to lift the boat back into the water with one of the wharf cranes, with Georgie crouched in the stern praying that she would float. In his plaster jacket, Georgie would have gone to the bottom of the river like a stone. She floated and Georgie sculled her up river to a mooring at Putney.

When Georgie was discharged he went back to work, and Dad fastened on the boat. He had a river inspector survey her, and she passed without question and was licensed to carry eight passengers. Dad named her *The Frog*. Joey and I spent practically every Sunday in her, pushing her, under Dad's instructions, up as far as Richmond lock and learning a new part of the Thames.

One weekday in the summer holidays when we had had *The Frog* for about four months, I wanted to go away. I wanted to sit on the sand by the sea. The river banks at low water were solid mud, except right outside the Tower of London, where they had dumped a bit of shingle for the kids to play on. I persuaded Joey to row there in *The Frog*. He had a friend called Benjie who wanted to come with us, so we cut our bread and jam, filled an empty bottle with water and set off, saying we were going up the park. I was thirteen, Joey one month off his eleventh birthday and Benjie just nine.

We walked to Putney and collected the bailer and the oars from the shed under the pub. *The Frog* was afloat and the tide on the ebb, so we let go and merrily pushed her down the river. It was easier for us to stand up in the boat and face forward to push the oars rather than sit down and row in the orthodox way, as Joey's feet hardly touched the floorboards when he sat on the rowing thwart. There was a bit of lively wind behind us which helped us on our way, and which we failed to take into account. We brought *The Frog* to the steps underneath Tower Bridge and tied her to a ringbolt. We messed about on the hard shingle and ate our bread, and after a very little while Joey noticed that the tide had turned. We shoved off and started back to Putney, with a bit of a flourish at first to show off, but only too aware of the distance we had to cover.

We got through the first couple of bridges all right but found that the wind had freshened. It was now blowing hard over the strong tide which threw up quite a pobble on the water. *The Frog* stood well out of the water and took a lot of notice of the wind, which blew her head towards the north Embankment wall. I swapped places with Joey and took the oar against the weather side as I was heavier and could push harder. The sun went in and it crew cold. Benjie sat huddled in the stern and Joey and I had to work hard, neither of us talking as we slogged together, pushing for all we were worth just to keep the bow pointing in the right direction. Tugs and lighters overtook us and we rolled and bounced in their wake. 'Tell you what Joey,' I panted, 'we'll find a place to hang on for a bit, and have a rest.'

It had taken us more than two hours to get as far as Waterloo Bridge, and Joey thought we should keep going. 'We got to get back to Putney on this tide,' he said. 'We'll never push her against this wind once the tide turns.' We battled on, looking far from capable as *The Frog* bucked and slapped her way under Westminster Bridge. We were in the stretch of angry grey water below the terraces of the House of Commons when motor boat came up behind us.

'Coppers!' shouted Benjie. The officious little boat idled alongside us, Joey and I continuing to row as if she were not there, hoping she would take a look at us and go away.

'What do you think you're up to?' a man's voice shouted at us.

'Goin' to Putney,' I yelled back, still pushing the oar.

'Whose boat you got?'

'It's our Dad's.'

'Give us your line.' The police boat edged nearer.

'We don't want a tow,' I cried. 'We can manage.'

'Hand it over,' ordered the copper. As they came alongside us Joey had to ship his oar out of the way, and one of the coppers leaned out of their cockpit and gathered an armful of our rope from the bow and made fast to a ringbolt. With a jerk the slack took up as the police launch put on speed, and one of the coppers pulled us up close to their stern so that we didn't yaw about. Moving so fast against the wind in our thin clothes made us feel cold, and *The Frog* smacked a bit of spray over her bows, so the three of us lay down on the bottom boards below the gunwale. I was shaking with exhaustion and thankfully watched the undersides of the bridges passing over my head. Joey closed his eyes, and Benjie was curled up like a wet little mouse. We didn't say anything to each other. I waited for the approach to Putney Bridge, and as soon as it came in sight I crawled up into our bow and called to the coppers.

'Mister,' my voice flew away in the wind. 'Let us go now, ay?'

There was no reply. The three coppers had their backs to me. 'Oi!' I yelled. 'Don't take us no further!' One of the policemen turned round and shortened the tow rope.

'What's up? he shouted.

'Cast us off 'ere,' I pleaded. 'Go on, mister. I don't want my Dad to know we've had a tow.' The copper turned his back and took no notice. We shot through Putney Bridge.

There was an eerie feeling under the bridges. The sound changed to the slapping of moving water on the buttresses and the tide sucked and swirled in evil dark eddies, brown and green. The river smell was stronger, a drainy smell like the bung holes of old sinks, and pigeons roosted above among the ledges and ironwork. Once through the bridge we were close to our moorings where many people would recognise us and witness the shame of the police bringing us back. I was so angry with the coppers that I didn't say thank you. We tied up *The Frog*, climbed over the railings and put the oars and bailer back in the shed. We didn't talk much on the way back to the buildings. We had not put up a very impressive performance for Benjie, and we knew it would be a miracle if Dad failed to hear of our escapade.

Nothing happened for a couple of days and I was beginning to hope that the incident had escaped Dad's notice. Joey and I were messing about in the yard and we saw Dad coming in. He jerked his head at us and pointed to the block entrance. Without a word to our mates we hurried up the stairs and waited for him in the living-room. He hung his cap on one of the pegs in the passage and entered the room without looking at us. Joey and I waited, eyeing each other. 'Have you had *The Frog* out?' he suddenly shot at us. Taken off our guard I said 'no' and Joey said 'yes' at precisely the same moment. 'Got yourselves mixed up with the bloody police as well,' Dad roared, banging his hand on the table. We did not answer, wondering how much he knew. 'Where did you go?'

'Tower beach,' I said.

'Where did they pick you up?'

'Westminster,' said Joey quietly.

'What the hell for?'

'I dunno,' I lied. 'We had the tide with us, but we had a head wind an' they just came alongside and scooped us up.'

'Bit bloody stupid wasn't it?' Dad's voice had lost its edge.

'Yes Dad,' we said together.

'Now look here,' Dad moved over to his armchair, sat down, and began to roll a fag. 'Don't ever put yourselves in a position where the coppers have to sort you out. Just let this be a lesson to you. You can take the boat out, but keep above Putney and don't go beyond Chiswick.'

'Yes Dad.'

'One more thing. You took a passenger?' We nodded. 'Well, cut that out. Drown your bloody selves, but I don't want any roosters knocking on our front door about their kids. Understood?'

'Yes Dad.' He picked up his newspaper and we edged out of the room and belted down to the yard.

'I think Dad was tickled pink,' grinned Joey.

'Yeh, I wonder who told him?' I said.

'We don't have to worry about not takin' Benjie,' said Joey. 'He says he wouldn't come with us again, not for 'undred pounds.'

'Windy,' I sneered.

'Don't blame him,' said Joey. 'How about taking *The Frog* out tomorrow?'

'Not 'arf,' I said.

ELEVEN

The Naylors Join Up

We now had a Cossor wireless set with a fretwork case and an accumulator at the back which stood on the sideboard in the living-room. After supper was cleared away I had the table for my homework while Dad listened to the BBC National Service. Mum, Lu and Dodie usually stayed in the kitchen after washing-up and got on with the washing or ironing, and I could hear the thump as Dodie lifted one flat iron off the gas ring with the toe of the other. Mum often did a bit of cooking for the next day and the three of them kept up a murmur of private talk. I became used to working while the wireless was on, but every single night at about eight o'clock Dad went out to the boozer, and then everything changed. The living-room was the thoroughfare between the kitchen and the bedrooms and everyone started moving about. Lu collected up all our shoes for cleaning and Dodie got out her knitting or sewing. Mum always had a little sit in Dad's chair, chatting to the girls and persuading one of them to pop the kettle on. Joey pottered between his bedroom and the kitchen carrying his snails one at a time for their ten minutes of freedom on the tiled wall, pointing out which one was tame and another which knew its name. I was conscious of what was going on and kept half an ear on the conversation. I now had at least three subjects set each night and was supposed to spend no more than forty minutes on any one of them, but I hardly managed to finish my work before I was hustled into bed around nine o'clock.

I stood my atlas round the candle in the bedroom so that the light would not be seen above the door through the glass fanlight, and sat up in bed to finish off my written work and catch up with the backlog of set book reading. I shared a single bed with Lu, and she usually stayed up with Mum and Dodie until Dad came in, to be certain that everything would be all right. When she came to bed and caught me still reading she told me off, and I had to put my books down and move over against the wall to make room for her. She sat up against her pillow with a tin pie dish of water and a bag of curlers on her lap, damping strands of hair and twisting them over little bits of black elastic with metal ends that clipped together. I had to lie still while she did this, because the pie dish slopped over if I so much as breathed too hard.

Lu had found herself a young man, which complicated all our lives. In the first place I had to put up with this nightly ritual, and she was for ever pestering Dodie to lend her something to wear. Dodie took care of her things and kept them ironed and mended, and Lu often tried to pinch something from Dodie's locker without asking. Mum knew about Lu's young man, but we had to keep him a secret from Dad, because we had only just recovered from a terrible row over Dodie.

On her way home from work Dodie had paused at the gate to chat for a moment to a man who lived in the buildings. Dad had happened to notice this trivial encounter but said nothing about it until he came home from the pub, and then he went berserk. To Dodie's astonishment he accused her of all kinds of dreadful things, calling her a guttersnipe and turning furiously on Mum when she tried to calm him down. Although Lu and Dodie were both over twenty-one he was not going to allow them to become involved with men in any way, and he made his attitude perfectly clear. He threw Lu's tiny tube of Tangee lip colour on the fire and said he would beat the living daylights out of her if she mucked about with her eyebrows again. This shook us a bit, because we thought Lu's newly affected fringe had successfully hidden the bristly red marks above her eyes. A thin pencilled line was all the rage, but Lu, over enthusiastic as usual, had plucked herself bald.

Lu first met Teddy when she worked in the factory canteen, but as she had changed her job they had to try to meet in the evenings. She invented plausible reasons for going out, pretending to go to the pictures with a girl friend or making out that she had to stop late at work. She had to be home by ten o'clock and as Teddy worked a late shift they could not meet until nine, so she had to wander about the streets for hours. She began to get careless and arrived home several times after Dad. Dodie and Mum grew anxious and Dad became suspicious. The next time it happened Dad turned out the gaslight and locked the front door. Dodie waited in the dark in our bedroom listening until she was sure that Dad had gone to bed, then she crept out and unlocked the door. When Lu came in there was a fiercely whispered argument in our bedroom, Dodie telling Lu off for causing us all such worry and Lu saying she didn't care.

Dodie and I had to keep a bit of carrot in our bedroom. Although it was against the rules, Joey kept a guinea pig in the kitchen. When we crept about in the dark to open the door for Lu, the guinea pig squeaked and rattled the bars of his cage, making a terrible din and giving the game away. The only way to shut him up was to stuff a bit of his favourite grub through the bars, so we always had to be prepared. One night we thought Dad had gone to bed, but he was still sitting in his chair in the dark. When Lu came in it was half-past eleven. Dad lit the gas and caught Dodie in her nightie and Lu fully dressed. This was the showdown, and it lasted half the night. Mum got up and so did I, and even Joey came out of bed to try to hang on to Dad's legs when he went for Lu. This was not the sort of row that would blow over after a few days. A new situation had arisen, and Lu would not give way for the sake of peace and quiet as we had all done in the past. For a few days there was a sullen atmosphere and then Dodie surprised us. In her quiet way she announced that she was leaving home. Mum understood and supported her decision, but the rest of us were frightened. We had never been separated and Dodie had always looked after us and been the stabilising influence. The thought of her leaving was not to be borne.

She rented a gloomy basement in a little street near the Worlds End and furnished it thinly with a few of her own things, a collection of boxes disguised behind bits of gathered curtain material, and an item or two of second-hand junk. She scrubbed it clean, but it retained the familiar smell of mouldy plaster and damp wood that the little fire in the grate could not dispel. It was bravely homelike with little bits of matting and a pot of flowers. Dodie put her books on a shelf and settled down with her own solitude. Now Lu had somewhere to wait when she was to meet Teddy.

We carried on in the buildings with a rebellious Lu, Georgie only coming home for the odd night and no Dodie. The writing was on the wall for Dad, his children were beginning to escape.

I was now well established into my fourth year at school and under the influence of a brilliant pair of teachers who taught art and music. They had arrived like the trade winds and blew gusts of life around us. Out went the neat water colour washes on minute bits of paper, and in came paint and talk and pictures. I went dotty over Renoir and Van Gogh, and when I saw a reproduction of his self-portrait with a bandage over his severed ear, I was haunted by his face. I had seen it before. It was old Deaffy, poor, scruffy, little old Deaffy who sold newspapers at the Worlds End, whom I had laughed at with the other kids when he hurled himself to the ground in an epileptic fit. I had seen him many times with scabs on his face and starved, half-mad eyes staring from under his bandaged head. After seeing the portrait I was filled with guilt and compassion for him.

I still could not read music, but it no longer mattered. I had a quick and retentive ear and looked forward to singing the Bach and Handel Cantatas and choruses from *The Messiah*. I flung myself more and more into school affairs, just keeping my head above water in my studies and involving myself in after school activities to delay the actual moment of having to go home. I stayed behind for games practice, drama, house meetings and even went carol singing. With a couple of other girls I polished the benches and cleaned the sinks in the lab and shifted chairs for the schoolkeeper. My contacts with my friends from the yard had gradually melted away. As we grew older I spent more and more of my evenings indoors grappling with homework, while my mates were leaving school. Occasionally I met one of the boys in overalls, a fag end behind his ear, coming home from work and we exchanged glances. Sometimes, in the evening, I was sent to the off-licence bar at the pub to get six penn'orth of main line in a jug for Dad, and I would see some of the girls going out of the gate. I wondered where they were going and I envied them. I was still in a drill slip, which was now a bit tight around the bosom, but my old friends had perms and handbags and ear-rings. We gave each other friendly smiles and said 'hallo', but they didn't stop to talk. We had lost touch with each other and no longer had anything to say. My reports said plenty. 'Rose must put more of her energy into her work', with the words 'energy' and 'work' underlined, was a comment from one of my more perceptive teachers, when I had volunteered to keep the chapel windows clean.

Our music teacher invited a few of us to a concert at the Aolean Hall, where she was to conduct the orchestra. The programme was to include much of the music she had already played to us, *Fingal's Cave*, The *Emperor Concerto* with Cyril Smith as the soloist, the *Unfinished Symphony* and a suite by Gordon Jacobs called *Uncle Remus*. I tried to persuade the girls to go to the concert in our school uniform but they would not hear of it. The most respectable thing that Lu possessed was a thin brown and white check macintosh. I took it out of the cupboard and put it on over my school dress, heaving it up over the belt to shorten it a bit. In her locker I found a thin navy blue scarf, so I tied it in a big floppy bow to hide the neck of my uniform. Just as I was leaving, Lu caught me and asked me what I thought I looked like. She turned me round then took off her shoes.

'For heaven's sake put these on,' she said handing me her little black numbers with bows on the front and fairly tall heels. 'You look like a district nurse in those clodhoppers.' She gave me enough money to get a bus to Bond Street and put a dab of Californian Poppy on my chin.

My blonde teacher walked to the rostrum in a pale gold evening dress and I was so proud of her I felt a sudden choke of tears. I looked quickly at the strange faces all around me to see if they were as delighted with her as I was, and I clapped hard and went on clapping to make them all join in. She lifted her baton and the orchestra began the overture. My only disappointment was that the lights did not dim as they did in the pictures. For the first time I saw the sharp black and white of evening dress laced with red and winking brown stringed instruments, the silver of trumpets and horns, the ranks of woodwind and brass topped by the great drums and the golden discs of the cymbals. There was a moment when they were all banging and blowing together, with rows of arms moving in fierce and exquisite unison over the violins, and my teacher spread out her arms to gather up the great wave of sound. After the thin dotted line in the pit at the Chelsea Palace, it was a revelation to me. I was thrilled and excited, and unconsciously moved on my hard chair. Lu's mac rustled. Each time I took a breath the macintosh crackled in response. I froze, and concentrated on sitting still instead of listening to the music. My feet began to thump inside Lu's shoes and I tried to ease one off with the toe of the other. The mac sent out a ripple of sound and the people around me began to murmur 'sh!' When the clapping started I whipped the shoes off and tucked my feet under the chair. Things went along wonderfully well after that.

We had been warned that it was wrong to talk or clap between the movements of a work, but I was getting worried about the time, and I mouthed a question at my friends. It was past nine o'clock, so I waited impatiently for the next break, scooped up my shoes and rustled out of the hall. I started off trying to run, but by the time I climbed up our stairs it was just after ten. I made sure I held the programme in front of me so that Dad would not think I'd been up to anything, but he narrowed his eyes as I walked in. I knew I was in for it.

One of my friends invited me to her fifteenth birthday party. It was an exclusive group that I was to join and I was flattered enough to be determined to go. Lu turned out the cupboard and we found a frock that Mum had brought home years before which Dodie had carefully folded and saved. It had a ladylike beige lace yoke and stiff shiny blue material fell in a solid straight line to the hem, which stopped about two inches above my ankles. The elbow length sleeves were trimmed with lace. I put it on, and anxiously watched Lu's face which remained totally blank. I feared the worst.

'It makes you look a bit older,' she said, as if she were trying to think of something nice. 'Turn round.' I moved ungracefully. 'I know what, love,' she said brightening, 'it's not the frock. You need some shoes. We got to lift you up a bit.' Mum said the stuff was lovely and must have cost a fortune. She splashed out at Blakies and bought me some black fabric dance shoes with straps.

The party was in a large house in Hurlingham and my friends might have been a chorus line. Silver shoes glittered beneath full length taffeta dresses that swirled from their waists, and little silver bags hung from wrists that emerged from butterfly sleeves. There were half a dozen or so young men who stood about clumsily and shuffled round the room with the girls to the latest songs on the gramophone. It was smart and dazzling, and I watched. All the evening I sat on the floor next to a fat leather arm-chair and talked to my friend's father, and I left before they served supper.

On the way home I had a bit of a snivel at first. I had looked silly and old-fashioned and I knew it, and I also knew that Mum and Lu had done their best for me. The truth about myself had been lurking around in my mind and the party brought me face to face with it. There was a gap a mile wide between me and the clique I so desperately wanted to be a part of, and I hadn't the sense to see that no matter what I did it would always be there. How many more times was I going to feel an outsider just for the pride I felt at being asked? I made up my mind to stop trying to be something I wasn't and decided that if ever I got another invitation I would have the nerve to say 'no.' I looked down at the terrible waste of my awful shoes and wondered how much they had cost Mum.

Before long Lu had become engaged and the time had come to confront Dad. Teddy was a handsome man with a cheerful and breezy manner, and he had no intention of being browbeaten. It was arranged that Teddy should call properly to take Lu out and that we would all keep out of the way so that he could have a talk with Dad. Lu tried to warn Teddy what to expect, but we had no idea how Dad would behave. The dreaded Saturday evening arrived. Mum gathered Joey and me into the kitchen, and when Lu had introduced Teddy she joined us, and Mum shut the door. We could soon hear Dad's voice, and Lu pressed her ear to the door, keeping her eyes on Mum. We tried to guess how they were getting on, and when we heard both their voices raised Mum jerked her head at Lu and she darted into the living-room. She was dressed ready to go out, and within a few moments we heard Lu and Teddy leave.

'What kind of bloody rooster has she picked up with?' Dad roared as soon as the front door had shut. Teddy had not made a good impression because he had been impertinent enough to put his trilby hat on the living-room table. Dad tore him to shreds and nagged and nagged at Mum as if it were her fault that Teddy existed at all. Eventually he slammed off to the pub and I knew that things would be worse when he came back, we had certainly not heard the last of this event. We had no Dodie, Georgie was away, and there would be fireworks when Lu came home, so I persuaded Mum that I was old enough to stay up with her. That night was one of the worst we had ever had.

I decided that I must act. I managed to get Mum to come with me to a magistrate's court to try for a separation from Dad. I had no idea how to go about such a thing, but I felt there must be *some* law or other to curb Dad's behaviour. Mum was worn out and left the talking to me. We saw a man behind a table in a very brown varnishy room, and he was not particularly interested. 'You must show marks of violence,' he said.

'There have been,' I answered him. 'Plenty.'

'No action can be considered,' he repeated, hardly bothering to glance up from the papers spread before him, 'unless there are visible signs.' Dismissed and somewhat crushed, I did not know what else to say, so we went home.

Teddy and Lu were to be married on Easter Sunday, and I thought it was the most exciting thing that had ever happened in my whole life. We seemed to be so different from other families. For one thing we didn't have a three-piece-suite and we never had visitors. We never had any special clothes for Sunday and we didn't have a knees-up at Christmas. There had been several weddings in the buildings, and I had watched from a distance when my friends scampered up and down the stairs in taffeta bridesmaid's frocks. I could not begin to imagine Dad permitting such a tremendous event as a wedding to take place in our family, but at last Lu had managed to bring us into line with everyone else.

Dodie made Lu's white dress and sewed net and artificial lilies-of-the-valley on to a white alice band. Teddy arranged for the reception to be held in the backyard of his mum's house. The idea of asking Dad if it could be held in our flat wasn't even considered, because of his distaste of being sociable and his disapproval of everything to do with Teddy. We didn't even know if he would give Lu away, and we wondered how he would behave towards Teddy's crowd of friendly, celebrating relations. I knew what I thought. He would be polite, superior and withdrawn, and when we got back home he would be critical and abusive. But it didn't matter! Lu was getting married. It was to be the biggest occasion we had ever had, and I didn't care what kind of row we had afterwards. After all, Lu wouldn't be there to hear it.

I got up early on Easter Saturday morning, and called at Dodie's, and we went to Covent Garden, where she carefully selected some freesias to make Lu's posy. We stood them up to their necks in a bucket of water in the basement. At the last minute Dad announced that he would come to the wedding and he looked quite distinguished in the suit. It had spent so much time in uncle's it was still quite presentable. When I saw Lu walking down the aisle, actually holding his arm, I couldn't help wondering what she was thinking. Dodie had pinned a pink flower on Mum's hat and bought her a pair of pink cotton gloves. With bright shining eyes, Mum stood up next to me in the church to watch Lu pass by, and nodded her head. Old Lu looked all right. Dad disappeared directly after the service, for which we were all thankful, but there were a lot of puzzled looks from Teddy's relations.

It was much quieter at home without Lu. I enjoyed having a bed to myself but mum missed her wages. As unexpectedly as Dodie had left us, she reappeared, giving up her little taste of independence to help us out and keep me at school. Her few months of absence had made a difference and she managed to maintain an element of freedom, paving the way for me.

I had little time for anything other than working for the School Certificate examinations, in which I was not to distinguish myself. Quite suddenly, in the middle of the term, new girls came to the school. The spoke hardly any English, and we soon discovered that they were Jewish refugees from Germany. Refugees to me were the dark-skinned people with bright clothes who lived in colonies near Putney Common. They had fled from the Spanish war, where I knew a few Englishmen had gone to fight. I heard the words 'fascist' and 'communist', but had little idea of their significance. Lonely people holding placards outside Walham Green station shouted angrily at passers by about the war in Spain, but no one stopped to listen.

On the newsreels I watched Hitler making speeches to thousands of people, and I saw rows of soldiers in steel helmets. In the newspapers there were photographs of shabby old men cleaning the gutters in German streets, and they wore marks on their clothes to show that they were Jews. Germany was a long way away, and I was sorry for the old men, but I had things nearer home to worry about. Now it was different. Seeing Elsa and Güdrun – who had been driven from their homes – every day at school made me realise what terrible and wicked things were happening. And nobody seemed to be doing anything to stop it!

Soon I heard about clashes between the fascists and communists in London. I got to know what Sir Oswald Moseley looked like because there were so many pictures of him speaking at blackshirt rallies. There were reports on the wireless news and in the papers about the fights between the blackshirts and the reds, whom some people called 'Bolshies' and others 'Commies'. I didn't ask Dad what it was all about, but I did talk to Mum. She rarely gave a thought to anything outside the family and told me not to worry. 'The coppers will soon sort all them rowdies out,' she said.

I did worry though, more than that, I became really frightened. Dodie and I went to the pictures one Saturday afternoon, and for sixpence each we sat through two films, a cartoon, the organist and a newsreel. In addition to all this, they screened a recruitment film for the Territorial Army. It was called 'The Gap', and it showed what would happen if the gap in our anti-aircraft defences was not filled by urgently needed volunteers. I sat and watched an aeroplane bombing a row of defenceless little houses, over and over again. The walls and windows crumpled in the blasts and roofs fell into the rooms. Nothing was there to stop the aeroplane, and I just could not believe it. It couldn't be as dreadful as that! War happened abroad, in Spain and Abyssinia. It happened to foreigners, to them, not to us. Dodie must have been as shocked as I was, because a couple of days later she volunteered for classes in air-raid precautions.

The war came a step nearer when Mum took Joey and me to queue up outside the Town Hall to receive our gas masks. Dad didn't come with us. He never conformed with any public duty in case they put his name on a list. It was growing dusk and people around us talked quietly, asking each other questions and knowing no answers. Newspaper sellers ran about shouting headlines, adding stabs of anxiety to the tension. 'The Gap' was still vivid in my mind, and the rubbery smell of the mask when I tried it on was suffocating. 'There won't be a war, will there Mum?' I asked, longing for reassurance.

'A' course not love.' Mum smiled, and added confidently, 'They won't let it happen!'

'Who do you mean by "they"?' I wanted to know.

'God,' she replied, 'an' the newspapers, an' the Gover'ment.'

For once Mum's magic formula of three didn't work, because there was a war and we were separated, never again to live together as a family. We were sent away, each in turn to survive alone, for which we had been well prepared. Georgie went straight into the Merchant Navy and Dodie to a munitions factory. Lu was to have her first baby while Teddy was in an army training camp. Joey joined the Royal Air Force in 1941 and I wanted to be a Wren. I thought I was well qualified to handle a boathook and row Admirals out to the fleet. But they wouldn't have me because my measly old eye was just about sightless. I finished up in a boy scout's hat and more bloody boots, up to my knees in Welsh cow-dung. It was the Land Army for me.

Joey had only just arrived home on leave on the night the buildings were bombed. Mum was making him a cup of cocoa when the whistling crunch of the bombs fell in a line across the four blocks. Many of our neighbours were killed, but Dad staggered through the smoke and dust into the glare of the burning gas main in his long underpants, clutching two bits of salvage – the canary in its cage and a bottle of beer.

Nothing was ever the same again. The war swept away life as we had known it and it disappeared for ever. When I drank my tepid mug of tea in a freezing cowshed before dawn, and dismally contemplated the value of my war effort, I always thought fondly of Mum, just 'popping the kettle on'. Tea, I reflected, had seen us through every crisis, and would see us through plenty more. I thought of her faith in 'God, the newspapers and the Government', and wondered which of the three had failed her. She would battle on though, it would take far more than a war to defeat Mum. After all, she had been fighting one all her life – single-handed.